Confucian Feminism

Bloomsbury Introductions to World Philosophies

Series Editor:
Monika Kirloskar-Steinbach

Assistant Series Editor:
Leah Kalmanson

Regional Editors:
Nader El-Bizri, James Madaio, Ann A. Pang-White,
Takeshi Morisato, Pascah Mungwini, Mickaella Perina,
Omar Rivera, and Georgina Stewart

Bloomsbury Introductions to World Philosophies delivers primers
reflecting exciting new developments in the trajectory of world
philosophies. Instead of privileging a single philosophical approach
as the basis of comparison, the series provides a platform for diverse
philosophical perspectives to accommodate the different dimensions
of cross-cultural philosophizing. While introducing thinkers, texts
and themes emanating from different world philosophies, each book,
in an imaginative and path-breaking way, makes clear how it departs
from a conventional treatment of the subject matter.

Titles in the Series:
A Practical Guide to World Philosophies,
by Monika Kirloskar-Steinbach and Leah Kalmanson
Daya Krishna and Twentieth-Century Indian Philosophy,
by Daniel Raveh
Māori Philosophy, by Georgina Tuari Stewart
Philosophy of Science and the Kyoto School, by Dean Anthony Brink
Tanabe Hajime and the Kyoto School, by Takeshi Morisato
African Philosophy, by Pascah Mungwini

Confucian Feminism

A Practical Ethic for Life

Li-Hsiang Lisa Rosenlee

BLOOMSBURY ACADEMIC
LONDON • NEW YORK • OXFORD • NEW DELHI • SYDNEY

BLOOMSBURY ACADEMIC
Bloomsbury Publishing Plc
50 Bedford Square, London, WC1B 3DP, UK
1385 Broadway, New York, NY 10018, USA
29 Earlsfort Terrace, Dublin 2, Ireland

BLOOMSBURY, BLOOMSBURY ACADEMIC and the
Diana logo are trademarks of Bloomsbury Publishing Plc

First published in Great Britain 2024

Series design by Louise Dugdale
Cover image © shuoshu / Getty Images

A catalogue record for this book is available from the British Library.

A catalog record for this book is available from the Library of Congress.

ISBN: HB: 978-1-3504-2616-0
          PB: 978-1-3504-2617-7
          ePDF: 978-1-3504-2618-4
          eBook: 978-1-3504-2619-1

Series: Bloomsbury Introductions to World Philosophies

Typeset by Integra Software Services Pvt. Ltd.
Printed and bound in Great Britain

For my late mother–in-law, Judith E. Rosen:
My feminist muse

Contents

Series Editor's Preface

Bloomsbury Introductions to World Philosophies will offer plural, hitherto unexplored pathways into the study of world philosophies. Instead of privileging a single philosophical approach as the basis of comparison, the series will provide a platform for diverse philosophical perspectives to accommodate the many different dimensions of cross-cultural philosophizing. While the choice of terms used by the individual volumes may indeed carry a local inflection, they will not foreclose critical thinking about philosophical plurality. The individual volumes will strike a balance between locality and globality.

Confucian Feminism: A Practical Ethic for Life is a novel and critical reappropriation of Confucian philosophy that can guide living. By infusing *ren* 仁 (humanness) and *xiao* 孝 (filiality) into care-ethics, as well as aligning Confucian *you* 友 (friendship) with the Greek *philia* and governance with *datong* 大同, Li-Hsiang Lisa Rosenlee boldly reimagines a Confucian-inspired interpretation of care-ethics in this volume. Her reading seeks to transform standard ways of understanding such Confucian core methods, tenets, and concerns, while simultaneously offering one transnational and transcultural instantiation of care-ethics.

Monika Kirloskar-Steinbach

Acknowledgments

This book in many ways is a sequel to my first monograph—*Confucianism and Women: A Philosophical Interpretation* (2006)—a project that started out as a way to answer to myself what it means to be culturally informed by Confucianism and be a feminist. In the end of that book, I promised to construct a substantiated account of a Confucian feminism. Now that promise is finally delivered. This is an inventive, philosophical project that intends to re-imagine Confucianism in a feminist fashion and thereby hybridizes both Confucianism and feminism. This project has been a long time coming and its coming to fruition fulfills more than an academic promise. It is as academic as it is personal. Through the process of writing and thinking through my own life experiences, now I can declare with confidence that I am not just a feminist happens to be an aspired Confucian, but that I am a Confucian feminist.

Carrying a hybrid identity, for sure, comes with its own risks. Along the way, I have encountered many who are skeptical of the possibility of a Confucian feminism. The reasons are wide-ranging: some object to the interjection of feminism into the "pure" study of Confucian thought; some point to the textual deficiency in Confucianism that is somehow diametrically incompatible with any "feminist" aspiration; and then there are those who are indifferent to feminist philosophy which is considered not "philosophy" proper. As a professional philosopher engaging in comparative feminist studies since my graduate years, I must say that it is rather challenging to try to publish works not just on feminism, but on Confucian feminism in the world of philosophy that is still predominantly Western and masculine oriented. Marginalization, skepticism, and rejection abound.

Luckily, I have also met some avid supporters—especially graduate students—at many universities where I have delivered the earlier drafts of this book; their enthusiasm for a much more inclusive, transnational feminism has given me a renewed sense of urgency to complete this monograph. Most of all, I would like to thank the editors of the Bloomsbury, Monika Kirloskar-Steinbach, Ann Pang-White, and Colleen Coalter who took a chance on me to publish this hybrid project, and the anonymous book reviewers for their detailed and constructive comments. Lastly, I would like to dedicate this book to my late mother-in-law, Judith E. Rosen, who inspired me to re-appropriate Confucian *xiao* and thereby helped cement my Confucian-feminist commitment to care.

I would like to acknowledge the use of materials from previously published works with permissions. First, "Why Care? Feminist Re-appropriation of Confucian *Xiao*" in *Dao Companion to the Analects*, edited by Amy Olberding, volume 4 of the series *Dao Companions to Chinese Philosophy*, pp. 311–34 (New York: Springer, August 10, 2013), copyright Springer Science+Business Media Bordrecht 2014, DOI 10.1007/978-94-007-7113-0_15, Print ISBN 978-94-007-7112-3, Online ISBN 978-94-007-7113-0. Reproduced with permission from Springer Nature. Second, "Confucian Care: A Hybrid Feminist Ethics" in *Asian and Feminist Philosophies in Dialogue: Liberating Traditions*, edited by Jennifer McWeeny and Ashby Butnor (New York: Columbia University Press, 2014). Copyright © 2014 Jennifer McWeeny and Ashby Butnor. Reprinted with permission of Columbia University Press. Third, "Confucian Friendship (*You* 友) as Spousal Relationship: A Feminist Imagination," *International Communication of Chinese Culture*, 2:3 (2015): 181–203. Reproduced with permission from Springer Nature. Fourth, "Multiculturalism and Feminism Revisited: A Hybridized Confucian Care Ethics" in *The Bloomsbury Research Handbook of Chinese Philosophy and Gender*, edited by Ann A. Pang-White (New York: Bloomsbury Academic, an imprint of Bloomsbury Publishing Plc, 2016). Fifth, "Ritual, Dependency Care and Confucian Political Authority," *International Communication of Chinese Culture* 4:4 (2017): 493–513. Reproduced with permission from Springer Nature. Lastly, "A Revisionist History of Philosophy," *Journal of World Philosophies* 5.1 (2020): 121–37. However, all of the previously published works have been revised in order to provide a greater sense of coherence and to include up-to-date works.

Many thanks to all my family, friends, and colleagues for their supports and encouragements as well as to my teaching institution, University of Hawai'i—West O'ahu, that provided flexible teaching schedules and course reductions in addition to a sabbatical leave in spring 2020 to make the completion of this project that much more feasible. All the remaining mistakes and shortcomings, of course, are entirely my own.

Prologue

Hybridity is a defining characteristic of the contemporary world where globalization is an irreversible historical fact and a way of life. Not only are goods and services but also are our cultural, ethnic, as well as gender expressions crisscrossing and transgressing the conventionally delineated boundaries in an ever more increasing pace, forming a complex web of human relations. A globalized world where goods are traded and cultural boundaries are redrawn is the world wherein we all live and wherein we anchor our hybridized Confucian feminism. This is not a return to a "pure" theoretical study of Confucianism, nor is it a one-sided "feminist" critique of Confucian patriarchy. Rather, this is an inventive, philosophical project to re-appropriate the Confucian textual tradition in a feminist image of herself as an attempt to merge Confucianism with feminism, and in their union both are uplifted to their mutual perfection where Confucianism is reimagined as feminist, and thereby feminist theorizing is enriched and expanded transculturally and transnationally.

This hybridized Confucian feminism is intended to provide viable theoretical tools based on characteristic Confucian terms, methods, and concerns in order to formulate a liberating feminist future for women—trans or born, queer or straight—anywhere and everywhere. In so doing, Confucian feminism—much like liberal feminism, Marxist feminism, existential feminism, radical feminism, and so on—also belongs to the pantheon of feminist theories aiming at liberating women from gender oppression and providing its own distinctive conceptual paradigm and practical approaches to women's issues, concerns, and experiences.

To reconceptualize Confucianism as a theoretical basis for a distinctive feminist theory might sound farfetched to some, not only those in the feminist communities, but also sinologists and philosophers alike. Many of the objections or skepticisms rest on the overt textual misogyny in the Confucian texts or the historical connections between Confucian teachings and gender oppression manifested in various social practices. Certainly, there are textual and historical connections between Confucianism and gender oppression. But what is less clear is why feminist theorizing that envisions a liberating future for women anywhere and everywhere should thereby be constrained by those historical and textual limitations.

After all, the theoretical construction of liberal feminism that typically traces its intellectual genealogy to Locke, Kant, and Mill is not thereby limited by, or rejected on the mere basis of, the textual or moral failings of these past thinkers. Nor is existential feminism limited or invalidated by the textual or moral failings of Nietzsche, Heidegger, Sartre, or Beauvoir.[1] Why then should the feminist theorizing of Confucianism be dismissed simply because of some misogynistic references in the Confucian texts or associations of certain social practices with Confucian teachings? The difference between feminist theorizing based on those canonical Anglo-European thinkers and our Confucian feminism is not that the former is entirely based on self-conscious feminist thinkers. Rather, it is this somnambulatory assumption that feminist theorizing using the terms, methods, and concerns articulated by canonical Anglo-European thinkers is a *natural* progression of making what is implied explicit. In contrast, this same natural progression is typically denied to Confucianism which is seen as a backwater ideology of the bygone era, and hence any progressive appropriation of Confucianism including feminist theorizing is foreclosed aprioristically.

Needless to say, Confucius was no feminist and there is ample textual misogyny littered all across the Confucian textual tradition. To construct a Confucian feminism is not the same as extending the feminist genealogy to Confucius, in the same way that to construct a liberal feminism is not the same as extending the feminist credential to Locke or Kant, since it is rather obvious that neither Locke nor Kant is a self-conscious, self-proclaimed feminist. Nonetheless, characteristic Lockean and Kantian terms, methods, and concerns are routinely incorporated into liberal feminism. It is in this long tradition of philosophical appropriation of past thinkers that our Confucian feminism situates itself.

Confucian feminism thus theorized here is, first and foremost, a philosophical project that seeks to tease out progressive, conceptual potential of the Confucian tradition centering especially on the pre-Qin and Han texts. These Confucian canonical texts are read philosophically, instead of historically; that is to say, the focus of this project is not on explicating the context, the origin, or the intent of the Confucian texts historically. Historical context, for sure, is useful and necessary for understanding a given text. This project, however, goes beyond offering a historical reading of the texts. It focuses on explicating progressive conceptual possibilities in the Confucian classical texts so as to help aid our own understanding of ourselves and solve our own contemporary issues.

Second, this is not a cultural recovery project; its focus is not on reclaiming the relevancy of an indigenous intellectual tradition against the hegemonic force of coloniality. Although it is true that there is a historical and cultural basis for the Confucian textual tradition, our Confucian feminism is not meant to be only applicable to certain geolocalities, let it be Beijing or Boston. This is so because the practice of philosophy, in part, aims at transcending the givenness of factuality including geolocality, temporality, and historicity. This hybrid feminist project is not constructed solely with the aim to liberate women who are presumed to be receptive to Confucian persuasion, however that receptivity is defined; rather it is a theoretical paradigm with Confucian characteristics for women, anywhere and everywhere. Much like Plato's *Republic* or Aristotle's *Nicomachean Ethics*, Confucianism belongs to the world as part of the shared repository of human wisdom.

Lastly, this is not a sociological project. Its focus is not on how any social institutions and practices intersect with Confucian teachings historically or presently, or the extent to which Confucian values still persist in a given society. In other words, this project makes no empirical claims on the applications of Confucian teachings in the lived reality both past and present, and the valence of Confucianism is not thereby assessed on its empirical efficacy, in the same way that the valence of various Anglo-European canonical texts is not measured on those historical or empirical bases. For instance, the valence of various Kantian terms, methods, and concerns that are prevalent in contemporary progressive projects—let it be on human rights, ethics, or feminism—does not rest on the applicability of Kantian concepts in Prussia historically or whether or not Kantian teachings still hold sway within the Germanic-speaking world presently. This project does not aim at laying claims that existing social movements in certain societies are derivative of their receptivity to Confucian persuasion. These sociological claims require in-depth field studies, which are beyond the scope of this philosophical project. However, some practical guidelines will be explored as an effort to apply the theoretical to the practical.

Just like any feminist theory, our Confucian feminism also carries with it a normative dimension of how things should be, even if that is not how things are. Its claim of universality here is a normative one instead of an empirical claim. The Confucian ideal thus constructed here rests on its internal conceptual coherence alone with the aim to better understand ourselves and the world through conceptual means that are ever more agile and dynamic. It is in this vein that our Confucian feminism offers its own ideality for women. Certainly, Confucian feminism by itself will not be able to bring about a fully liberating future for all women from all gender-based oppression. But it does assert that one possible way to confront the issue of gender oppression is through the utilization of characteristic Confucian terms, methods, and concerns.

Why Confucianism?

The often-asked question of why using Confucianism as a theoretical basis for the progressive, contemporary movement of feminism, I would argue, is itself borne out of the somnambulatory assumption that the West—broadly construed—is the sole rightful heir to the progressive future of humanity. Modernity is oftentimes seen as synonymous with the West, and hence non-Western intellectual thoughts have only historical, ethnic, or religious values that belong to the realm of the historical past, the descriptive, or the non-rational. The field of Asian and Comparative Philosophy is assumed to be populated by substandard *philosophants* or is treated as a natural by-product of Western influence on the non-Western world that retroactively applies the label of "philosophy" to their own intellectual traditions. Hence to take Confucianism as a theoretical basis for feminist theorizing immediately arouses suspicion, prompting additional justifications so as to demonstrate not only the "philosophical" aspects of Confucianism, but also the "compatibility" of Confucianism with modernity. Curiously, no such additional justifications are needed, or even asked for, whenever a canonical Western thinker or text is anachronistically integrated into contemporary progressive projects.

So this hybridized project of Confucian feminism will not begin with a justification. Just like the canonical tradition of the West, Confucianism—an enduring intellectual tradition—can also offer a great well of conceptual resources that are not yet fully explored. This imaginative, feminist project begins with taking Confucianism as a philosophy and seeks philosophical insights available within this complex, textual tradition to formulate a viable feminist theory to address the problem of gender oppression and to envision a liberating future.

In the vast majority of human textual traditions, being a "woman" itself is a liability historically and presently. For not just textually, but also politically, socially, economically, culturally, and religiously, in the gender binary of man and woman, man is oftentimes positioned as the nobler one who is fit to rule, to lead, and to offer his guardianship to woman who is either less emotionally restrained, less intellectually inclined, less authoritatively endowed, less resolved in her will, or less expansive in her proper domain. Being a "woman," in other words, is being the "lesser" gender, however the "lesser" aspect is expressed in different textual traditions. Given that patriarchy and misogyny are a shared feature in the vast majority of human textual traditions, to incorporate Confucianism, on the face of it, should encounter no more difficulties than it is to incorporate the Western canon into contemporary feminist theorizing.

However, a quick survey of feminist scholarship in monographs, anthologies, or journal publications shows that textual misogyny in non-Western traditions including Confucianism is still by and large seen as a disqualifier for their incorporation into feminist theorizing. This hybrid project intends to fill that void and to venture into a theoretical frontier where few have boldly gone before. In short, despite its textual misogyny, as I see it, Confucianism can also be a wellspring for feminist theorizing. Distinctive Confucian terms, concepts, and concerns such as *ren* 仁 (humaneness), *xiao* 孝 (filiality), *you* 友 (friendship), *li* 禮 (ritual), and *datong* 大同 (great community) can also be viable conceptual tools for women to navigate the existential contour of gender oppression and construct a feminist liberating future.

The time is ripe for such a transcultural, transnational project that does not linger on the superficial critique of the sexist Confucian tradition conventionally conceived, but one that takes the next step into the unknown, yet constructively imagined theoretical horizon of a Confucian feminism. As Robin May Schott points out back in 2003, Western feminists by and large have gone through and are done with the phase of negative critiques of the Western canon and are now much more engaged in the phase of positive construction of feminist theories emerged out of the ashes of those canonical texts.[2] Here I am arguing for the same move for Confucianism. Through a feminist re-imagination of Confucianism, my chief purpose is to provide women—anywhere and everywhere—with viable conceptual tools to navigate the actual contour of human experiences.

Project Outlines

In order to provide the colonial background information for the once contested issue of multiculturalism in the feminist discourse, Chapter 1: The Politics of Feminism begins with an introduction to the roles that Western canonical thinkers such as Hume, Kant, and Hegel play in constructing and cementing an exclusively Western genealogy of philosophy where the rational and the philosophical are seen as an Anglo-European intellectual prerogative. In the feminist debate over the compatibility between multiculturalism and feminist liberation, the so-called "liberal exit" strategy is once touted as the only genuine solution to gender oppression for the so-called "third-world" women who are supposedly entrenched in their "traditional," "illiberal" cultures. Western liberal intervention is seen as a necessary pre-condition for the liberation of those "third-world" women, seemingly echoing those canonical thinkers' Eurocentric, hegemonic worldview with a racialized, hierarchical developmental logic.

Susan Okin's now infamous essay "Is Multiculturalism Bad for Women" (1999) that sees the Western, liberal culture as the least oppressive form than all the rest is a case in point. This totalizing effect of liberalism, broadly construed, in turn makes the emergence of any non-Western feminist theorizing impossible. Feminist encounters with non-Western cultures have long been uni-directional: Feminist criticism of misogyny globally. In the context of Confucianism, Chenyang Li's (1994) comparative piece on the incorporation of Confucian *ren* 仁 into feminist care ethics can be seen as the inception of a rare, positive, bidirectional engagement between Confucianism and feminist theorizing. However, the initial debate on the theoretical compatibility between Confucian *ren* 仁 and care ethics at times has veered into a political debate on the worth of a culture mirroring its colonial predecessor's assessment of the colonized.

Once we move past the issue of compatibility between Confucianism and feminism, in Chapter 2: When Care Ethics Encounters *Ren* 仁 and *Xiao* 孝, we proceed to infuse Confucian *ren* 仁 (humanness) and *xiao* 孝 (filiality) into care ethics in order to strengthen its theoretical grounding and expanding its theoretical horizon to meet the often-raised objections to care ethics. Specifically, the social and political dimension of *ren* 仁 helps to address the structural changes needed to transform a personal care to a social and political care where reciprocal deference underlines the performance of ritual and where the state authority is measured based on its caring capacity for the most vulnerable. Furthermore, the moral dimension of *ren* 仁 that begins with the cultivation of *xiao* 孝 helps expand the paradigmatic maternal care to include elder care. The intergenerational caring labor of *xiao* 孝 that grooms each of us, as it were, from the ground up is the perfect embodiment of the understanding that our inevitable interdependency must then lead us to our moral reckoning to care for those near and far.

As many of the early critics of care ethics point out, by promoting a care-oriented ethic without at the same time addressing the burden of care, care ethics may in fact further the oppression that women already are forced to endure; now women must also care for the needy before they care for themselves. And there is nothing more transparent of women's disproportionate caring labor than in the roles of wife and mother. In order to address the issue of disproportionate caring labor, we must first address the gender roles of wife and mother as well as the institution of marriage.

Even though marital relationship is not the only intimate relationship available to women nor is the marriage institution the only socially recognized institution to express the enduring nature of an intimate relationship, women's disproportionate caring labor is most acutely expressed in the institution of marriage. Hence to reconceptualize the marital relationship along with the institution of marriage is urgently needed. Both Chapter 3: Marriage and Perfect Friendship and Chapter 4: Hybridity of *Philia* and *You* 友 intend to propose a hybrid concept of friendship incorporating both Greek *philia* and Confucian *you* 友 (friendship) to reconceptualize modern marital relationship. By replacing spousal relationship with moral friendship, we would be able to rehabilitate the institution of marriage and to enable all to live a fully flourishing and ethically satisfying life so that in a marital union both spouses can become greater than they once were.

Another perennial critique of care ethics is that it offers no structural changes that one can implement in the larger social or political institution. The Confucian concept of *datong* 大同 that grounds the state's political authority on its ability to care for the vulnerable—the young, the old, the sick, and the disabled—is able to offer care ethics that much needed political dimension, making caring an essential function of a *ren*-based state, instead of a private burden irrelevant to the political discourse, or worse yet a private burden for women to bear alone. Confucian *datong* 大同 is an inclusive state of compassionate care, but in order to foster a shared culture of care, first we will need to reconceptualize what constitutes the self, citizenry, and political authority. Infusing modern democratic system with Confucianism provides such a plausible possibility.

In Chapter 5: Democracy and Its Limits, we take up the ongoing contestation over various proposed blended systems of Confucian democracy focusing especially on Joseph Chan's (2013) Confucian perfectionism service thesis and its critics. Much like the earlier debate on the compatibility between Confucianism and feminism discussed in Chapters 1 and 2, the perceived incompatibility between Confucianism and democracy rehashes the same kind of objection and critique of Confucianism. It is my take that much like the Western canonical texts, Confucian texts can also progress beyond their original historical and social contexts to not only be in sync with the modern world, but also be able to provide viable solutions to our very modern problems.

In Chapter 6: Ritual, Common Good, and Social Cohesion, we provide an in-depth study on Confucian *li* 禮 (ritual)—along with its associated concepts of *quan* 權 (weighing) and *he* 和 (harmony)—as a means of good governance. Confucianism with its sustained emphasis on ritual as the shared social, political, and spiritual bond and its deep commitment to caring for the vulnerable as the basis of political authority is able to provide us with a much more wholesome picture of an inclusive, compassionate state going beyond a rights-based citizenry limited by punitive laws. Richard Haass's *The Bill of*

Obligations (2023) is a fresh reminder of the inadequacy of a rights-based citizenry in our own democratic state. Ritual, as a quintessential Confucian means of governance, is able to provide us with a deeper, social, and spiritual bond to hold all of us together beyond our self-centric concerns in our democratic state.

In Chapter 7: A Practical Ethical for Life, we further explore how Confucianism conceptualizes the issue of dependency care not just as a woman's issue, but as a political issue, an issue that deserves the first consideration in a *ren*-based state. In going beyond the theoretical, we propose a dual lens of family and care as characteristic Confucian-feminist paradigm to theorize both the root of gender oppression and its liberation. The proposed dual lens is first used to provide some practical guidelines in dealing with the issue of elder care in our increasingly greying world. In addition, it is used to interrogate the popularized notion of the "leftover woman" *shengnu* (剩女) (China's equivalent of a spinster) and the commercialized notion of the "light-mature woman" *qingshounu* (輕熟女) (Taiwan's equivalent of a financially independent woman delaying marriage) along with some implications for the LGBTQIA+ communities that are contra to the assumed heteronormative way of life. As part of the pantheon of feminist theories, Confucian feminism is able to provide its own explanation for gender oppression and envisions its own distinct liberating future.

In the Epilogue, this project is closed with a reflection on my own feminist journey in search for an ethically satisfying life and my own eventual commitment to filial care for my late mother-in-law. My hope is that this imaginative, hybrid project of Confucian feminism could be used as a living guide for women to navigate the existential contour of their lived experiences without borders.

Conclusion

As promised in my previous monograph on *Confucianism and Women* (2006), this hybrid project is the sequel that lays out a comparative feminist theory based on characteristic Confucian terms, methods, and concepts. It is now also possible to envision a progressive, feminist future infused with Confucian *ren* 仁, *xiao* 孝, *you* 友, *li* 禮, and *datong* 大同, a future where caring for others is a moral basic, a mark of humanity, where human interdependency is not seen as an obstacle but is instead what makes a flourishing, ethically satisfying life possible, where spousal relationship is no longer hinged on gender-based hierarchy or gender-based division of labor but instead is marked by virtuous friendship as the internal good of a feminist marriage, where the ritualized self is ever more porous and deferential to the needs of others, and where caring for the social dependent is no longer brushed aside as a private matter but instead is seen as the political priority of a *ren*-based state. In short, this is a Confucian-inspired feminist care ethic practical for life, and in their union, both Confucianism and feminism are uplifted to their mutual perfection.

1

The Politics of Feminism

In Chinese gender studies, there has been a long running tradition where feminists criticize Confucianism for its victimization of women. As Terry Woo writes back in 1999, the relationship between Confucianism and feminism "has largely been a one-sided affair: feminist criticizing the status and treatment of women determined by Confucianism."[1] But feminists are not the first ones to attribute the ills of China including gender oppression to Confucianism. In the genre of colonial literature, the "status of women" is a familiar trope used to contrast the civility of the colonial power with the barbaric "natives." And due to its prominent status in Chinese civilization, Confucianism, more or less, is linked to the historical understanding of the ills and gains of the Chinese people, including gender relations. The Anglo-European representation of Confucian teachings fluctuates from being the emblem of high culture and civility in the seventeenth century to a backwater ideology by the nineteenth century. Missionaries and travelers' observations of the impact of Confucian teachings on the lives of women generally reflect this oscillating evaluation of Confucianism from civility to barbarity.

The practice of footbinding, in particular, has become emblematic of the misery of Chinese women from the nineteenth century onward. The foreign crusade against footbinding comes to a focus especially after the Opium wars (1839–42 and 1856–60) when the last dynastic court of Qing was forced to open up its seaports to colonial powers. Footbinding remains as one of the favorite examples in feminist literatures demonstrating the severity and moral depravity of gender oppression faced historically by Chinese women.[2] Even though there is no direct textual connection between Confucianism and the practice of footbinding, the prolonged co-existence between the two for a thousand years by itself has made Confucianism a moral suspect to many feminists.

In the late Qing and early Republic eras, anti-Confucian sentiments ran high. Confronted with countless defeats and humiliations at the hands of the colonial powers, the gentry dissents belonging to the Reform movement in the late Qing and to the May Fourth movement in the early Republic era during the late nineteenth and early twentieth centuries also capitalized on the inferiority and the unspoken miseries of Chinese women as part of the emerging nationalistic discourse on the ills of Old China. A total purge of Confucianism was completed during the Cultural Revolution by the early 1970s. Both the Reform/May Fourth movement and the Cultural Revolution radically rejected Confucianism, seeing it as the root of Old China's malaises, and that, in turn, laid the foundation for the feminists' representation of Confucianism as antithetical to women's liberation.

Beginning in the 1970s–80s, there was a surge of interest in Chinese gender studies abroad. The surge of publications on the conditions of Chinese women formed part of the grand feminist movement toward constructing a global history of women, intended to provide a validation for feminists' defiance against the patriarchal social structures as well as the social constructs of gender. By going outside of the Anglo-European sphere, feminists intended to provide an empirical proof of the urgency and the ubiquity of gender oppression, while expanding their sphere of concern to include their less fortunate sisters in the "third-world." Confucianism, through the lens of universal patriarchy, is often portrayed as the cause of Chinese women's oppression historically and presently. Or, as Julia Kristeva in her book on *About Chinese Women* (1977) simply titles her chapter on the misogynistically vile nature of Confucian teachings as "Confucius: An Eater of Women."

Needless to say, the early feminist assessment of Confucianism is highly inflammatory and misguided, which more or less is aided by their somnambulatory assumption that the cultures in which the "third-world" women are born are inherently and irredeemably patriarchal both past and present. Hence the status of the "third-world" women is usually measured on a sliding scale of universal victimhood with Anglo-European women being the most liberated, the most gender-conscious, and the most self-determined. Anglo-European feminists see gender-based oppression faced by non-white women as "similar but much worse," treating their cultures as the worsening factors aggravating the suffering of the "third-world" women.[3] The posture that feminists have adopted so far in their encounter with other cultures is an enlightened savior coming to rescue "third-world" women from their deeply rooted misogynistic and patriarchal way of life. The Anglo-European world is no longer just one culture among many, but instead occupies the unique vantage point of meta-culture, against which all other, parochial cultures must be measured.

The hierarchical ranking of cultures in early feminist discourse, in part, owes its origin to the eighteenth-/nineteenth-century race theory facilitated and consolidated by many Western canonical thinkers, such as Hume, Kant, and Hegel, equating the civilized and the rational with whites, and the unreasonable and the barbaric with non-whites. Unfortunately, this colonial worldview that contrasts the West as the progressive future of humanity with the patriarchal, oppressive nature of the non-Western world continues to find its way into feminist discourse on the "third-world" women. In order to understand this somnambulatory assumption of the non-Western culture, in the following we will take a detour into the making of an exclusively Western genealogy of the history of philosophy starting in the mid-eighteenth century during the height of the so-called European Enlightenment.

A Revisionist History of Philosophy

Indeed, it is perplexing as to why the theoretical possibility of constructing a Confucian feminism has not yet been fully explored by philosophers, feminists, or sinologists alike, given how prominent Confucianism has been historically and given how early on Chinese Classics have been studied and made available to the Western audience initially via the accounts of the Jesuits in the late sixteenth to the early eighteenth century. For instance, father Matteo Ricci's fluency in the Chinese language both in the written and spoken forms and his erudition with Chinese Classics has made this long-running and complex intellectual tradition accessible to the Western audience, albeit through the lens of his own theological convictions. Nonetheless, a fair amount of Chinese Classics have been studied and translated by the Jesuits from the late sixteenth century onward. Leibniz's voluminous writings on China constitute one of the most in-depth cross-cultural works by philosophers during the European Enlightenment era. In fact, in many *philosophes'* accounts including Christian Wolff, Francois Quesnay, and Voltaire, Confucianism represents a viable, civil, and at times, superior, alternative ethics to Christianity.[4]

Contrary to the contemporary wrangling over the classification of Confucianism and Confucius, a dispute that is still ongoing, for the seventeenth-century Jesuits who first provided the window into the complexity of Chinese Classics and Confucius's teachings to the European audience, the classification of Confucius as a philosopher and Confucian teachings as primarily an ethical and political system of thought seemed rather obvious. Europeans' interest in Confucianism as an intellectual tradition however declined precipitously by the late eighteenth century and the perception of Confucianism took a radical shift from a philosophical system to an ethnic religion by the early nineteenth century. The creation of the academic subject of anthropology and the emergence of the conceptual distinction between religion and non-religion (i.e., secular) in the late eighteenth and early nineteenth centuries help drive non-Western intellectual traditions including Confucianism out of the category of philosophy into the category of religion where the "pre-rational" belief systems are housed as part of one's anthropological observations of the native. By the early nineteenth century, philosophy has become synonymous with the West whose intellectual development is said to begin with ancient Greeks and then continuously unfolds itself exclusively in the Anglo-European world.[5] The genealogy of philosophy is a story of the West's rational and self-conscious development of its intellectual tradition presumably above all other ethno-beliefs that are labeled as "pre-rational," "religious," or simply "unphilosophical." Thus, non-Western intellectual traditions including Confucianism are routinely deemed as outside the study and the practice of philosophy.

Even today, the field of Asian and Comparative philosophy sits on the margins of the discipline of philosophy: Only 10 percent of the 118 graduate programs of philosophy in North America teach Chinese philosophy, and only a handful of institutions have a compulsory requirement on non-Western philosophy in their philosophy programs. The discipline of philosophy, in fact, has the most Anglo-Euro-centric curriculum in the field of humanities other than specifically named area studies.[6] The inquiry into the systematic exclusion of non-Western philosophies including Confucianism from philosophy might seem pedantic; its answer does hold the key to understanding the root of various objections regarding feminist theorizing based on Confucianism. After all, if Confucianism is not considered a philosophy—as it is still not so considered in the vast majority of the academies in North America today—then it hardly makes any sense for philosophers to study it, let alone constructing a Confucian feminism envisioning a liberating future for women anywhere and everywhere.

Thanks to Peter Park's (2013) exhaustive study on the systematic exclusion of Africa and Asia from the history of philosophy, now we know that the claim of the Greek origin of philosophy also has its own historical origin. It is in fact a revisionist claim in the face of ample contrary textual evidence historically available to the eighteenth- and nineteenth-century philosophers such as Hegel who engaged in a revisionist effort to construct an exclusively Western genealogy of philosophy, which then is echoed by the twentieth-century philosophers such as Heidegger, Husserl, Gadamer, Derrida, among many others. Their effort obviously has been successful, since this revisionist history of philosophy has been preserved and perpetuated in nearly all of the academies in the Anglo-European world, and has now become intuitively true to many of us philosophers.

Take a quick look at the compulsory requirements for philosophy majors, one is bound to find the requirement on the history of philosophy, which usually has three components: Ancient, Medieval, and Modern philosophy;

and all these courses are taught strictly and exclusively Western, as if the practice of philosophy by passing the rest of the world only started with ancient Greeks and straightly moved onto the philosophical developments in the Anglo-European world. Little did we know that the seemingly "natural" progression of philosophy as exclusively Western is in fact, a revisionist claim, constructed by canonical thinkers such as Hegel who see the rational, philosophical thinking as a Western intellectual prerogative.

For instance, in his introduction to the lectures on the history of philosophy, Hegel contrasts the rational, progressive nature of the world spirit unfolding itself in the history of philosophy with the stagnation of the Chinese who supposedly have already achieved all they could possibly have achieved two thousand years ago. As Hegel writes:

> [W]hat the history of philosophy displays to us is a series of noble spirits, the gallery of the heroes of reason's thinking. [...]The content of this tradition is what the world of the spirit has produced, and the universal spirit does not stand still. But it is with this universal spirit that we have essentially to do here. It may indeed be true of one people that its culture, art, science, its spiritual possessions generally, make no headway, as seems to be the case with the Chinese, for example, who may two thousand years ago have got as far in everything as they have now. But the spirit of the world is not engulfed in this unconcerned peace. This follows from what it simply is, because its life is act.[7]

To Hegel, what separates mere opinions from philosophy is that the latter is a true science that aims at discovering Truth, and hence the history of philosophy should not be a survey of opinions, or what he calls "a gallery of downright follies" in the course of time.[8]

Hegel sees the history of philosophy as the same as the progressive, rational unfolding of the world spirit itself. The emergence of the rational self-consciousness of the world spirit, for Hegel, begins with a separation of the spirit from nature, from "its immersion in matter, in intuition, in natural or non-rational willing"; this stage of the world spirit's self-immersion in nature properly speaking is not yet a true developmental stage of the world spirit. To Hegel, this preliminary stage is not only "the lowest, the least true" and "not produced by spirit itself"; it is a stage that characterizes "the nature of the Oriental world in general." In contrast, "the first form of free and spiritual self-consciousness, and therefore the beginning of philosophy, is to be found in the Greeks."[9] In sum, philosophical thinking as a rational unfolding of the world spirit itself, for Hegel, belongs exclusively to the West.

Hegel's rejection of non-Western philosophies is, however, not solely due to a lack of access or his own ignorance. As noted earlier, through the Jesuits' translation efforts during the late sixteenth to eighteenth century, Chinese Classics were well received by many of the *philosophes* during the eighteenth century. And prior to the early nineteenth century, non-Western intellectual thoughts were routinely included in the history of philosophy texts.[10] In addition, Hegel himself also studies and writes about Indian philosophy. So it begs the question as to what transpires this radical shift in the West's perception of the non-Western world in the early nineteenth century that leads to the expulsion of non-Western intellectual thoughts from the rank and practice of true philosophical thinking.

Obviously, to pinpoint a definitive cause would be impossible. But what is certain is that Hegel's revisionist construction of the history of philosophy is informed by and made possible through his race theory in which humanity is divided into four distinct races of African, East Asian, American, and European. Each of the four races is then generalized with a set of developmental characters corresponding to the sort of social and political institutions that are deemed possible given their inherent racial characters.[11] In other words, Hegel's exclusion of non-Western philosophies from true philosophical thinking is premised on his race theory clothed in a developmental logic where Europeans represent the paragon of humanity in a perpetual, progressive mode in contrast with the stagnation of the rest of the world hierarchically ranked, from the lowest ladder of the perishing, feeble American savages, to the slavery nature of Africans, then to the despotic, intuitive Asians.[12] As it will become clear later, the same type of racialized developmental logic, unfortunately, is also echoed in feminist thinkers such as Harriet Taylor Mill's (1852) and Beauvoir's (1949) assessment of women's situation globally. In the once-contested issue of multiculturalism, liberal feminists also tactically employ the same type of hierarchical, developmental logic in formulating their so-called "liberal exit" strategy for the "third-world" women.

Hegel however is not the first one to articulate such a racist view. The "scientific" concept of race, in large part, is made possible through the nearly four decades of teaching and writings of Kant. Kant deliberately chooses to write about races and writes about it in a certain way, despite being confronted and challenged by his contemporaries. His first race essay "Of the Different Human Races" (1775/7) was initially written as a course announcement for physical geography, a course Kant taught from his first year of teaching in 1756 till his retirement in 1796. In 1772, Kant started to offer anthropology as a separate course from physical geography, both of which were immensely popular courses taught most frequently by Kant—surpassed only by logic, metaphysics, and moral philosophy, which were however required courses.[13] It is worth noting that Kant helps to construct physical geography and anthropology, two new academic subjects in the mid-eighteenth century. And it is through teaching these courses that Kant first develops his race theory, in which the seemingly infinite diversity in human sub-groupings is summarily organized into four distinct races that are hierarchically and teleologically ranked, a view that he holds till his last known manuscript, *Opus postumum*, completed in 1801 and published posthumously as a series of journal essays in 1882–4.[14]

Kant lays out four races correlated with four distinct skin colors (white, black, red, yellow) and four geographical localities (Europe, Africa, America, India) as a result of climate adaptation at the early stage of human migration. Racial characters are hereditary and are not subject to change in the second transplantation. But the manifestations of one's racial characters are not just limited to the physical forms, but also one's dispositions and temperaments. In Kant's estimation, the red race is a weak, perishing race and the negro race is "lazy, soft and trifling."[15] The white race diverges the least from the original human formation and is well adaptive to all subsequent transplantations.[16] In positioning the white race as the most perfect human form, Kant is laying the ground for the realization of his later proposed cosmopolitan ethical community where Europeans "will probably someday give laws to all the others"[17] and where Christianity as the only true religion will provide the moral legislations for humanity to realize "the (moral) kingdom of God on earth."[18] A long story short, the concept of race for Kant is a regulative concept that we impose onto nature so that it is possible for us to grasp the world as a system. That racialized system then forms the basis for Kant's progressive concept of world history with a cosmopolitan aim, and provides an empirical evidence for the validity of his teleological judgment in the third *Critique*, which, in Kant's own words, is the completion of his "entire critical enterprise."[19]

Despite the depth of Kant's racism (as well as misogyny), there is no shortage of philosophers using Kantian terms, methods, and concerns to engage in contemporary progressive movements including feminism. In fact, Kant's race theory has been vigorously defended, whitewashed, or brushed aside by many contemporary philosophers who maintain that the *core* of Kant's philosophy remains intact, unperturbed by the *expose* of Kant's extensive writings and teachings on race as if they were merely minor glitches in an otherwise brilliant philosophical system.[20] This is true for other Western canonical philosophers as well.

For instance, Hume's infamous footnote appended in 1754 to his essay on "Of National Characters" (1748) and then carefully revised and retained in its

1777 posthumous edition was hugely influential during his time and beyond. As Hume writes in this lengthy footnote in 1754:

> I am apt to suspect the negroes and in general all other species of men (for there are four or five different kinds) to be naturally inferior to the whites. There scarcely ever was a civilized nation of that complexion, nor even any individual eminent either in action or speculation. No ingenious manufactures amongst them, no arts, no sciences. On the other hand, the most rude and barbarous of the whites, such as the ancient GERMANS, the present TARTARS, have still something eminent about them, in their valour, form of government, or some other particular. Such a uniform and constant difference could not happen, in so many countries and ages, if nature had not made an original distinction between these breeds of men. Not to mention our colonies, there are NEGROE slaves dispersed all over EUROPE, of whom none ever discovered any symptoms of ingenuity; though low people, without education, will start up amongst us, and distinguish themselves in every profession. In JAMAICA, indeed, they talk of one negro as a man of parts and learning; but it is likely he is admired for slender accomplishments, like a parrot, who speaks a few words plainly.[21]

As an avid reader of Hume, Kant repeatedly cites Hume's footnote on Black inferiority in support of Kant's own race theory and racial hierarchy.[22] And yet, contemporary scholars continue to defend Hume's writings as being *racial* instead of being *racist*, and similarly, Hume's *racialism* is said to be irrelevant to Hume's *core* philosophy and furthermore can be easily remedied by Hume's own philosophy on the universality of human nature and our original equality.[23] But the same cannot be said of non-Western philosophies that are routinely excluded aprioristically from contemporary progressive discourse due to their overt textual misogyny, "feudalistic" mode of thinking, or other perceived connections to historically and socially oppressive practices.

Multiculturalism and "Third-World" Women

Unfortunately, the same type of racial and cultural hierarchy that first cemented by those eighteenth- and nineteenth-century canonical thinkers continues to find its way into feminist scholarship on cross-cultural studies where Anglo-European women are said to be the most liberated, the most progressive, and the most self-conscious feminists compared to all the rest.

Susan Okin's now infamous essay "Is Multiculturalism Bad for Women?" (1999) discussing the rights of women in the context of group rights for minority cultures within Western nations where the liberal West is said to be far less patriarchal than nearly all the rest is a case in point.

As Okin writes, "[w]hile virtually all of the world's cultures have distinctly patriarchal pasts, some—mostly, though by no means exclusively, Western liberal cultures—have departed far further from them than others."[24] For those cultures that contain oppressive practices against women, they should alter themselves according to liberal values or should perish. Okin argues against granting "group rights" to minority cultures within the Western nations, and instead proposing the "liberal exit" strategy as a solution to gender oppression for minority women. As Okin writes:

> It is by no means clear, then, from a feminist point of view, that minority group rights are "part of the solution." They may well exacerbate the problem [....] Indeed, they *might* be much better off if the culture into which they were born were either to become extinct [...] or, preferably, to be encouraged to alter itself so as to reinforce the equality of women [...].[25]

In short, the rigid colonial dichotomy of the progressive West vs. the patriarchal non-Western world continues to manifest itself in the post-colonial era under a feminist guise.

In Okin's view some cultures (mostly Western liberal ones) are plainly and simply better than the rest, and the worth of all cultures should be assessed according to liberal principles and values. Minority cultures (and most of them in Okin's view are antithetical to liberal values and principles) do not have any intrinsic values of their own. Hence granting minority group rights, according to Okin, might not be part of the solution, but might in fact exacerbate the problem of gender oppression. Okin's world is neatly divided into liberal and illiberal, Western and non-Western, feminist and patriarchal. With the West representing the pinnacle of human achievement, what the non-Western world has left to offer is compliance and conformity to Western liberal values and principles. Following Okin's hierarchical, developmental logic, minority women can be liberated if and only if they are assimilated into Western liberal culture through voluntary abandonment of their own culture identity or through cultural extinction.

The dichotomizing worldview implied in the "liberal exit" strategy for minority women mirrors its colonial predecessors that see the world as merely composed of *Europe and the People without History* as theorized in Eric Wolf's anthropological study (1982/97), where Europe dictates not just the future trajectory of the world, but also the way in which human past is assessed. History is then written in a language of segregation, where the culture of the inferior must be first dismantled and then reconstituted in accordance with the image of the superior West. Cultural extermination and coerced assimilation into the dominant culture were routinely practiced during the colonial era; even John Stuart Mill, a self-proclaimed defender of women's rights, uses liberal values and principles to justify British colonialism in India and around the globe.[26] It is indeed nothing short of astonishing that feminists such as Okin should arrive at a similar conclusion regarding the worth of non-Western cultures hundreds of years later.

It is clear that global sisterhood is impossible, if feminist consciousness is only and exclusively premised based on the hegemony of the liberal West, however "liberalism" is construed. But if feminism is to be relevant to women on the ground, then culture must be prima facie valuable in its own right. Any discussion involving "Third World Feminism," as Chandra Talpade Mohanty (2003) writes, must address these two simultaneous projects: "[T]he internal critique of hegemonic 'Western' feminisms and the formation of autonomous feminist concerns and strategies that are geographically, historically, and culturally grounded."[27] If feminism is to be truly without borders, it must, among other things, also be culturally grounded as well. Non-Western cultures must be relevant in feminist discourse, not just as something to be discarded, but as a fundamental analytic tool to understand the manifestations and meanings of gender that is geographically, historically, and culturally specific.

Culture, if seen thickly and pervasively, offers a distinct pattern of ways of life encompassing both public and private, ranging from spiritual, political, social, economic, educational, to aesthetic. In short, culture is that through which one first becomes conscious of one's being as a particular. Or, to put it in a Heideggerian idiom, we are thrown into the world with a particular worldhood that has a specific temporal and spatial locality. Culture—as the shard worldhood in which our particular being is always a being-with-one-another—is what gives us the tools to imagine what else is possible. As Avishai Margalit and Joseph Raz (1995) write in support of the rights of minority cultures, "[f]amiliarity with a culture determines the boundaries of the imaginable."[28]

To exit from one's culture is commonly termed as an acceptable solution among liberal scholars to the problem of gender oppression in minority cultures.[29] In order to balance the rights of the individual and the rights of minority groups, liberal scholars generally agree that individuals should be granted the right to exit a particular group in question when its rules or practices become intolerable. However, it is not clear as to what it means to "exit" one's culture, if culture is seen thickly and pervasively. This is not to say that cultural practices cannot be changed or one cannot take on more than one cultural identity, but this so-called "liberal exit" strategy does raise questions regarding the nature and the meaning of culture.

To some liberal scholars, such as Jeremy Waldron (1995) and Chandran Kukathas (2003), culture is seen on the same footing as any voluntary association that an individual may choose to join in or to exit from. This sort of trivialization of the importance of cultural belonging is indeed reflective of the liberal tendency to view one as an atomic individual to whom relationality is externally constituted and therefore can be discarded at will. Cultural identity thus viewed is merely one external relation among many, such as one's membership in a workout gym or a book club. And when the club rules become unreasonable, one is free to leave and pick another club with more palatable rules. This portrayal of culture, obviously, misses the mark of culture, but more importantly, it helps foster a false sense of openness of the so-called "liberal" culture in contrast with all other self-enclosed, static, illiberal cultures that one should freely exit from.

The open and self-determinant character of the Western self is made clear in transnational feminist discourse where women in the non-Western world are often said to be blind to their own sexist cultures due to the effect of socialization. Or, as Anne Phillips (2007) puts it, Okin's characterization of women in the non-Western world echoes the anthropological distinctions "between an 'egocentric' Western self, characterized by a clear differentiation between self and other, and a 'sociocentric' non-Western one."[30] The Western self is seen as in full possession of itself, whereas the non-Western self is hopelessly enmeshed in social relations.

The "exit" strategy for "third-world" women who are enmeshed in their supposedly socio-centric self will need to be premised on the liberal intervention to restructure that given minority culture first. As Okin (2002) comments on the realistic rights of exit for minority women, "without a cultural context that allows one to develop a sound sense of self, it is difficult to imagine a woman being able even to conceive of exit as an option."[31] In other words, women raised in non-Western cultures have a deficient, distorted sense of the self, and hence the liberal exit strategy that requires a sound sense of the self would not even be imaginable to minority women, let alone realistic. Liberal intervention is then the only option left for Okin in order to provide a realistic exit strategy for women globally.

Non-Western cultures thus conceived not only are disposable, but necessarily so, especially from the liberal standpoint. It is all too often that non-Western cultures are assessed as ethically unworthy, and hence the discussion of non-Western cultures in the feminist communities is, by and large, one of rejection and condemnation. Under the Western colonial eyes, progressive change belongs to the West, whereas the rest of the world if left to its own devices is immune to change. As Uma Narayan (1997) puts it precisely in her discussion of "third-world" feminism:

> From the viewpoint of colonizing Western power, an important "difference" between "Western culture" and various colonized cultures was the alleged singular openness of "Western culture" to historical change—cast, not surprisingly, as "progress." Colonized cultures were conversely often represented as victims of a static past of unchanging custom and tradition, virtually immune to history.[32]

Hence any change that occurs in these "traditional" societies such as the rise of feminist consciousness is invariably read as a sign of "Westernization." In this way, "progressive humanity," "feminism," and "West" are all synonymous.

Okin's stark contrast between the progressive liberal West and the eternal patriarchy of minority cultures is well situated not only in the long history of colonial literature, but also in celebrated feminist writings. For instance, Simone de Beauvoir in her landmark feminist work *The Second Sex* (1949) discounts the need to study the evolution of man's attitude toward his wife anywhere else but the West, since gender relation has not progressed in the non-Western world where women have lived in a state of slavery since the beginning of time. As she explains, albeit in a footnote, "we shall study that evolution in the West. The history of woman in the East, in India, in China, has been in effect that of a long and unchanging slavery."[33] In other words, the non-Western world is frozen in time, and hence no study is needed in assessing possible changes to women's slavery state of being in the East, in India, or in China.

Beauvoir's characterization of the retarded state of non-Western women mirrors the Western colonial perception of its colonized in regard to the savage condition of women around the world compared to the higher state of Anglo-European women. This sort of racialized, developmental ladder employed in assessing women's condition globally is also reflected in Harriet Taylor Mill's noted feminist work, "The Enfranchisement of Women" (1852), roughly a century prior to Beauvoir's *The Second Sex* (1949). As Taylor Mill writes:

> In the beginning, and among tribes which are still in a primitive condition, women were and are the slaves of men for the purposes of toil. [...] The Australian savage is idle, while women painfully dig up the roots on which he lives. An American Indian, when he has killed a deer, leaves it, and sends a woman to carry it home. In a state somewhat

more advanced, as in Asia, women were and are the slaves of men for the purpose of sensuality. In Europe there early succeeded a third and milder dominion, secured not by blows [...] but sedulous inculcation on the mind.[34]

Racial hierarchy is plainly shown in Taylor Mill's characterization of women around the world in an ascending order with the savage state of Australian women on the bottom, up next to the servile state of Native American women, then to the somewhat higher state of Asian women who, instead of toiling out in the open, toil solely in the bedroom. In comparison, European women are oppressed in a milder form—not physically or sexually—that is, only in their habits and thoughts, representing the highest stage in women's quest for equality. The West, in short, is the ideality for progressive humanity.

In the context of the once-contested issue of multiculturalism, it is clear that for feminists like Okin Western liberalism is positioned as the meta-culture to which all other parochial, patriarchal, illiberal cultures must pay homage. Contrary to this liberal pretension, granting a basic respect to non-Western cultures should be the starting point for any cross-cultural encounter. Otherwise, no genuine intercultural exchange would be able to get off the ground.

Any enduring culture, as Charles Taylor (1995) eloquently argues, must have something valuable to offer. As he writes precisely on the politics of recognition:

> [O]n the human level, one could argue that it's reasonable to suppose that cultures that have provided the horizon of meaning for large numbers of human beings, of diverse characters and temperaments, over a long period of time [...] are almost certain to have something that deserves our admiration and respect [....] Put it another way: it would take supreme arrogance to discount this possibility a priori.[35]

To grant a basic sense of respect and recognition to any enduring culture is not only a reasonable thing, but more importantly a human thing to do. Just as the presumption of the dignity of humanity, the presumption of equal worth and equal dignity of culture should not require an additional burden of proof of its equal perfection. Granting equal respect for culture, however, doesn't mean that all cultural practices have equal values, nor does it mean that one cannot embody more than one cultural identity. But it does mean that only through cultural appropriation is change even possible at all. Culture, as it were, is the filter through which reality and possibility come to be for us. The boundaries of what is real and what is possible constantly change through intercultural exchanges and intracultural contestations, but change is never made outside the bound of culture, as if it came from Thomas Nagel's vantage point of *The View from Nowhere* (1989). A contextualized viewpoint is the order of the day for even the claim of detachment and transcendence.

A transnational, transcultural feminism cannot be formed based on the assumption that women in the non-Western world are bearers of inferior cultures as implied in the so-called "exit" strategy championed by the liberal community. The choice thus framed would seem to be a discrete, yet morally unambiguous either/or: either one is liberal *and* Western, or one is patriarchal *and* non-Western. Under this purview, no one is capable of being a bearer of a non-Western culture and being a feminist of any sort at the same time. If we find such a liberal pretension and complacency unbearable, then what we need instead is a culturally informed, contextualized feminist theory that enables women to give new and viable meanings to their lived experiences.

To reimagine Confucianism feminist is not an attempt to whitewash its textual misogyny, which, for better or worse, has already been well explored, and more often than not, in a highly inflammatory fashion. The attempt here is to view Confucianism through the lens of gender so that a progressive movement can also take hold within this long running intellectual tradition with respect to gender. To accomplish this, our feminist theorizing of Confucianism must go beyond the mere negative critique of Confucian texts, but take the next step to conceive feminist possibility intra- and inter-culturally to formulate a feminist theory with characteristic Confucian terms, methods, and concerns. Feminists have not taken this step precisely because by merely raising the issue of compatibility between feminism and Confucianism they have at times been met with outright rejection or, worse yet, deadening silence from the feminist communities.

Issues of Compatibility

Chenyang Li's (1994) pioneering piece on the compatibility between care ethics and Confucian *ren* 仁 (humaneness) which then sets off a series of fierce debates is a case in point. Ever since Sara Ruddick published "Maternal Thinking" (1980), care ethics has emerged as a significant contender in the field of ethics, serving as a viable (and some would argue the only genuine) feminist alternative to the Kantian-liberal approach to normative ethics.[36] Carol Gilligan's *In A Difference Voice* (1982) and Nel Noddings's *Caring: A Feminine Approach to Ethics and Moral Education* (1984) paved the way for fruitful discussions on issues such as the compatibility between care-based thinking and justice-based thinking, the applicability of the mother-child dyadic relationship to the civic realm, and the feminine stereotyping of care-based thinking.[37] In its early stage, discussions surrounding care ethics were by and large confined to Western theories. In 1994, Chenyang Li's comparative piece, for the first time, extended the scholarly engagement to Confucianism.

The question of compatibility between Confucianism and care ethics has since been rigorously contested.[38] But what is being contested goes beyond the conceptual compatibility between care ethics and Confucian *ren* 仁. At times, it becomes a question of feminist identity and the ethical valence and relevancy of Confucianism to modernity. In other words, the debate in part becomes a debate on what can or cannot be properly counted as "feminist" and in part becomes a debate on the worth of Confucianism in this modern world. Whether Confucianism has anything valuable to offer to all sorts of progressive project including feminism depends on one's assessment of the ethical valence of the Confucian tradition, which, for better or worse, is interwoven with Chinese culture. Hence a seemingly theoretical assessment inevitably becomes a political debate on the worth of a culture.

Against the long tradition of the one-sided feminist criticism of Confucianism, Li's 1994 comparative piece can be seen as the first step toward resetting the terms of engagement between feminism and Confucianism. The main tenet of Li's argument is that the Confucian concept of *ren* 仁 that takes filial care in the parent-child relationship as the basis of its moral paradigm shares significant common grounds with care ethics, which also anchors its moral paradigm in the non-contractual, maternal thinking at home. Li then concludes with the following optimistic note: "Since, as we have shown, Confucianism and feminism share important common grounds, it is possible to reconstruct Confucianism to be feminist. If this is the case, then it seems more likely for feminism to prevail in a form of new Confucianism."[39]

Li's reconciliatory effort has been met with excitement as well as furious objections within the Asian and Comparative philosophical communities, but has been virtually ignored within the feminist communities, which by and large remain immune to the influence of non-Western, philosophical traditions. Few care ethicists bother to go beyond a brief mention of Confucianism.[40] And for a few who do engage Confucianism, they see no positive value in incorporating Confucianism into feminist theorizing. For instance, Virginia Held in her *The Ethics of Care* (2006) briefly but decisively rejects the compatibility between Confucianism and feminism, seeing Confucian ethics as a non-feminist form of care. Nel Noddings follows suit; in her *The Maternal Factor: Two Paths to Morality* (2010), she lays out the improbability of Confucianism converging with feminism, given its patriarchal roots and its reliance on social roles and tradition. In other words,

Confucianism seems to be too deeply muddled to have a plausible chance to positively intersect with feminism.

Although both Held and Noddings's objections to the compatibility between Confucianism and care ethics are quite brief, the significance is twofold. First, Held and Noddings are one of the few prominent care ethicists who actually engage Confucianism in their writings, and hence their mentioning of Confucianism, even though it is casted in a negative light, could serve as an important dialogical beginning between Confucianism and the feminist communities. In this respect, both Noddings's and Held's brief, but decisive, dismissal of Confucianism in their discussion of care ethics, nevertheless, is a welcoming starting point. Second, even with the rise of Western scholarship on Confucianism, positive assessment of Confucianism in the context of feminism remains marginal, and hence both Held's and Noddings's blunt characterization of Confucianism as patriarchal and anti-feminist serves as a fresh reminder of the colonial politics of feminism at play within the Western academy in which non-Western intellectual traditions are frequently assessed as ethically unworthy.

Held's (2006) rejection of the compatibility between Confucianism and feminism is familiar. Citing Daniel Star (2002) and Lijun Yuan's (2002) objections to Li's article (1994), Held implies that Confucianism is fundamentally incompatible with feminist care ethics due to its role-based categories of relationship and its inherently patriarchal nature. Even if Li is correct in arguing for theoretical common grounds between Confucian *ren* 仁 and care ethics, Held believes that it is unacceptable to call Confucianism feminist. As Held writes, "[a] traditional Confucian ethic, if seen as an ethic of care, would be a form of care ethics unacceptable to feminists [...]."[41] Noted here, Held is not so much disputing whether Confucian *ren* 仁 is a form of care ethics, but what matters to her is that Confucianism does not merit the name, feminist.

This is true for Noddings (2010) as well, who sees Confucianism as synonymous with patriarchy and its reliance on social roles and tradition as fundamentally anti-feminist. As Noddings writes:

Let's turn briefly to Confucianism's endorsement (or acceptance) of male domination. It may happen, as Li suggests, that Confucianism will gradually embrace female equality or at least not speak out authoritatively against it. But [...] if a religion (ideology or philosophical school) does not explicitly reject the doctrines that support domination, these doctrines remain quietly embedded in the religion and are thus available to those who would reactivate them. Confucianism would have to admit that it was wrong to claim the inferiority of women, and, then, patiently locate and repudiate all the doctrines based on this claim. This will be extremely difficult for an ethic that puts such emphasis on social roles and tradition.[42]

It goes without saying, for Noddings as well as for Held, Confucianism, Chinese tradition, and its social roles are all misogynistic. The debate on theoretical compatibility, hence, easily becomes a referendum on the ethical worth of a culture.

Without a doubt, Confucianism was not originally a feminist tradition, nor did it take interest in promoting women's well-being particularly. But if any theory that is contaminated with a patriarchal past is deemed unworthy of the name "feminist," then that exclusion must not only extend to the vast majority of theories both Western and non-Western, but also apply to the very notion of care. For one might argue that the practice of (maternal) care has been historically performed under a patriarchal social structure and therefore must in some way contribute to the continuous oppression of women in the private domain and functions as a major impediment to women's autonomy and liberation. In fact, this suspicion is shared by numerous early critics of care ethics. Care ethicists are fully aware of that objection; for instance, Held argues that "the practice of care to be recommended were not those conducted under patriarchal oppression but those to be sought in postpatriarchal society."[43] If the practice of (maternal) care could be uncoupled from the social conditions in which it has historically found itself, then the same thing could be done for Confucianism as well. One can employ the same methodology uncoupling Confucianism from the sexist social conditions with which it has been historically entangled.

Nonetheless, a progressive reading of non-Western classical texts or what some call "indigenous feminism" immediately arouses suspicion. The concern partly is rooted in the perceived danger of its being easily co-opted by conservative, nationalistic efforts. For instance, Vrinda Dalmiya (2009)— in her assessment of the compatibility between care ethics and Confucianism using India as an example—writes: "Postcolonial attempts to revitalize the Hindu tradition in India consequently become 'Trojan horses of the Hindu right.'"[44] In order to avoid the same negative impact of the Hindu revitalization on Indian women's lives, Dalmiya cautions visionaries of Asian feminist movements to consider the impact of a revitalized Confucianism on Chinese women's lives. As she writes, "a revival of a theoretically revised tradition needs to worry about how such reclamations affect the fabric of social life *on the ground*."[45] For Dalmiya, the potential adverse effect of a Confucian feminism as applied to Chinese women's lives is much more at stake than the theoretical disputes over whether Confucian *ren* 仁 is or is not feminist.

To conceive a "feminist" possibility in classical sources, as Dalmiya puts it, may "pique the intellect,"[46] but the ultimate test is how it affects women's lives on the ground. The potential impact of a revitalized non-Western canonical tradition is clearly assumed to be adverse to women.

Yet, it is perplexing to see why the assumption of an adverse effect is usually not present whenever Anglo-European texts are invoked in feminist theorizing. For instance, Aristotle's sexist remarks on women are no less appalling, but that does not prevent Martha Nussbaum from revitalizing Aristotelian tradition in her capacities theory. In fact, as Dalmiya points out in the opening of her essay, "[p]ointing out the misogynist statements that Aristotle makes about women would, for example, be an odd critique of Nussbaum's capacities theory!"[47] Also, as Dalmiya acknowledges, feminists, such as Iris Young, often publically "raid" Western sexist texts to further their feminist theorizing.[48] One wonders why such a borrowing cannot be applied to Confucian texts as well.

For sure, there is a certain amount of risk involved in revitalizing classical texts and its being co-opted by the far-right nationalist movement is real. Confucian texts, just as Hindu scriptures, carry potent symbolic meanings to its people and much of what has been done in their names is harmful to women, but there are also great wells of untapped resources within Confucianism that one can use to further women's liberatory movements. Or, to borrow from Annette Baier (2000) as she reflects on some feminist impulse to discard all Western canonical texts:

> [T]o dismiss as hopelessly contaminated all the recorded thoughts of all the dead white males, to commit their works to the flames, could be a self-defeating move. At the very least we should [...] examine each work we are tempted to burn to see if it does contain anything that is more worth saving than patriarchal metaphysics.[49]

One should hope that no less generous spirit should be applied to Confucian texts as well. The incorporations of Confucianism into feminist theorizing, by itself, should not be a sign of a clear and present danger to the feminist liberatory movements.

Conclusion

In this contemporary world, hybridity and interculturality are the proper way forward for the feminist liberatory movements. Revitalizing Confucianism through the lens of gender is less about arousing some sort of cultural pride than it is an act of broadening the scope of feminist theorizing. A hybrid feminist theory infused with Confucianism is neither East nor West; instead it is a blended possibility intended to help women think through their own lives and find viable conceptual tools to change the existing patriarchal socio-political structures. Is Confucianism alone able to address all women's problems? Not likely. But then, no ethical theory is able to do that.

Yes, the bottom line is to better the lives of women. But it is not just Chinese women's lives that are at stake here. Confucius is not just a Chinese philosopher studied by the Chinese only. Just as is true of Plato, Aristotle, Kant, or Hegel, Confucianism belongs to the pantheon of human intellectual traditions ready to caution, to aspire, and to propel us into the not-yet defined future, or the futurity of Dasein in a Heideggerian dictum. After all, what is a philosophical activity, if it is not to generate new ideas out of the old and to tease out the possibility of a given idea at hand? As Confucius puts it precisely in the *Analects* 2.11, in order to realize the new, we must first rekindle the old (溫故而知新).[50]

The ability to rethink and to transcend what is given to us is a hallmark of feminist thinking. As Held points out, feminist philosophy is a rethinking of thinking in the history of philosophy about how to live and organize our worlds and what we take as true and what our values are.[51] Held believes that feminist thinking can reorient our conventional thinking guided by the masculine model of autonomous individuals and can begin to find what is valuable in women's experiences. As she writes, "[o]ne often fails to find what one is not looking for, and scientific research that has been looking for female weaknesses and passivities has often failed to pay attention to women's strengths. Feminist thinking is changing what is looked for and what is found."[52] In the same spirit, one could argue that feminists must look beyond the confines of Western canon and change what is looked for and what is found in Confucian texts in order to pave the way for an inclusive feminism. Once we move past the politics of feminism, we are now able to start the actual construction of a Confucian feminism, beginning with the care ethics' encounter with *ren* 仁 and *xiao* 孝.

2

When Care Ethics Encounters *Ren* 仁 and *Xiao* 孝

In this chapter we begin our actual construction of Confucian feminism by infusing *ren* 仁 (humaneness) and *xiao* 孝 (filiality) into care ethics so as to strengthen its theoretical grounding. Chenyang Li's (1994) pioneering piece on the similarities between Confucian *ren* and care ethics and its early critics with a focus on Daniel Star (2002) and Lijun Yuan (2002) will serve as our initial point of entry into this hybrid project of a Confucian-inspired care ethics. Yuan in her later work *Confucian Ren and Feminist Ethics of Care* (2019) has since modified her previous stance (2002) and (2005) to partially embrace both Confucian *ren* 仁 and care ethics as feminist, but that partial embrace of Confucianism is still by and large limited to the Asian and Comparative philosophical communities decades after Li's 1994 comparative piece. Under this light, it is worthwhile to revisit the initial debate on the possibility of a feminist theory anchored in Confucian *ren* 仁.

Revisiting Confucian *Ren* 仁 and Care Ethics

Both Star (2002) and Yuan (2002) reject Li's optimistic, concluding note on the possibility of a new form of Confucianism that is feminist based on the similarities between Confucian *ren* 仁 and care ethics, even though their reasons vary. Li, Yuan, and Star respectively represent the following responses to the possibility of a Confucian feminist care ethics: first, Confucian *ren* 仁 is a form of care ethics and is compatible with feminism; second, Confucian *ren* 仁 is a form of care ethics, but is not compatible with feminism; and third, Confucian *ren* 仁 is not a form of care ethics and is not compatible with feminism. Li constitutes the first response, Yuan (2002) the second, and Star the third.

To substantiate his claim, Li cites three shared characteristics between Confucian *ren* 仁 and care ethics: (a) both hold care as the highest moral ideal; (b) both are not principle-based; and (c) both care with gradations. Furthermore, according to Li, it is not contradictory to hold a doctrine that has a caring characteristic, yet is oppressive in its application. Li compares the failed application of the liberal doctrine of equality to white men only with the failed application of Confucian *ren* 仁 to learned men only.[1] All in all, the Confucian concept of *ren* 仁 is faulted in its empirical application, not in theory, and hence theoretically Confucian *ren* 仁 is compatible with feminist care ethics. By extending Confucian *ren* 仁 to women in responding to the feminist concern of gender parity, a new form of Confucianism that is feminist and Confucian will likely prevail, as Li concludes.[2]

In rejecting Li's reconciliatory effort to bring together Confucianism and feminist care ethics, critics such as Yuan (2002), provide familiar objections to both care ethics and Confucianism. For Yuan, Confucianism is a form of care ethics, but both care ethics and Confucianism are bad for women, since both fail to meet the bare minimum criteria of feminism. In her view, both care ethics and Confucianism encourage unnecessary self-sacrifice and silencing; both fail to address the issue of justice within family; both focus on women's roles instead of women's rights; and finally both fail to provide adequate conceptual tools to criticize all forms of male dominance, which for Yuan is a necessary condition that makes an ethical theory feminist.[3]

Differing from Yuan, Star, in his objection to the compatibility between care ethics and Confucianism, maintains that care ethics is distinct from Confucian ethics, which he calls "role-focused virtue ethics." And due to the Confucian emphasis on hierarchal role-based relationships and its reliance on patriarchal tradition such as its constant references to the father-son relationship, Confucian *ren* 仁, in his view, is not compatible with feminism. Furthermore, in Star's view, Confucians "will oftentimes not *really* care."[4]

Li's rebuttal to both Yuan and Star can be summarized as follows. First of all, Star's insistence on the distinctiveness between Confucian *ren* 仁 and feminist care ethics does not negate the possibilities of similarity. As Li points out, similarity itself implies differences and the degree of similarity and difference all depend on the context. So in Li's original context of comparing care ethics with Kantian ethics, care ethics and Confucian *ren* 仁 share significant common philosophical grounds. Second, even if Star's assessment of Confucian ethics as a role-based virtue ethics is correct, Confucian ethics, which Li calls "role-based care," is not necessarily incompatible with feminist care ethics, since one can still exercise care through one's performance of social roles.

As for Yuan's objection to seeing Confucianism as feminist, Li disputes Yuan's claim that Confucianism can be reduced into a set of patriarchal rituals and practices; instead, the core of Confucianism, according to Li, is the teaching of *ren* 仁, which is capable of revising existing rituals through the concept of *yi* 義 (righteousness) for the sake of doing what is right and appropriate in a particular context. And lastly, Yuan's characterization of both Confucian *ren* 仁 and care ethics as feminine ethics that do not provide conceptual tools to criticize all forms of male dominance is debatable. As Li points out, this criterion might be useful in constructing an ideal feminist theory, but it cannot be used to assess whether a given theory is feminist or not. All normative feminist theories such as liberal feminism and Marxist feminism can be said to be inadequate in some way in criticizing all forms of male dominance, but they are all feminist nevertheless.[5]

Setting aside whether Confucian *ren* 仁 can be a form of care ethics or not, it is worthwhile to first examine what makes a theory "feminist" in the first place and whether or not Confucianism and care ethics can be considered feminist. According to Virginia Held's (2006) definition, a genuine feminist ethics must take caring experiences and activities at home as the basis for our normative, moral thinking. If one adopts Held's criterion, then Confucian *ren* 仁 is feminist through and through. For, first of all, unlike the dominant moral theories based on a masculine model of abstract reasoning, force, and confrontation, Confucianism takes the activity of reciprocal care in unchosen relationships such as parent-child relationship seriously. As sinologists generally agree, Confucianism bases its moral core in the private realm of filial affection and familial responsibility. In Confucianism, since the private familial excellence of filiality (*xiao* 孝) is not seen as different in kind from the public excellence of *ren* 仁, reciprocal care and relational personhood have always been taken as paradigmatic.

Furthermore, for Held, moral thinking must begin with the standpoint of human children whose survival must presuppose the activity of care being performed. Held claims that the value of care is, therefore, empirically and ontological prior to all other values.[6] Similarly, in Confucianism, the importance of filial care (*xiao* 孝) is justified on the ground that we were cared for by our parents when we were young. As Confucius says to his disciple in the *Analects* 17.21, he who questions the necessity of observing the mourning ritual for his deceased parents really neglects the fact that he was cared for by his parents when he was young. Hence, much like Held's care ethics, Confucianism with its emphasis on filial care as the basis for its highest excellence of *ren* 仁 cannot be said to neglect the work of care in unchosen private relationships or the relatedness of human existence. In sum, Confucian *ren* 仁 mirrors feminist care ethics in that it takes the work of care in private unchosen relationships as the core of our moral thinking.

But of course, critics of care ethics disagree with Held's definition, arguing instead that care ethics is not yet a *feminist* theory since it accentuates the stereotype of women as naturally caring and burdens women with caring labor. Claudia Card's (1990) rather harsh review of Noddings's *Caring* (1984), where the emphasis on care not only is insufficiently feminist, but more importantly perpetuates evil, is especially illuminating in this regard. Marilyn Friedman (1993) also argues that care ethics with its emphasis on performing care for others might do more harm than good to women by bolstering "some of the practices and conceptions that subordinate women."[7]

The common objections to care ethics can be summarized as follows: first, care ethics is silent on the moral imperative to care for oneself and to be reciprocally cared for by one's peers; second, care ethics is unable to deal with the issue of violence due to its emphasis on the caring relations regardless of the quality of the relations; third, care ethics neglects wider social, economic, and political institutions due to its emphasis on the mother-child dyadic relationship. Care ethicists, such as Held, are well aware of this sort of objection. For instance, Held seeks not to eliminate, but to incorporate other moral values, such as the value of justice, into her all-encompassing metaphor of moral tapestry where care ethics forms the wider framework. As Held writes, "[i]t is plausible to see caring relations as the wider and deeper context within which we seek justice and, in certain domains, give it priority."[8] It is with this inclusive spirit that I seek to incorporate Confucian *ren* 仁 into feminist care ethics' overarching moral tapestry to further strengthen its theoretical grounding.

As will be argued more fully later on, just as care ethics, Confucian *ren* 仁 begins its moral thinking from the dyadic relationship between parent and child in the private realm, but it doesn't stop there; the spiritual discipline of one's whole self must continue outward from the family, the community, to the state, and beyond. Confucian *ren* 仁 is both the familial excellence of filiality (*xiao* 孝) and the civil excellence of benevolent governance. *Ren* 仁 is a caring ideal but also a perfect excellence that encompasses all other particular excellences such as courage, wisdom, and righteousness, trust, etc. So a full range of human excellences along with filial care as the foundation of moral thinking and culminated in the wider realm of social, political, spiritual harmony in Confucianism is able to provide that moral imperative for women not only to care for themselves, but also to actualize their utmost potential in the realm of ethics as well as politics, and beyond.

Insofar as our exemplary, moral conduct is primarily expressed through ritualized, communal norms, the concept of *li* 禮 (ritual) is essential to the actualization of *ren* 仁. The incorporation of the concept of ritual into a feminist liberatory ethics might seem counter-intuitive, since a feminism (of any sort) to a large extent is suspicious of communal norms, especially those based on gender. And empirical gender norms in Confucian writings are by and large reflective of a patriarchal tradition. Yuan (2002), Star

(2002), and Noddings (2010) in their rejection of the compatibility between Confucianism and feminism certainly express such a sentiment.

Confucian ritual (*li* 禮), as it will be argued fully in later chapters, is not an impediment to genuine care; instead, ritual provides an internal mechanism to ensure a cohesive, harmonious society by making oneself ever more other-regarding and responsive to the needs of others, especially the social dependent. Confucian *li* 禮 that structures as well as informs the socially appropriate needs and expressions of care, as Kelly Epley (2015) argues, is indispensable to an effective care. In order to meet the needs of other, one must, first of all, learn to recognize the needs and, second, learn to render socially recognizably appropriate care. Since, as argued earlier in Chapter 1, one's sense of the self is tightly wrapped in one's cultural identity, one's needs are structured and informed by what is socially appropriate. Proficiency in ritual—the social grammar through which needs and caring labor are expressed—hence is the very first step to an effective care.

All in all, Confucian *ren* 仁 is not only compatible with care ethics, but also able to provide the kind of conceptual and practical grounding that care ethics needs to strengthen its theoretical foundation and to extend its applicability from the personal, to the social, the political, and beyond. This hybrid care ethics is at the same time Confucian and feminist, since it is a kind of normative ethics infused with Confucian *ren* 仁 that dictates an outward extension of care from the family to the world community, and it is a kind of feminism that seeks structural changes to foster a cooperative environment in which reciprocity and mutual trust characterize all human relationships in private as well as in public. A Confucian, contrary to what Star (2002) says, will not only care, but will care rather efficaciously without borders, as a feminist should.

Personal Autonomy vs. Filial Obligation

The actualization of Confucian *ren* 仁 must begin with *xiao* 孝, a form of familial caring labor, starting at home but continuing onto the social and the political realm intra- as well as inter-generationally. By integrating Confucian *xiao* 孝 into care ethics, the theoretical horizon of care ethics is strengthened and broadened as caring labor expands both horizontally and vertically. In the following we will take an in-depth study on Confucian *xiao* 孝 as the foundation of *ren* 仁. But before we get into the core of the argument, here is a bit of a divergence on the background that helped formulate the reasoning for me personally as well as academically.

As we sometimes do, when we commit to a project we procrastinate till the last minute, and as the deadline approached, I had a rather peculiar dilemma: Should I do everything humanly possible to complete the project that I have promised to do or should I care for my mother-in-law, who is now quite ill and requires daily assistance? The issue of elder care is no doubt an existential question all must ponder, especially for those of us with increasingly frail parents and demanding careers. But this is even more so for me not just personally, but academically. As you see, the subject that I intend to dissect is precisely the dilemma that I am facing: Why should I care?

In fact, according to the convention of liberal-individualism, no one is obliged to care for my mother-in-law, not her husband, not her two sons, let alone her two daughters-in-law. A quick glance at Anglo-European theories where the issue of familial care is by and large absent shows that familial care simply is not considered a "moral" issue worthy of rigorous scholarly attention. Part of the neglect is due to the purported conflict between familial obligation and the liberal principle of voluntarism and self-determination. Since familial relationships are involuntary and familial obligation cannot be rationally determined, it follows that there is no familial obligation at all. As Christian Sommers observed back in 1989:

> The contemporary philosopher is, on the whole, actively unsympathetic to the idea that we have *any* duties defined by relationships to which we have not voluntarily entered [....] Because the special relationships that constitute the family as a social arrangement are, in this sense, not voluntarily assumed, many moralists feel bound in principle to dismiss them altogether.[9]

One's familial obligation, if there is any at all, belongs to the realm of the personal, the subjective, and the sentimental, which in turn is outside the consideration of the rational and the ethical. So, according to this liberal convention, my relationship with my mother-in-law, that is derivative and involuntary, by itself doesn't give rise to any sort of special moral obligation. Indeed, according to Sommers, this liberal insistence on self-determination and voluntarism "undermines the network of mutual obligations that characterizes the family and its members."[10]

At best, one's familial obligation can only be subsumed under the model of voluntary, peer friendship as first proposed by Jane English (1979) where the extent of one's filial duty is determined solely by the strength and the duration of the friendship one has with one's parents. In the event of estrangement, the adult child, as English argues, has no obligation to care for his parents beyond his "general duty to help those in need."[11] In other words, one has no special duty to care for one's parents with whom one is no longer friendly, and the general duty to care for those in need applies equally to one's parents and strangers on the street. The familial tie that binds oneself to one's parents, at face value, renders no moral obligation at all. As English writes simply, in response to her own essay title—"What Do Grown Children Owe Their Parents?"—"I will contend that the answer is 'nothing.'"[12]

Nicholas Dixon's (1995) revival of English's friendship model continues to assert the voluntary aspect of familial obligation that rests solely on the strength of one's friendship with one's parents. The extent of one's obligation to one's parents is the same as to one's peer friends, both of which are determined by the strength of existing friendly relations. As Dixon writes, "[c]entral to the friendship model is the extent of filial obligation is determined by the extent of our friendly relations with our parents. Exactly the same holds in the case of peer friendships, where deeper friendships generate more extensive duties of friendship."[13] Simply put, one cares for one's parents voluntarily the same way as one cares for one's friends, but there exists no filial duty as such.

In the case of my mother-in-law, my care for her, under the voluntary friendship model, can only be justified based on the strength of our friendship. And if it so happens that there is no friendly relation existing between us, I am free to walk away. Or, worse yet, if the choice is between caring for my peer friend and caring for my mother-in-law, based on this friendship model my obligation to help must gravitate toward my peer friend. After all, few of us are our in-laws' BFF! This liberal friendship model, in fact, not only undermines the presumed mutual obligations of familial relationships, but furthermore makes a mockery of it by asserting the moral priority of caring for one's peer friends over one's family.

Beyond the friendship model, there is also the "special goods theory" that attempts to provide a different sort of justification for filial obligation while accommodating the liberal demands of voluntarism and self-determination. Simon Keller (2006), for instance, grounds our filial obligation to care for our parents on the unique position that we occupy to provide special goods to as well as to receive them from our parents. The sort of goods that our parents have provided us is incomparable to all others. The kind of care, love, and nurturance that our parents have bestowed on us are not just beneficial and indispensable to our growth and well-being, but more importantly, they are constitutive of our sense of the self. That we are who we are, by and large, is a function of the unique position that we occupy in the parent-child relation; our parents through the kind of care and support that they have bestowed on us shape the kind of person we are today.

Reciprocally, by virtue of our relationships with our parents, we are also in a unique position to provide the sort of care, assistance, and comfort that are incomparable to all others. When a child performs care, she is able to provide her parents the kind of healing and satisfaction that is often not possible when the care is performed by an equally competent stranger. The sort of special goods that a child is able to provide the parents with is integral to the parent-child relation and hence one has a reciprocal familial obligation to one's parents. But there are limits to this "special goods" model.

Keller sets up two restrictions on filial obligation, and if either condition obtains, our filial obligation to care for our parents ceases to exist. "First, the child's duties to provide special goods to the parent should not be such as seriously to impede the child's ability to live a good life."[14] The ability to make autonomous choices about the shape of one's own life, according to Keller, "is regarded in contemporary Western culture as being, a central component of the good life and a central entitlement of the individual."[15] In other words, the concern about living a good life for oneself trumps filial obligation. Second, not all children have a special obligation to care for their parents. Filial obligation depends on the following conditions: (a) whether the parents have proven to be undeserving; (b) whether there is a personality conflict; (c) whether one has a limited ability to provide special goods to the parents.[16] In short, our filial obligation in part must be earned by our parents, and in part is conditioned on our willingness and ability to deliver care to our parents. Once again, personal autonomy is the supreme value, against which all other values, including one's filial duty, must be ranked accordingly.

For Keller, as it is for English and Dixon, caring for one's family has no prima facie moral valence and is not integral to the development of one's moral sense. Just like the "friendship" model, this "special goods" model sees filial care as something extra that one might or might not choose to perform depending on one's concept of a good life. Living a good life for me should be my central concern, and my moral reasoning of what constitutes a good life rests on a detached, de-subjectivized viewpoint. Intimate, familial relationship by itself has no moral weight in my deliberation. So in the case of my mother-in-law, either there exists no special filial obligation for me to care for her, or the obligation is conditioned on whether she has "proven" herself to be worthy of my care, whether her personality has meshed well with mine, and whether I can find time to provide her care. Under this liberal purview, there is really no compelling moral reason for me to care.

As far as morality is concerned, one's family and strangers on the street have an equal weight in one's moral deliberation; one's affective attachment to one's family, in and of itself, simply has no moral pull over one's own person. In other words, my rational, noumenal self where moral deliberation takes place, as Kant insists, is completely unencumbered by my affective, phenomenal self. My contingent relationship with my mother-in-law, hence, does not oblige me in any special way to care for her in times of need, and my indifference to her needs in turn does not diminish my moral sense of the autonomous self.

Of course, my mother-in-law has a right to seek medical care, but no one is compelled, on the liberal-individualism ground where personal autonomy reigns supreme, to care for her beyond the care provided by the medical institution or hired personal assistance at home. The sons or the daughters-in-law need not be involved in caring for her. In fact, she has already had a number of falls and cuts because she was left alone to navigate through the challenges of mundane everyday living. So considering all this, what should one do? Do I leave her to die in a slow and self-destructive way since no one expects anything of me, or should I step in and make a case for Confucian *xiao* 孝?

My choice is clear: I choose to care. And my caring choice is not premised based on whether she has proven herself to be deserving, whether caring for her impedes my autonomy, or whether we do get along. Rather my caring choice rests on my understanding of what constitutes a moral self. I can honestly say that my eventual commitment to caring for my mother-in-law is, by and large, propelled by my understanding of Confucian *xiao* 孝, a moral vision that sees human interdependency as a strength in, and not a distraction from, human flourishing. It is my take that, echoing the words of Confucius in the *Analects* 1.2, *xiao* 孝 is the root from which humanity grows. Or, as said in the beginning chapter of *Xiaojing* 孝經 (*Book of Filiality*), *xiao* 孝 is the root of excellence and whence comes the birth of moral education (夫孝, 德之本也, 教之所由生也).[17] In other words, one's moral sense grows from one's genuine feelings and care for one's intimate relationships in the family.

It is worth noting that Confucian *xiao* 孝 is not a mere, contractual response to our parents' prior care of us, nor is it a proportional response to an existing friendly relationship between the adult child and her parents. Rather, the practice of *xiao* 孝 is grounded in something more fundamental: It is the necessary beginning of a moral personhood. Unlike the liberal-individualism model, morality for Confucius simply cannot bypass one's affective ties in the familial realm. Caring for the needs of the dependent in the personal realm is the beginning of one's moral thinking. Confucian *xiao* 孝 is the root, the beginning, of one's cultivation into the moral maturity of *ren* 仁. Caring for my mother-in-law, therefore, is constitutive of my sense of the self; it forms part of my life's journey to self-realization, not only in the realm of morality, but also in the realm of feminism.

A Confucian self, just as a care ethicist would suggest, cares naturally, starting with an attentive and productive response to the needs of one's loved ones. Confucian *xiao* 孝 captures the essence of a Confucian care at home: The young is raised by the old with affection and the old in turn leans on the young to move forward. A Confucian self, just as advocated by care ethicists, recognizes that vulnerability and interdependency characterize human existence. Hence, to productively meet the needs of others in the way we would want our own needs to be met constitutes the starting point of the moral self that owes its beginning to the care of others.

Xiao 孝 and Its Modern Revival

To talk about Confucian *xiao* 孝 to some, in this day and age, may seem quite antiquated. A quick survey of some popularized perceptions of Confucian *xiao* 孝 shows disdain and incomprehension. For instance, Bertrand Russell (1922), in his assessment of the problems of China in the early twentieth century, writes: "Filial piety, and the strength of the family generally, are perhaps the weakest point in Confucian ethics, the only point where the system departs seriously from common sense."[18] Russell considers the necessary reforms that China must undertake in order to face the impending challenges of modernization at the turn of the twentieth century, and concludes that Confucian ethics emphasizing family feeling and the authority of the old "make it a barrier to necessary reconstruction."[19]

The perception of Confucian *xiao* 孝 as morally perverted, obsolete, and fanatical continues to find its way into later scholarships. For instance, Walter Slote (1998), in his psychocultural analysis of the Confucian family, counts *xiao* 孝 "the principal instrument" through which Confucianism as a form of authoritarianism is established and maintained.[20] Donald Holzman (1998), in his textual survey of *xiao* 孝, calls it a "peculiar passion," a kind of "extreme devotion" to parents that is characteristic of China, and yet is unknown or very uncommon in the West.[21] Holzman then compares Chinese attitudes toward *xiao* 孝 with religious fanaticism in the West. As Holzman concludes from his observation of popular Chinese filial anecdotes:

> I believe the sometimes exaggerated and fanatical behavior we have seen in the anecdotes above show us that we are in the presence of the kind of fanaticism we are more familiar with in the West as associated with religion and, in particular, with the actions of Christian saints who attempt to show their absolute devotion to Christ and to God by performing acts of total self-abnegation and altruism, acts that are

often at least as shocking and or as repulsive as those performed by the
Chinese saintly sons and daughters [...] we have just seen.[22]

Chinese attitudes toward *xiao* 孝 in Holzman's estimation are as fanatical,
irrational, and extreme as those associated with a religious cult.

Similarly, Ranjoo Seodu Herr (2003) in her effort to assess the
compatibility between care ethics and Confucianism sees the constant
demand of Confucian *xiao* 孝 placed on the adult child as a rather bizarre
feature of Confucianism. As she writes, "[i]f we consult the *Analects* and the
Mencius, the central question with respect to intimate relationship is how to
express love and respect for one's *parents*. In contrast to the almost complete
silence with respect to parents' obligations toward children, the constant
demand for filial piety seems almost bizarre."[23] Just as is true for Russell and
Halzman, for Herr the Confucian emphasis on *xiao* 孝 on the ethical plane
seems inscrutable.

Lisa Raphals's (2004) reflection on the nature and nurture aspect of *xiao*
孝 in a rather comprehensive anthology on filiality, unfortunately, also
characterizes Confucian *xiao* 孝 as an archaic as well as a gendered mode
of cultural expression. Through her study of the Warring States and Han
texts, Raphals considers *xiao* 孝 "as a specifically Chinese emotion that is
gendered in very different ways for men and for women" and then offers
her speculative suggestion that Confucius and his disciples valorized *xiao*
孝 "as a very culturally specific variant of love, and considered it a natural
emotion. For men."[24] In other words, Confucian *xiao* 孝 is construed here as
a culturally gendered, yet natural, emotion for men. Raphals then proceeds to
compare *xiao* 孝 with medieval *accidie*, an archaic mode of religious emotion,
and asks rhetorically in the concluding sentence: "Is filiality, like *accidie*, an
emotion whose time has come and gone, artifact of a strongly hierarchical
Confucianism that is obsolete? Or can (and should) it be reconceived in ways
yet to be determined, and is it being done, as we speak here?"[25] In comparing
xiao 孝 with *accidie*, the answer to Raphals's own question is rather obvious:
Confucian *xiao* 孝—a culturally specific emotion for man—is as obsolete as
accidie.

All in all, *xiao* 孝 is conventionally seen as an archaic, fanatical cultural
expression of the Chinese that is morally irrelevant to modernity. Despite all
this, the effort to revive Confucian *xiao* 孝 is under way. For instance, Roger
Ames and Henry Rosemont's (2009) philosophical translation of *Xiaojing* 孝
經 (*Book of Filiality*) provides a starting point for the revitalization of *xiao*
孝; by studying Confucian *xiao* 孝 as a viable alternative to our own ethical
sensibilities, their hope is that a more inclusive, cross-cultural understanding
can emerge.[26] As a self-proclaimed feminist, I take a step further and make

the revitalization of Confucian *xiao* 孝 not only an ethical movement, but also a feminist one. Far from being an oppressive mode of cultural expression or inscrutable religious fanaticism, Confucian *xiao* 孝 with a blend of care ethics can provide an ethical guide for all to navigate the terrains of life where each and every one of us is intractably interwoven in the fabric of interdependency and vulnerability.

Life begins and ends in dependency, and hence any ethics that overlooks or minimizes the centrality of human interdependency that makes life possible in the first place will distort the existential experiences and therefore be inept in charting the actual contours of life's challenges. Care ethics, unlike other canonical ethical theories, takes the caring labor in the context of mother-child relationship seriously and thereby brings forth the ethical valence of caring for the needs of the dependent. Much like care ethics, Confucian *xiao* 孝 also recognizes the importance of caring for the dependent, but it takes caring a step further and extends that caring labor intergenerationally. *Xiao* 孝 is an intergenerational labor of love, or to borrow from Eva Kittay (1999, 2002), it is love's labor, that begins at home and culminates in the harmonious world of *datong* 大同 (great community), as the highest Confucian political and spiritual aspiration.

In contrast to the ethical traditions nested in liberal-individualism that often neglect and marginalize the issue of family care, caring for one's family has a central importance in the Chinese moral sense. As various historical studies have shown, the centrality of *xiao* 孝 in the Chinese moral sensibility predates the rise of Confucianism.[27] Indeed, *xiao* 孝 is a shared ethos in various textual traditions including *Daodejing*, *Zhuangzi*, and *Mozi*, not just Confucianism.[28] But the ethical importance of *xiao* 孝 in Confucianism is also indisputable. As it is said in the *Analects* 1.2, *xiao* 孝 and *ti* 弟 (deference) constitute the root of *ren* 仁, the ultimate state of virtuous living. Or, as said in both Chapter 9 of *Xiaojing* 孝經 (*Book of Filiality*) and the "Jianben 建本" chapter of *Shuoyuan* 說苑 (*Garden of Persuasions*), "[a]mong human practices, none is greater than *xiao* (人之行, 莫大於孝)." *Xiao* 孝, in short, not only is the starting point of Confucian *ren* 仁, but more broadly constitutes a uniquely Chinese moral sense, or what Holzman calls a "peculiar passion" of the Chinese.

Although the specific content of *xiao* 孝 varies throughout history, the general form of *xiao* 孝 as a concerted devotion to the welfare of one's family, nevertheless, remains constant.[29] One's devotion to *xiao* 孝 is premised based on the understanding that one owes one's existence to the care of one's parents and those who came before.[30] As shown in the *Analects* 17.21, one's genuine grief for the departed parents is a sensible response to the parental affection and care that one has once received when one was young. In this instance,

Confucius uses the vulnerability of the child in need of care as the starting point of our moral thinking. Confucian self takes the affective human attachments as a constitutive component of morality.

Echoing Confucius in seeing *xiao* 孝 as the root of one's moral education, Mencius also sees that to practice *xiao* 孝 is one's most basic moral duty. As shown in the *Mencius* 4A19, "[t]here are many duties one should discharge, but the fulfillment of one's duty towards one's parents is the most basic. There are many things one should watch over, but watching over one's character is the most basic."[31] Confucian *xiao* 孝 is practiced for the sake of cultivating the goodness of a moral self, and at the same time, one's moral self cannot simply bypass the realm of the personal for the sake of the realm of the disinterested and the universal. Morality is located in everyday life, and how to productively respond to the affective ties to which one's existential self is invariably attached is the beginning of Confucian moral living.

One's journey to moral cultivation must always begin with *xiao* 孝, which, among other things, involves genuine love and respect for one's family. To merely provide material comfort in accordance with social convention is not yet *xiao* 孝. As Confucius observes in the *Analects* 2.7, "[t]hose today who are filial are considered so because they are able to provide for their parents. But even dogs and horses are given that much care. If you do not respect your parents, what is the difference?" Laboring for one's parents fulfills only the form of *xiao* 孝 dictated by social convention, but the meaning of *xiao* 孝 hinges on one's genuine care and respect. As Confucius responds to Zixia's query on *xiao* 孝 in the *Analects* 2.8, "[i]t all lies in showing the proper countenance. As for the young contributing their energies when there is work to be done, and deferring to their elders when there is wine and food to be had—how can merely doing this be considered being filial?"

Being *xiao* 孝 is not the same as being obedient to parents' every command. When the parents go astray, Confucians recognize that remonstration is in order. To remonstrate against parents' morally questionable conduct is widely articulated as a necessary part of the practice of *xiao* 孝.[32] To be complicit in parents' unreasonable behavior, on the other hand, is seen as antithetical to *xiao* 孝. As recorded in the *Zuozhuan* 左傳 (*Zuo's Commentary*), a fourth-century BCE text that recounts the story of Duke Zhuang of Zheng (*c.* 722 BCE), Duke Zhuang was faulted for his constant pampering of his mother who later on became bold and incited a rebellion against the Duke. The unfortunate event of exiling the mother after the rebellion, according to all the commentators, is caused by Duke Zhuang's tolerance of the mother's unreasonable behavior in the first place, and hence he is at fault for being unfilial.[33] When parents' malevolent intent is known, one doesn't simply comply at the expense of one's well-being.

Furthermore, as recorded in the "Liuben 六本" chapter of *Kongzi jiayu* 孔子家語 (*The School Sayings of Confucius*), disciple Zengzi was scolded by Confucius for taking a severe beating from his violent father without protest. In short, in the face of violence and abuse, Confucian *xiao* 孝 would not require complicity or compliance.

The end of practicing *xiao* 孝 is to bring forth the moral goodness supposed in the parent-child relationship in which the parents are affectionate and the children filial. As shown in the *Mencius* 4A28 and 5A4, King Shun—the ultimate personification of *xiao* 孝—through his tireless filial persuasions is able to lead his wicked father to see the light of moral goodness embodied in the role of father and thereby helps shape the moral character of the son. *Xiao* 孝 not only substantiates the affective tie between parent and child, but also provides a moral rectitude in the familial relationship in which father fathers and son sons. As discussed in the *Analects* 12.11, having a rectified familial relationship in which father is affectionate and son filial is also indicative of a well-governed, effective state where the ruler rules and the minister ministers. The Confucian self is a moral self that expands outward through strengthening and rectifying those existential ties, from the familial, the social, to the political, and beyond.

Generally speaking, without anchoring one's self in one's existential, affective ties is to be without a sense of the self, since one's attachment is what gives substance, or what gives "weight" so to speak, to the self. The Kantian noumenal self that only thinks from the vantage point of the rational and the universal unattached to this phenomenal world of relations and affections is unrecognizable to any of us who are someone's mother, daughter, spouse, friend, or neighbor. Those affective ties are the fabric in our tapestry of life and the anchor of life itself. To discount those existential attachments is to flee into the realm of Kantian abstraction where the self is with neither sense nor substance. As Bernard Williams (1981) puts it in his famed "wife rescuing" scenario in which a rescuer deliberates impartially whether or not to save his wife over a stranger, this sort of moral deliberation is really "one thought too many."[34]

In the same way, to deliberate whether one has a filial obligation to one's parents is also one thought too many. One's affective attachment to another person is what gives life substance in the first place. And the parent-child attachment is one of the deepest attachments that one is able to experience. Perfect detachment and neutrality demanded by the Kantian impartial moral law hence can only have an imperfect hold on oneself. As Williams goes on to argue, one's affective attachments to others might run the risk of offending against impartial moral law; "yet unless such things exist, there will not be enough substance or conviction in a man's life to compel his allegiance to life itself."[35] Furthermore, "[l]ife has to have substance [...] but if it has substance, then it cannot grant supreme importance to the impartial system, and that system's hold on it will be, at the limit, insecure."[36]

Just as Kant observes in the realm of knowledge that thoughts without content are empty and intuitions without concepts are blind, one might say that affective attachments are what gives life its content and without which life is also empty. And when life is devoid of affective attachments, it also loses its hold on one's commitment to life itself. Rae Langton's (2000) piece on the correspondences between Kant and Maria von Herbert provides a rare glance at the sort of challenges possible to Kant's detached moral will on the existential level, demonstrating the inadequacy of impartial moral law's hold on one's self when one's affective ties are in tatters.

Maria von Herbert is a sister of Baron Franz Paul von Herbert and she is a keen Kantian reader seeking Kant's moral guidance on the permissibility of suicide during a time of personal desolation. In his initial response, Kant advises Herbert to follow the universal moral law of truth telling without taking into account the consequential impact on her friendship with her male suitor from whom she has concealed a previous, intimate relationship. Once the truth was discovered, the male suitor lost interest in Herbert and she was left living in a state devoid of passions, contemplating suicide. Kant insists that the loss of affective ties should not impede one's ability to act morally, since the moral will demands a complete detachment from inclinations. To Kant, it is not only that one's moral will must be made in the absence of corresponding inclinations such as sympathy, but more so that one must follow the moral law with a sense of "moral apathy" which Kant describes as a state of divine bliss, a state of "completely independence from inclinations and desires."[37]

But as a keen reader of Kant, Herbert in fact finds following the moral law too easy in a life without passions, since moral imperatives are obeyed by default. Without the presence of passions, Herbert sees no point in living. She then proceeds to ask what sort of life Kant leads: "I would like to know what kind of life your philosophy has led you to—whether it never seemed to you to be worth the bother to marry, or to give your whole heart to anyone, or to reproduce your likeness."[38] Kant's indifference to the pursuit of familial, affective ties is a puzzle to Herbert who now finds life without passions empty of content and her commitment to life itself consequently slipping. Kant, after classifying Herbert's condition as feminine hysteria over romantic love, didn't respond to the query further, and Herbert then committed suicide. It is clear that, to Kant, affective ties are not only morally irrelevant, but an impediment to morality. Yet without affective ties to anchor one's sense of the self, one also loses conviction in life itself. Unlike

Kant, Confucius understands the importance of human relations, and to substantiate familial, affective ties with moral rectitude is what makes life worth living in the first instance.

Xiao 孝—that is, building and maintaining the affective tie between parent-child first and foremost—is the beginning of morality, but Confucian ethics does not stop at the door of one's household. Just as is true of care ethics, Confucian ethics also aims at providing a normative ethics beyond the personal. A hybrid Confucian care will extend the moral demands of familial care to wider social and political relations. Confucian moral cultivation, although it begins at home, must extend outward to encompass both familial and non-familial relations as indicated in the Confucian five core relations: Father-son (familial), ruler-minister (political), husband-wife (spousal), older-younger (communal), friends (social). The Confucian self is a moral self that grows ever more inclusively in the web of human relationships both familial and non-familial. Unlike its transcendental Kantian counterpart where the self is defined by its rationality in the noumenal world, the Confucian self is decisively an existential one whose moral perfection is achieved only through one's continuously productive responses to the needs of one's affective ties in this human-all-too-human phenomenal world.

Ren 仁 and Inter-subjective Care

The interrelationality of the Confucian self is clearly demonstrated by its interchangeability with the concept of *ren* 仁, perfect humanity. As stated in the *Mencius* 7B16 and both Chapters 20 and 25 of *Zhongyong* 中庸 (*Centrality and Commonality*), "*ren* 仁 means person" and "to realize oneself is *ren* 仁."[39] *Ren* 仁, the most prominent Confucian concept, etymologically is composed of the character person (*ren** 人) and numerical two (*er* 二), denoting the ethical effort in sustaining and expanding complex human relations in achieving the perfect virtue of *ren* 仁.[40] To be *ren* 仁, at the most basic level, is to have compassionate feelings toward others. As recorded in the *Analects* 12.22, Confucius responds to the query on the meaning of *ren* 仁 by saying simply: "Love others." Or, as said in the *Mencius* 4B28: "The person of *ren* 仁 loves others." Generally speaking, cultivating affective ties constitutes the practice of *ren* 仁, and the virtue of *xiao* 孝 that displays one's genuine care for one's familial ties is the starting point of one's moral cultivation.

Xiao 孝 is only the starting point, not the end point of *ren* 仁. *Ren* 仁 as an inclusive sense of perfect humanity encompasses all particular excellences that govern human relations such as *qin* 親 (affection) in the parent-child relation, *xin* 信 (trustworthiness) in friendship, *yi* 義 (righteousness) in ruler-subject relation, and *bie* 別 (distinction) in spousal relation. Unlike the Kantian supreme moral law that can only be deliberated by a rational will unattached to the phenomenal world of relations and affections with moral apathy, Confucian *ren* 仁 must be realized through the expansion of the web of human relations in which one is intractably embedded. A self structured by the Kantian principles of personal autonomy and de-subjectivized rationality is a self that is unattached to anyone, depends on no one, and is not morally obliged to reciprocate care in the most basic, intimate parent-child relation. By contrast, a Confucian self not only recognizes the inevitability of dependency and vulnerability of human existence, but also is morally obliged to extend its sphere of caring concerns from the personal, the social, to the political, and beyond.

In a contextualized personhood, the substance of one's self is necessarily and essentially dependent on the extent of the existential relationships that one is able to sustain qualitatively and quantitatively with moral rectitude. Taking care of others, especially those social dependent and vulnerable ones, is seen as a strength, not a distraction from human flourishing. The well-being of others is intrinsically intertwined with one's own, and hence the journey into one's moral education must be made inter-subjectively. As said precisely in the *Analects* 6.30: "*Ren* 仁 persons in seeking to establish themselves establish others, in seeking to promote themselves promote others." It is only through one's caring labor inter-subjectively that one is able to realize moral maturity within.

Confucian ethics is not a familial ethics; neither is care ethics. Care ethics infused with Confucian *ren* 仁 seeks comprehensive care for all by, on the one hand, expanding one's sphere of concern motivated by one's recognition of the interdependency and vulnerability of human existence, and, on the other, expanding the social and political capacity to care for all. This expanded care is clearly delineated in the celebrated Confucian ideal society of *datong* 大同 where political authority is measured by its capacity to care for the dependent and vulnerable (the concept of *datong* will be fully elaborated in later chapters).

Confucian expanded care resonates well with Kittay's (1999, 2002) triadic concept of "*doulia*" where society must assume commitment to preserve the well-being of the relation between the caregiver and the cared-for. "*Doulia*," derived from Greek meaning slave or servant, is repurposed by Kittay to denote "a caregiver who cares for those who care for others."[41] The principle of *doulia* recognizes the importance of the preservation of a caring relationship between the cared-for and the care-giver, and hence it demands that the public provides a condition in which the care-giver can give and thrive at the same time. Sustaining the caring relationship must also be a public responsibility. The cared-for, care-giver, and a public commitment to care for the care-giver form the triadic concept of *doulia*. For both care ethics and Confucian ethics, maintaining caring relations is seen as a moral good for both the interdependent self and society at large; the caring labor performed at home must be aided by the communal, social, and political support, so that the care-giver and the cared-for can both thrive. The greatness of society is then measured by the sort of commitment it makes to sustain that caring network to care for the vulnerable at home and beyond.

The centrality of family—as Ames and Rosemont (2009) in their translation of *Xiaojing* point out—permeates all areas of Chinese history including the socio-political, economic, metaphysical, moral, and religious.[42] Family, however, does not need to be defined biologically or by marital relations solely, since, as said in the *Analects* 12.5, by deferring to others with the same familial sense of moral rectitude, within four seas all are one's brothers (四海之內, 皆兄弟也). For Confucianism, family is an inclusive metaphor that exerts moral pull on oneself to incorporate distant others into the intimate circle of mutual trust and care first by direct interaction and then by moral extension through sympathy.

Confucian ethics emphasizes the moral nature of the human heart in its encounter with or in its anticipation of human suffering as seen in the famed example of seeing a child about to fall into a well discussed in the *Mencius* 2A6 and 3A5. In the same way, care ethics also emphasizes the imperative to care extending from the understanding that infants' survival depends on our willingness to respond to their needs. Life like ours begins as a vulnerable dependent. As Held puts it, we all start out as "human children" or as Kittay writes, "we are all some mother's child."[43] Confucian care sees caring for others as a spontaneous act of the moral heart that internalizes the needs of the dependent and vulnerable others, and hence can respond to it with utmost sincerity.

In order to broaden the scope of one's caring concerns, all human relationships in Confucian care are viewed as only different in degree, but not in kind. As is evident in all five Confucian social relations, all relationships are characterized by reciprocity and mutuality including the parent-child relation (parental care will be discussed fully in later chapters). Confucian care views human relations as a continuum with strangers on the one end and intimate loved ones on the other. The difference between strangers and family is only one of degree, since strangers have a potential to be made intimate through marriage or friendship, for instance. The ultimate moral aim for Confucian care is to incorporate others into one's inclusive metaphor of family where *xiao* 孝 in the non-voluntary familial relationship is the moral origin for all voluntary relationships. Once again, as said both in the *Analects* 1.2 and 1.6 and Chapter 1 of *Xiaojing* 孝經, Confucius takes *xiao* 孝 as the root of all moral excellences and urges his disciples not only to be filial at home, deferential in the community, but also to be trustworthy in one's words and "love the multitude broadly." Confucian care is extensive in its scope and at the same time is solidly grounded in the intimate relationships at home.

For the Confucian, extending the love and respect that one has for one's family outward is not just a good moral guide in one's private life; rather, it is the key to good state governance. As said in the *Mencius* 1A7, "[t]reat the aged of your own family in a manner befitting their venerable age and extend this treatment to the aged of other families; treat your own young in manner befitting their tender age and extend this to the young of other families, and you can roll the Empire on your palm." Likewise, as said in the *Mencius* 7A15, "[l]oving one's parents is *ren* 仁, respecting one's elders is *yi* 義. What is left to be done is simply the extension of these to the whole Empire." In short, the moral as well as political challenges, for the Confucian, are to find ways to extend one's familial care and affection outward, so as to seamlessly expand the scope of one's caring concerns in the web of human relations.

The point is that strangers are not completely outside the purview of one's moral compass for Confucian care. Instead, precisely because strangers are defined by a lack of intimate relationship with oneself, the Confucian self that grows in the web of human relations seeks to extend intimacy to strangers so as to transition strangers to acquaintance, to friends, and ultimately to family. Our colloquial expression that refers to our best friends as our family is indicative of the permeability of the boundary between the familial and the non-familial as well as the centrality of family in our conception of the most endearing and intimate attachment that one can possibly experience existentially.

Caring Labor and Gender Rectification

In its intersection with feminism, Confucianism will have to rectify its gender-based roles, since feminism as a whole aims at abolishing gender-based oppression. The spousal relationship, as one of the five cardinal social relations, governed by the concept of *bie* 別—the gender-based division of labor—will have to give way to a genuine sense of cooperation based on mutually beneficial task sharing that enhances both partners' long-term capacities instead of diminishing them. Feminism brings gender into a laser focus in any intercultural dialogue, and the way a "woman" is fashioned into a gendered being often significantly limits her practical abilities to experience the world, to share in cultural capitals, and to fully thrive and flourish beyond the dictates of gender roles. Care ethics, in particular, sheds light on the importance of caring labor, but also the disproportionate amount of burden that women shoulder in caring for others at home as well as in the work place. Confucian ethics, if it is to be relevant to women, will have to come to terms with that.

As mentioned earlier, Kittay's triadic concept of *doulia* is helpful here to alleviate the burden placed on women by making caring for the caregiver a societal commitment. The Confucian's contribution of *xiao* 孝 further normalizes the existential facts of interdependency and vulnerability in human existence, acknowledging that the young is cared for by the old who in turn leans on the young to move forward. But none of these caring tasks should be gender specific; that is to say, women should not be the only ones who care for the young, the old, the sick, and the disabled, while men are free to choose whether or not to care. There has to be a better solution, and both Confucian ethics and care ethics must go beyond the emphasis on the importance of caring for others by dealing directly with the inequity between men and women in performing actual caring labor.

To urge women to abandon their caring tasks, however, is not the solution. As Kittay who has a disabled child writes passionately:

> Someone must care for dependents. If men do not take up the role, women will not simply abandon it. Feminists may persuade women that liberation and equality demands refusing nonreciprocated affective labor directed at fully functioning adults [....] But no feminist movement would, could, or should urge women to neglect the needs of their dependent children, or those of their disabled, ill, or ailing family members and friends.[44]

No ethical theory, feminist or otherwise, should advocate voluntary abandonment of meeting the caring needs of the vulnerable simply because equally capable others will not take up the task. Like care ethics, Confucian *xiao* 孝 is a life-long commitment that one has toward one's family, both living and dead. To advocate for a voluntary abandonment of one's filial obligation is equally unthinkable for the Confucian. Confucian *xiao* 孝 is an intergenerational labor of love, or as Kittay reflects on her care for her chronically dependent daughter, it is love's labor. And no one should walk away from that. Life is based on mutual, cooperative assistance starting at home. Men no less than women should cultivate that sense of care for the young, the old, the sick, and the disabled starting at home and beyond.

The difficulty, however, lies in how to effect an equitable share of caring value in both men and women. As Kittay writes, "[i]t seems to me that the difficulty is, first, to cultivate in men a sense of care as deep and extensive as we find today in women [...] and second, to join the sense of care with the sense of justice."[45] Leaving aside the issue of whether Kittay genderizes care and justice, the inequity between men and women in performing actual caring labor is a practical problem. On what ground, can men be mandated to be caring, or be "urged" into performing caring labor?

Just as in most traditions, Confucian tradition also relies on women to perform most caring labor. As delineated in the "Neize 內則" chapter of *Liji* 禮記 (*Book of Rites*) regarding the two different sets of educational curricula, boys are to receive both extensive literary and ritual education while girls are instructed on domestic skills and household management.[46] Similarly, as said in the *Mencius* 7A22, the caring labor to keep the aged fed and warmly clothed on a daily basis falls on women. This sort of gender-based roles is the beginning of the inequity of caring labor. And nothing is more pronounced than the caring labor performed by mothers and wives. As stated earlier, gender-based division of labor in the spousal relationship will have to give way to a genuine sense of cooperation that mutually benefits both partners in enhancing their long-term capacities instead of diminishing them. In my estimation, spousal relationship will have to give way to moral friendship in order to address the problem of inequity in caring labor. Gender-based division of labor will have no role to play in spousal friendship, since a shared sense of moral goodness is its only *raison d'etre* (the spousal friendship model will be fully argued in following chapters).

One cannot walk away from caring for the vulnerable, but one can definitely demand help from other equally capable adults to contribute to the growth of a productive web of human relationships. The Confucian concept of ritual (*li* 禮)can definitely play an effective role in "urging" free riders to do their fair share by instilling a much more porous sense of the self that is receptive to the needs of others (the effectiveness of *li* 禮 will be fully argued in later chapters). And if all things fail, the less effective means of laws and social policies can then serve as the last corrective measure for a short-term gain. As Confucius says in the *Analects* 2.3 in regard to effective governance, "[l]ead the people with administrative injunction (*zheng* 政) and keep them orderly with penal law (*xing* 刑), and they will avoid punishments but will be without a sense of shame. Lead them with excellence (*de* 德) and keep them orderly through observing ritual propriety (*li* 禮) and they will develop a sense of shame, and moreover, will order themselves."

In other words, Kittay's *doulia* that mandates social policies to care for the caregiver is only part of the solution. To form a culture of care should be the main task at hand, a culture where to care for the dependent and to be cared for as the circumstances demand is no longer seen as contrary to one's wholesome self. To cultivate a sense of Confucian *xiao* 孝 as an intergenerational dependency and care at home should first be the starting point. By embodying Confucian *xiao* 孝 intergenerationally, one is thus fashioned into a caring being responsive to the needs of the vulnerable starting with one's loved ones at home.

Conclusion

In the end, caring for my mother-in-law is as much about meeting her needs as it is about meeting my moral self, face to face. As Kittay so powerfully observes, no feminist movement would, could, or should urge women to voluntarily abandon the needy. I, too, will not walk away. Learning from Confucian *xiao* 孝, I understand that intergenerational dependency is an existential given. The asymmetry of dependency between my mother-in-law and I is not the sole determinant of the extent of my caring labor, since I, too, stand in asymmetry with my own now already departed parents for whom I can no longer care to reciprocate all the goods that have been bestowed on me. In a real sense, I can only pay it forward. And in a broader sense, we all are recipients of all the social goods that we have enjoyed thus far.

The quintessential image of Confucian *xiao* 孝 as the old leans on the young to move forward crystalizes the centrality of intergenerational dependency in the making of one's moral self that perpetually stands in asymmetry with those who cares for oneself and whom one cares for. Paying it forward intergenerationally, as dictated by Confucian *xiao* 孝, seems not only fair and reasonable, but moral as well. And through my caring labor, I see my own feminist self in the making.

3

Marriage and Perfect Friendship

Marriage, along with the roles of wife and mother, has long been a subject of considerable discussion within the feminist communities with some advocating for a "philosophy of evacuation," or a complete abolition of the legal institution, which to many is the root of female servitude and her continuous affliction. Women's subjection in the institution of marriage is well documented. Well into the mid-nineteenth century after the abolition of legal slavery on both sides of the Atlantic Ocean, women by law were still subject to their husband's authority. As John Stuart Mill impassionedly writes in *The Subjection of Women* (1869), "[m]arriage is the only actual bondage known to our law. There remain no legal slaves, except the mistress of every house."[1]

Not every wife was abused by her husband, but when abuse did take place, there was no legal recourse for the wife. The infamous English common law—"rule of thumb"—that sanctioned wife-beating as long as the switch is no larger than a man's thumb practiced well into the nineteenth century on both sides of the Atlantic Ocean is a case in point.[2] Even when such outdated law is no longer on the books, domestic violence against women continues to be treated as a lesser form of civil offense. As late as 2015, the then rising NFL star, Ray Rice, received only a fine of $125 and an anger management counseling with the criminal charges dropped afterwards for knocking his then fiancée unconscious.[3] One could only imagine such a leniency would be unthinkable if the assault were to take place between strangers.

Legal leniency also applies to marital rape; no husband was convicted for raping his wife in the United States until 1979, and not until 1993, did all fifty states criminalize marital rape, albeit with ample legal loopholes still standing in various states as late as 2019. Prior to the criminalization of marital rape, a seventeenth-century English court opinion was commonly cited to support marital exemptions that a husband could not be guilty for raping his wife, since it was understood that "by their mutual matrimonial consent and contract the wife hath given up herself in this kind unto her husband, which she cannot retract."[4] In other words, a woman, by consenting to a marriage, has been seen by the law as relinquishing her rights as a person; she becomes an appendage to her husband subject to his will and authority in all matters including sexual access in whatever form that might be. It is no wonder why the institution of marriage practiced thus far has been a site of considerable contentions among feminists.

Love, that now is synonymous with marriage, is indeed a relatively modern phenomenon. Marriage for women in the long history of humanity was primarily an economic necessity. With no legal representation, no property rights, and no access to meaningful educational and employment opportunities, women had no place to turn to but marriage for basic survival. Or, as J. S. Mill puts it, marriage for women as late as the mid-nineteenth-century England was still very much a "Hobson's choice"—that is, "that or none."[5] Women married primarily for financial security and social standing, and men in return were promised of sexual access, offspring, and household management. This sort of *quid pro quo* was written into civil and religious laws, and was tacitly understood well into the 1950s. Partnership in this marital transaction however is not one between two social equals. The supposed marital unity that is so beautifully articulated in the wedding vows used in the 1552 Church of England Prayer Book—and is still in use today in many wedding services—has always been achieved at the expense of the wife. After all, in the original vows, the wife promises to obey and to serve in addition to love and to cherish the husband.[6]

As late as 1971, the superiority of the husband was still codified in Georgia's State Marriage Law: "[T]he husband is the head of the family and the wife is subject to him; her legal civil existence is merged in the husband, except so far as the law recognizes her separately, either for her own protection, or for her benefit."[7] The required marital subordination, no doubt, is rooted in the long-standing belief that woman by nature is inferior and in need of male protection and guardianship. From the Biblical command to the long history of philosophy, female subordination in marriage in exchange for protection and financial support has been seen not only as factual, but also good for women. As in the order of nature where the body should be subject to the rule of the mind, woman should be subject to the rule of man, and by submitting to the rule of the superior, the unity aiming at the common good is thereby achieved. In other words, marital subordination is seen not just as a practical outcome of the social conditions where women were barred nearly from doing anything else, but indeed as the order of nature good for both genders.

Even with all the political, legal, and social gains in recent history, women continue to suffer at the hand of the marriage institution. The uphill battles that women have to fight are paramount and are further compounded by the duty of child-rearing and household management. Numerous sociological studies—ranging from Arlie Hochschild's *The Second Shift*

(1989), Ann Crittenden's *The Price of Motherhood* (2001/2010), to Sheryl Sandberg's *Lean In* (2013)—illustrate the difficulties of combining work and family even for highly educated, successful, and wealthy women. The roles of wife and mother continue to define the essence of female identity and hence the burdens of child care and household management continue to hamper women's achievement. The social sentiment that a woman's first call of duty is the household regardless of what else that she might also choose to do explains the persistent achievement gap between genders. Now more women than men are in college and about half of the medical as well as law degrees are awarded to women; yet women only account for 38 percent of the lawyers and 36 percent of the medical doctors, not to mention that only around 10 percent of the CEOs in the Fortune 500 are women in 2023![8]

Even though nowadays women represent a slight majority of the workforce, overwhelmingly positions of power and wealth are still very much held by men. The root cause of this persistent absence of women in the leadership positions, in part, has to do with the household duty including child-care. A 2004 report where only 38 percent of women graduating from Harvard Business school remain in the workforce full-time in their child-rearing years and only 15 percent of the high power married couples surveyed have the wife remained in the full-time workforce. Ten years later in a 2014 report from *Harvard Business Review*, it shows that the traditional expectation of child-rearing as women's primary responsibility persists even among Harvard alumni, among whom around "28% of Gen X and 44% of Baby Boom women had at some point taken a break of more than six months to care for children, compared with only 2% of men across those two generations."[9] These surveys of Harvard alumni from whom the next generation of leaders oftentimes emerge offer a glimpse into the root cause of highly educated, capable women going off track from the leadership positions. Ann-Marie Slaughter's (2012) public confession in "Why Women Still Can't Have It All" detailing her struggle in combining her leadership position in the State Department and her family life says it all. Yet, this sort of public confession is rarely seen, if any at all, from men of power and wealth.

Combining family and career has always been a precariously balancing act for women, even at the best of times. The devastation brought by the Covid-19 pandemic—with the school and daycare centers closing and with the increased household chores of having all the family members constantly at home—had a disproportionate impact on women, and the result was a mass exodus of women from the workforce, four times higher than men during the height of the Covid-19 pandemic.[10] It is clear that women today continue to be on the receiving end of the cost of marriage and parenthood. The sacrifice that is required of women in the roles of wife and mother is undeniable.

So given all these, is it still possible, or even worthwhile, for feminists to rehabilitate the institution of marriage? Or, as Jeffner Allen (1984), Susan Okin (1989), and Claudia Card (1996, 2002, 2007) argue, the best course of action for feminists is to recognize that motherhood and marriage are by nature oppressive to women and should be left behind as remnants of the patriarchal past. If Allen's pronouncement of motherhood as the death of women and Card's advocacy of the abolition of marriage institution seem extreme as well as impractical—given that far from being abolished the marriage institution with the US Supreme Court's historic ruling in *Obergefell v. Hodges* (2015) is now further expanded to same-sex couples in all fifty states—what then would be a more productive way for feminists to reconceptualize the institution of marriage and the spousal relationship? For sure, no one should be compelled to enter the marriage institution and the marital relationship is not the only enduring, intimate relationship available to us. But if one so chooses to enter the marriage institution, how then should a feminist response be, beyond rejection and condemnation? In short, how should feminists reconceptualize the internal good of marriage?

Fuzzy Love and Absolute Equality

In the US Supreme Court's historic ruling *Obergefell v. Hodges* (2015) on the constitutionality of same-sex marriage, the meaning of marriage is sublimely contemplated in the majority opinion where marriage as one of the oldest institutions is seen as the embodiment of the transcendent ideals of "love, fidelity, devotion, sacrifice and family," and "[i]n forming a marital union, two people become something greater than once they were." It is these transcendent appeals that same-sex couples seek for themselves as well, and hence marriage should also be accessible to those consenting adults regardless of their sexual preference. According to the US Supreme Court, the choice regarding whether or whom to marry is one of the most intimate decisions that one can make and is entailed in the concept of individual dignity and autonomy. The intimate association in marriage is unlike any other in that it allows two individuals to form a supposedly insoluble bond through which new freedoms are found. As the majority of the US Supreme Court opines in its historic ruling *Obergefell v. Hodges* (2015), "[t]he nature of marriage is that, through its enduring bond, two persons together can find other freedoms, such as expression, intimacy, and spirituality." In other words, these new forms of freedom are unique goods of marriage in which both spouses are mutually defined by their intertwining, everlasting marital bond.

There is no doubt that this is what marriage should be, but as numerous sociological studies have shown, in marriage women are still the ones making a disproportionate amount of devotion to their family, and as a result, their personhood less valued and their human capacities less flourished than once they were before marriage. Although the doctrine of coverture codified in the State Marriage Laws till 1971 treating marriage as a singular legal entity represented by the husband is no longer legally binding, the husbandly primacy remains as a social practice, since married women are still struggling to realize the mutually enhancing transcendent ideals promised in marriage. It is more often than not that the wife is the one who is merged into the husband to form a singular marital union: Her personhood is now mediated by the husband's and his pursuit and aspiration supersede hers.

Love, as recognized by the US Supreme Court as one of the many transcendent ideals promised in marriage, for many is the defining feature of marriage. After all, in their push for equal rights, activists for same-sex marriage positioned the social movement as a quest for equal love. However a marriage built based on love, while essential, doesn't quite offer a clear conceptual tool for us to navigate through the difficulties women encounter in the roles of wife and mother. Oftentimes, love is used as an all-encompassing blanket response to the disproportionate devotion and sacrifice that women are expected to offer in marriage. It is only with women's willing self-sacrifice, men are able to move ahead, continuing to occupy nearly all positions with substantial economic, social, and political consequences while at the time enjoying their family life seen as a private retreat from their public pursuits.

As the saying goes, "behind every great man, there stands a woman." Women continue to stay behind so that men can move ahead. Take the Obama first family as an example: Both Obamas graduated with a law degree from Harvard and both practiced law in the same firm prior to marriage; yet, one is elected to occupy the most powerful position on earth and the other continues to play the same auxiliary role that women are expected to play for eons. This example illustrates the disproportionate pull of the household duty on women of all colors, classes, and educational levels. Indeed, feminists are in a dire need for practical conceptual tools that enable women to enter the marriage institution while continuing to have their personhood valued and human capacities flourished in the fullest sense possible, so that spouses may become something greater than once they were prior to marriage. Love should be part of the reason that women flourish, not a shield for men to deflect the feminist demands for gender equity.

In marriage, just as with everything in life, one can expect compromise, adjustment, and reorientation in goals and values, but how much sacrifice in the name of love is acceptable and reasonable that one should render in marriage to another capable consenting adult with whom one is supposed to unite into one everlasting soul? Traditionally, marital unity is built based on the required subordination of the wife to the husband, and thus marital unity amounts to a unity of the husband unto himself; his aspiration becomes hers and his life achievement is premised based on her willing sacrifice to stay behind. Now that the wife's natural inferiority is no longer accepted, how then should feminists reconceptualize the supposedly everlasting marital relationship?

Equality is usually what is stressed by feminists such as Susan Okin (1989) and Alix Kates Shulman (1993), but how far should we take the numerical equality as a measuring stick for fairness in marriage without degrading it into a purely contractual agreement? If a perfect 50/50 split is the goal in marriage, then it is hard to see how that marital unity can hold when it falls short of that demand. It is also difficult to conceptualize how an everlasting unity is achieved when a clear 50/50 split is its goal, that is, how do two individuals form one everlasting unity when an equal split forms the basis of that relationship?

The transcendent nature of marriage so sublimely articulated by the Court in *Obergefell v. Hodges* (2015), where a marriage is said to "allow two people to find a life that could not be found alone, for a marriage becomes greater than just the two persons," clearly would be impossible conceptually, if two people continue to be distinctly 50/50 in every aspect of marriage. The feminist demand for absolute equality hence not only is conceptually at odd with the supposedly transcendent nature of marriage, but practically becomes an all-or-nothing approach, an impossible goal to achieve for most of us mortals. Inevitably a sense of resentment and failure arises. When that absolute equality fails to obtain, women once again are forced to accept that either in marriage women are auxiliary to men, or no marriage is worth our while. A reconceptualization of marriage beyond fuzzy love and absolute equality is clearly needed.

Companionate Marriage and Perfect Friendship

In the next chapter, we are to explore the possibility of using a hybrid concept of friendship incorporating both Greek *philia* and Confucian *you* 友 to reconceptualize modern spousal relationship and thereby rehabilitate the institution of marriage to enable women to live a fully flourishing life while sidestepping the pitfalls of absolute equality and fuzzy love. But first we begin with the concept of "perfect friendship," the most intimate and highly praised relationship between male peers, as traditionally conceived, in the history of Western philosophy. In many ways, the union of modern marriage, a perfect medium through which two people are made intimate by forming a supposedly insoluble bond, resembles the union in perfect friendship. And yet, for the most part in the history of Western philosophy, only men are seen as capable of forming this sort of eternal relationship and consequently making marital relationship an inferior form of intimate relationship.

In order to remedy the exclusion of women along with marital relationship from the much cherished form of friendship—perfect friendship—we need to not only undo the assumed inferiority of women and the traditionally functional, contractual nature of marriage, but also make room for eroticism in perfect friendship. As it will become clear through the following conceptual evolution of friendship from Plato to Kant, this hybrid feminist marital friendship is not so much a new invention as it is a return to the once forgotten tradition of friendship where *eros* forms part of *philia*.

However, friendship between the sexes was, in fact, socially unacceptable prior to the nineteenth century. In the vast majority of human history, marriage is the only socially acceptable context for unrelated adult men and women to associate with one another, and marital relationship for the most part is conceptualized as a contractual, functionary, sexual relationship for child-bearing and household management. In other words, marriage is between two social unequals with defined functional utilities where the wife serves and the husband provides. Friendship didn't enter the social lexicon of marital relationship until the emergence of "companionate marriage" in the seventeenth century. A wife, for the most part, was acquired for the sake of propagation, not friendship. And perfect friendship, as theorized in the long history of Western philosophy as the highest form of intimate relationship, was out of reach of women.

The social evolution of friendship between the sexes, according to William Deresiewicz (2007), goes as such: Friendship between the sexes in ancient times was virtually non-existent; during the Middle Ages it was confined to the spiritual communities and was rare in the post-Renaissance literary world; then began in the nineteenth-century men and women learned to be friends in marriage. That marital friendship was later extended to pre-marital sexual relationship as in "boyfriend" and "girlfriend" (terms established in the 1920s) and then further extended to non-sexual relationship between the sexes.[11] However, marital friendship in the so-called "companionate marriage" emerged in the seventeenth century—emphasizing affection, intimacy, and companionship—is far from being a relationship between two equals. In companionate marriage of the old, a married woman not only manages the household duties as she should, but also must become a worthy companion to her husband, as an added value for the husband; husbandly superiority and wifely subjection remain squarely intact. That is to say, even though the wife and husband might begin to refer to each other as "friends," this newly introduced "friendship" was not meant to challenge or replace the long-standing husbandly authority and primacy. Clearly, this is not the kind of reciprocal perfect friendship that is long celebrated in the history of Western philosophy.

Mary Wollstonecraft in *A Vindication of the Rights of Woman* (1792) is the first one in the Anglo-European tradition to write about equal marital friendship in that the wife should strive to be the friend, not the servant to the husband. As she writes, "the woman who strengthens her body and exercises her mind will, by managing her family and practicing various virtues, become the friend, and not the humble dependent of her husband."[12] In order to be worthy of friendship with men, women must then be allowed to develop their rational faculty and virtues and be recognized as rational beings. The marital bond, for Wollstonecraft, must become a relationship between two equals. However as seen above, even in her advocacy for equal marital friendship, Wollstonecraft continues to see household duties as the natural domain of women.

This is also true for J. S. Mill, who impassionedly condemns women's subjugation in marriage and advocates for what he calls "reciprocal superiority" in equal marriage.[13] And yet, at the same time he also affirms that household management should be a married woman's first call of duty regardless what else she also chooses to. As Mill writes, "when a woman marries, it may in general be understood that she makes choice of the management of a household, and the bringing up of a family, as the first call upon her exertions [...] and that she renounces [...] all which are not consistent with the requirements of this."[14]

Whether the wife and the husband are conceptualized as equals or not, household duty continues to be the wife's first call of duty. This was true even for strong women's rights advocates such as Wollstonecraft in the late eighteenth century and Mill in the mid-nineteenth century, and is unfortunately still true today, given the disproportionate pull of household management and child-rearing duties on women from the working class to the materially well-endowed. As shown earlier, women's mass exodus from the workforce—four times higher than men—during the height of the Covid-19 pandemic is a clear case in point. Marital friendship described thus far obviously falls way short of both the feminist insistence on gender equity and the long-cherished philosophical concept of perfect friendship.

A History of Friendship: From Plato to Kant

The concept of "perfect friendship," most famously articulated by Aristotle, undoubtedly is conceptualized between two social equals and is reserved for male peers only. However, the concept of friendship goes a long way and its origin diverges significantly from our modern conception of what is entailed in "friendship." In the Anglo-European tradition, the word "friend" from ancient times down to the nineteenth century primarily applied to "relatives, kinsfolks," especially those who rendered mutual aid to oneself. Hence, the scope of who counts as a "friend" is far wider than what the modern concept of "friend" allows.[15] This is certainly true in Aristotle's writings on friendship where *philia* applies not only to social equals, but also to unequal familial relationships such as father-son, husband-wife, and brothers as well as to contractual relationship in commerce and in political citizenship and association.[16]

Adding to the wide range of mutually beneficial relationships covered under the umbrella of "friend" is Plato's erotic *philia* where friends are, first and foremost, understood as an erotic attachment between two lovers.[17] Eroticism under discussion here is primarily limited to males only in keeping with ancient Greek's pederastic tradition. Marital relationship between the sexes doesn't even come close to the blessed friendship between two male lovers who are given a head start in their winged ascendant to Olympus after death, a divine gift unparalleled to what one might get from non-lover friendships.[18]

Now by reconceptualizing marital relationship in terms of friendship, one might say that it is not so much of an invention as more of a revitalization of what came before in the forgotten tradition where erotic attachments and familial relationships—far from being antithetical or an impediment to a long-lasting friendship—are in fact compatible with, if not the origin of, friendship. But what is new here is that the hybrid form of friendship incorporating both Greek *philia* and Confucian *you* 友 (discussed in the next chapter) will now be applied to marital relationship replacing the patriarchal authority in matrimony and thereby providing women a new set of conceptual tools to navigate through the contour of the supposedly everlasting marital bond.

The problem in applying friendship to marital relationship is not so much that friendship and marriage have different natures and purposes, or that universality in ethics stands in conflict with partiality in friendship. Given the root of friendship, the first objection is moot; familial relationship is conceptually compatible with, if not the origin of, friendship. Befriending one's spouse is no more and no less odd than befriending one's peers. As for the perceived conflict between universality and partiality, this second point is also irrelevant in the most cherished type of friendship—friendship of virtue—where friendship is the consequence of a virtuous disposition. After all, even for Kant, friendship is a duty of virtue, an honorable duty commanded by reason.[19]

Rather, the problem in the marital relationship practiced thus far is that friendship has been long lopsided tilted in men's favor. The wife is the one bearing most of the cost of marriage for the sake of the husband—his well-being, his aspiration, his family—but that good will is rarely reciprocated. In this way, the wife is never treated as a true friend by the husband, since no one seeks substantial sacrifice from one's true friend without at the same time willing to do the same, and that relationship then sooner or later degrades into a relationship of exploitation. As it stands now, the wife and the husband have yet to learn to be true friends to one another.

"Perfect friendship," as Aristotle understands it, is a friendship of virtue; that is, the *philos* is loved on the ground of virtue as opposed to utility or pleasure. And perfect friendship is only possible between two symmetrically similar men in their virtuous character as well as social status. In other words, perfect friendship, first and foremost, takes the form of symmetrical equality. As Aristotle repeatedly stresses, equality is the mark of friendship.[20] After all, a friend is another self; that similitude between one's self and one's true friend is literal, not just in a figurative sense. As Aristotle understands it, friendship proceeds from a man's relation to himself, and his love for his friend "is linked to one's love for oneself."[21] In addition, only a virtuous man is able to achieve unanimity within himself. Only a virtuous man is able to love himself consistently and truly and thereby loves his friend—a second self—consistently and truly as he loves himself.[22] This required similitude, not to mention the assumed female inferiority as articulated by Aristotle in various writings, obviously excludes woman from forming perfect friendship with man by becoming his second self whom he loves truly and consistently as he loves himself.[23]

Although friendship for Aristotle also applies to marital relationship, it is a friendship of a different sort—a friendship based on utility and pleasure. In one passing remark, Aristotle does briefly mention the possibility of marital relationship based on virtue, if both parties are good.[24] But clearly for Aristotle, due to women's inherently inferior nature and flimsy rationality, the sort of virtues that women are capable of would be different in kind from the ones conventionally applied to men. Women's virtue lies in obedience and submission. As Aristotle repeatedly analogizes, the marital relationship between husband and wife is akin to ruler-subject in the political constitution of aristocracy.[25] There should be no doubt as to who is the one rules and who is the other obeys. Perfect friendship is imagined as between two good men, literally.

Just like other unequal friendships, marital friendship is excluded from a virtue-based friendship; utility and pleasure instead form the basis for unequal friendships. This doesn't mean that perfect friendship is not useful or pleasant; on the contrary, a virtue-based friendship is not only good and desirable, but also most pleasant and useful in the truest sense. A good man is not only good, but also useful and pleasant to himself as well as to his true friend who is, after all, a second self and vice versa. Equality hence implies mutuality in perfect friendship. This mirroring effect of a true friend is unavailable to unequal friendships including marital friendship where equality can only be mimicked through proportionality, that is, the inferior must love the superior proportionally more.

In the case of marital friendship, the wife by virtue of her inferiority owes the husband proportionally more in return than the husband to the wife. As Aristotle writes, in all the various forms of unequal friendship:

> [T]here is not at all, or at least not in equal degree, the return of love for love. For it would be ridiculous to accuse a god because the love one receives in return from him is not equal to the love given him, or for the subject to make the same complaint against his ruler. For the part of a ruler is to receive not to give love, or at least to give love in a different way.[26]

Since marital relationship is analogized as ruler-subject, it is clear that the wife should love the husband more in honor of his nobility and her love for him should not be equally reciprocated. This lack of reciprocation is still eerily true in most marriages today, as women continue to bear the disproportionate burden of the household management and child-rearing duties in sustaining marital unity.

Perfect friendship, although it is based on virtue, is not entirely limited to intellectual pursuits. The degree of intimacy that Aristotle requires of this sort of true friendship is extensive and in many aspects resembles marital intimacy. Besides having equal excellence and mutual good will, true friends also wish to live and die together, delight in each other's company, and share things in common including taste, joy, and sorrow. By living and dying together, Aristotle doesn't mean occasional association. Aristotle's "living and dying together" means a thorough sharing of all aspects of human experiences and activities—both intellectual and mundane—with one's *philos*. Sharing is the key here, and one wishes to share all things in common with one's *philos*, which is another self. As Aristotle writes in the *Nicomachean Ethics* (*NE*) 1171b32-1172a8:

> For friendship is a partnership, and as a man is to himself, so is he to his friend [....] And whatever existence means for each class of men, whatever it is for whose sake they value life, in that they wish to occupy themselves with their friends; and so some drink together, others dice together, others join in athletic exercises and hunting, or in the study of philosophy, each class spending their days together in whatever they love most in life; for since they wish to live with their friends, they do and share in those things as far as they can.

Philosophical contemplation is only one among many activities that one shares with one's *philos*. And who could be more intimately sharing all aspects of life experiences and activities with oneself than one's spouse, with whom one is supposed to unite into one everlasting, single soul, till death do we part?

Spousal relationship would have been the best form of *philia*, if not for the alleged natural inferiority that Aristotle attributes to women. As Martha Nussbaum (1986) reflects on the shortcomings of Aristotle in her discussion on Aristotelian friendship, "[i]f he had not had his views about female inferiority, he would very likely have preferred this sharing to extend into the sphere of the household as well: thus an even more perfect *philia* would be a good marriage, in which the full range of the aspirations and concerns that make up a human life might be accommodated."[27] In other words, Aristotle's prefect friendship in which "true friends are a single soul"[28] would have been more perfectly realized in marital relationship—a supposedly everlasting union sharing all aspects of human experience, both intellectual and mundane, in good times and bad, in sickness and health, and for better or worse.

What is more is that in marital friendship, the neglected aspect of *eros* by Aristotle in the discussion of *philia* can thus be recovered. As a heterosexually inclined man, Aristotle excludes *eros* from the discussion of *philia*. The absence of *eros* in Aristotle's writings is clearly a subjective omission, given how prominently *eros* figures in Plato's numerous writings.[29] The trouble with *eros* as Aristotle sees it, apart from his own subjective inclination, is that it overwhelms *prohairesis*.[30] But for Plato, it is precisely the madness of *eros* that enables us to transcend our human limitations. Erotic attachment, as Plato sees it, is the beginning of a long-lasting friendship; without that intense erotic desire first drawing two souls together and merging them into one unitive love, non-lover *philia* remains hollow, lacking that awe-inspiring divine madness shown in erotic friendship. It is no wonder that the dialogue *Lysis*, subtitled "On *Philia*," begins with Hippothales's desperate love-sickness for Lysis. In analogizing a skilled lover as a hunter over his prey in his advice to Hippothales on how to effectively win over Lysis—a beautiful young boy with a noble lineage—Socrates clearly evokes eroticism as the entry point into the discourse on *philia*.

Uncharacteristically, Socrates, who professes his own ignorance on nearly all subjects, boasts his god-given expertise on love. As he says to Hippothales who blushes at the questions of who is the best-looking boy, in the opening of *Lysis* 204b5-c2: "Aha! You don't have to answer that [....] I can see that you are not only in love but pretty far gone too. I may not be much good at anything else, but I have this god-given ability to tell pretty quickly when someone is in love, and who he's in love with." Likewise, in the *Phaedrus* 257a5-b2, Socrates again states his expertise on love as a divine gift to him. If one takes Socrates's word at face value, then *eros* must be an important philosophical subject that Socrates claims expertise on and is integral to the concept of *philia*. Even though the sort of *eros* as well as *philia* under discussion are decisively directed at men, the centrality of erotic *philia* in Plato helps reorient our modern concept of both friendship and marital relationship.

Marital relationship, among other things, is also sexual in nature, and as Plato has taught us, erotic attachment is neither different in kind nor an impediment to a long-lasting *philia* of virtue. In fact, erotic friendship inspired by divine madness surpasses all other kinds of friendship. As Socrates says in the *Phaedrus* 255b6-8, once the beloved comes of age and accepts the lover, he realizes that "all the friendship he has from his other friends and relatives put together is nothing compared to that of this friend who is inspired by a god." Erotic friendship between lovers is, hence, the highest kind of *philia*. Non-lover friendship, as Socrates goes on to explain in the *Phaedrus* 256e3–8, "is diluted by human self-control; all it pays are cheap, human dividends, and though the slavish attitude it engenders in a friend's soul is widely praised as virtue, it tosses the soul around for nine thousand years on the earth and leads it, mindless beneath it." Aristotle obviously disagrees with Plato, since Aristotle's highest form of *philia* is one without *eros*. But for Plato, *eros*—a divine gift—in a sense ennobles the mere human bond; the lover's god-inspired madness for the beloved itself, in turn, becomes awe-inspiring.

Eros, as Socrates explains in the *Phaedrus* 238b9-c4, is an unreasoning, overwhelming desire to take pleasure in the beauty of human body. There is a sense of involuntariness when it comes to our love of beauty; our sight is intuitively drawn to physical beauty. As Socrates says in the *Phaedrus* 250d1-8, our sight is the sharpest of our senses and physical beauty is the most visible among all objects. Our love of physical beauty, in time—as said in both the *Symposium* 206dff and *Phaedrus* 256a7-b5—can and should give way to our love of beautiful wisdom as lovers come together to help deliver beautiful ideas from their pregnant souls by living a blessed philosophical life. Nevertheless, the journey into our love of the soul begins with our erotic attachment to our beloved.

Eye, as Socrates sees it, is the natural gateway into the soul. It is through the eye that the lover's desire for the beloved overflows from the lover's into the beloved's soul, and the beloved then fills love in return as if the beloved has caught "an eye disease." The beloved's return of love, as Socrates goes on to say in the *Phaedrus* 255d6-e2, is called "backlove," which the beloved "neither speaks nor thinks of it as love, but as friendship." In other words, the friendship bond between the lover and the beloved becomes established only when love is reciprocated through the mirror-image of the beloved himself in the lover's eye. Love is contagious spreading from the lover to the beloved, and the beloved then loves the lover in return through the mirror image of himself in the lover or backlove. This sort of reciprocating act of love and backlove is the closest to the melting of two individuals into one unitive love as one can possibly get. To a modern reader, Plato's account of erotic *philia*, no doubt, brings to mind the deepest sense of romanticism in a sexual relationship where lovers long to merge with one another in an endless stream of reciprocating love and backlove.

Friends, as Socrates explains in the *Lysis* 222a2-4, naturally belong to each other, since the lover "would not desire him or love him passionately or as a friend unless he somehow belonged to his beloved either in his soul or in some characteristic, habit, or aspect of his soul." Erotic *philia*, as discussed in the *Lysis*, is then the desire to consummate with our original other half which belongs to us but is taken away from us. This account of erotic friendship resonates with the account in the *Symposium* 192b8-c3 where lovers desperately seek out each other after being split into halves by Zeus, and when one "meets the half that is his very own [...] something wonderful happens: the two are struck from their sense by love, by a sense of belonging to one another, and by desire, and they don't want to be separated from one another, not even for a moment." Erotic *philia*, in short, can be seen as an act of self-recovery where lovers are united by their sense of mutual belonging in their souls. As discussed in both the *Symposium* 209d and *Phaedrus* 255b6-8, the lovers' bond surpasses all earthly ones, even the bond between parent and child. Erotic *philia* that begins with the yearning for the consummation of the beautiful bodies is culminated in the lovers' consummation of the beautiful souls in their everlasting friendship bond.

Whether Plato sanctions actual physical consummation between the lovers is beside the point; for instance, contrary accounts can be found in *Phaedrus* and *Law*.[31] However, eroticism in Plato's account of the highest *philia* is unmistakable. Aristotle's omission of *eros* from his exhaustive account of *philia*, unfortunately, sets the tone for the subsequent philosophers who see *eros* as irrelevant, if not diametrically opposed, to true *philia*. Especially, after the effect of Christianization, *eros* now belongs only to the sexual relationship between the sexes. This separation of *eros* and *philia*, among other things, also means that spouses will never be the sort of friends that two men can possibly be since *eros* always stands in the way.

At most, erotic *philia*, far from its glorious days of Socrates and Plato as the highest form of *philia*, is now limited to the sexual relationship between the sexes legitimized by marriage. Following Aristotle, the subsequent Christian tradition oftentimes analogizes marriage as a friendship of pleasure or utility. Marriage is a medium through which certain functional utilities are realized, and erotic, sexual pleasure is one among them. However, erotic love has long been seen as morally problematic by Church fathers such as Augustine and Aquinas due to its unpredictability and irrational nature, and it is also associated with the disorderly desire that led to the fall of humanity.[32]

For both Augustine and Aquinas, there are only two ways to render sex morally and spiritually permissible: To procreate or to pay the "conjugal debt."[33] To speak of marital sex as a debt, it brings to mind the transactional nature of matrimony where it is generally understood that in exchange for financial support and security, the wife promises, among other things, sexual access. In consenting to marriage, the wife is seen as contractually having given herself to the husband, a promise that she cannot retract. After all, not until 1993, was marital rape criminalized in all fifty states of the United States but still with ample legal loopholes as late as 2019. Furthermore, one recalls the Biblical teaching in *Genesis* 3.16 where part of Eve's punishment for the fall is her desire for Adam and her subjection to his rule.[34] So in this biblical as well as social context, who is the debtor and who is the debtee seem quite clear. Erotic love itself is sinful except when it serves some definitive purposes in marriage: To procreate or to pay the marital debt.

In fact, not just *eros* is problematic for Christians, the Greek concept of *philia* is also deemed as incompatible with the theological virtue of charity. Aquinas is one of the few exceptions seeing the compatibility between Aristotelian *philia* and the theological virtue of charity.[35] At face value, charity—a fellowship of God and man—runs counter to Aristotelian *philia* of equal virtue and equal standing. In fact, for Aristotle, when the disparity is so great, friendship becomes unsustainable, and the friendship between god and man is of such nature. As Aristotle writes in *NE* 1158b32-1159a1, "[t]his becomes clear if there is a great interval in respect of excellence or vice or wealth or anything else between the parties; for then they are no longer friends, and do not even expect to be so. And this is most manifest in the case of the gods; for they surpass us most decisively in all good things." Furthermore, as Aristotle writes in *EE* 1245b14-19, god has no need for friends to contemplate with or otherwise, since god is its own good, superior to thinking of anything else. Indeed, some heavy-duty conceptual maneuvering is required to fit the Aristotelian circle of *philia* into the theological square of charity. Nevertheless, Aquinas sees values in preserving the intimate partiality of *philia* while transcending its exclusivity to better align with the Christian theological virtue of charity.

Unlike Aristotelian *philia* as among the greatest external goods that we can acquire, charity is not something that we can obtain through human effort, nor is it a natural phenomenon. According to Aquinas in the *Summa Theologiae*, charity is a divine grace, an infused virtue, given by God, and our participation in that divine love for us is charity.[36] Our gratitude for that divine grace then is extended to all rational human beings who participate in the love for God. The sinner and the faithful, the wicked and the good alike, we love them by virtue of our love for God who loves all indiscriminately. In loving one's neighbor, Aquinas seeks to incorporate Aristotle's intimate partiality where one loves one's *philos* more intensely. Aquinas justifies that partiality by quoting *Leviticus* 20.9 that transgression against some is a more grievous sin than others such as against one's father and mother. As Aquinas reasons, in wishing others well, all are equal—that is, we wish all the everlasting happiness—but in action, partiality is permitted since we cannot do good to all equally. Thus, we ought to love those who are closer to us more than others.

Friendship for Aquinas is a type of love, and love is a unitive force that seeks to unite the lover with the beloved. The effect of a unitive love, as Aquinas puts it so sublimely, is the "mutual indwelling" of the lover in the beloved so as to penetrate into the beloved's heart and soul.[37] There are, however, two kinds of love: The love of concupiscence as reference to the appetitive power and the love of friendship as reference to understanding. The difference is that in the love of concupiscence, the beloved is loved to satiate the lover in the form of physical pleasure, whereas in the love of friendship, the beloved is loved for the beloved's own good in the form of apprehending what is good or evil to the beloved as one's own.

It is not surprising that spousal love falls under the love of concupiscence. As Aquinas uses the possessive nature of the husband over his wife as an example to explain the love of concupiscence, "[f]or in love of concupiscence he who desires something intensely, is moved against all that hinders his gaining or quietly enjoying the object of his love. It is thus that husbands are said to be jealous of their wives, lest association with others prove a hindrance to their exclusive individual rights."[38] This possessive, marital love of concupiscence is then put in contrast with the higher kind of love, the love of friendship, where a man is zealous on behalf of his friend to repel all that stands in the way of the friend's good. Once again, the purer type of love of mutual good will belongs to men only; after all the wife who is only an object of enjoyment, an object over which the husband has an exclusive claim.

Even though Aquinas does occasionally use the concept of friendship in his discussion of marital relationship, calling it the "greatest friendship," marriage remains marginal in his writings on love, friendship, and charity.[39] In his commentary on Aristotle's *Nicomachean Ethics*, Aquinas also echoes Aristotle's brief comment on the possibility of forming a marital relationship based on virtue.[40] But it would be hard to imagine that as a keen scholar of Aristotle, Aquinas had modeled the sublime love of friendship after the unequal marital relationship. Rather, it is more likely that the love of friendship that Aquinas had in mind was one between two equals much like the Aristotelian perfect friendship of equal virtue and equal standing, and by analogy, the unequal marital relationship could also obtain a small measurement of true friendship. The love of friendship, if it is applied to marital relationship, then could only be imperfectly realized, due to the assumed female inferiority. Unlike equal friendship, marital union is decisively one of dependency and permanent guardianship for the wife. As Aquinas notes, it would be contrary to the order of nature if the wife were able to leave the husband, "because a wife is naturally subject to her husband as a governor, and it is not within the power of a person subject to another to depart from his rule."[41]

Nevertheless, the marital bond, despite the inequality in intellect and power between the husband and wife, should remain "friendly" by the order of charity. Charity, as pointed out earlier, is a fellowship of man for God. Contrary to the prevailing opinions, Aquinas sees charity as a type of friendship, but unlike Aristotle's *philia* with three possible ends—virtue, utility and pleasure—charity has only one unified end: The goodness of God. But how can man and God be friends? In order to establish the conceptual link between charity and friendship, Aquinas applies Aristotle's mutual good will to the God-man relationship in which through grace, man is invited to participate in God's beatitude for the fellowship of everlasting happiness.[42] This sort of communion between God and man however imperfect it might be, in Aquinas's view, gives charity the same flavor of the Aristotelian mutual good will in *philia*. It is from this primary fellowship of man for God that all other human relationships derive their meanings. It is by the order of charity that man loves himself as well as his neighbor so as to wish the highest spiritual good of everlasting happiness to all including his wife.

Despite Aquinas's tremendous theoretical maneuvering, for the most part in the Christian tradition, both *philia* and *eros* are seen as pagan vices confusedly disguised as virtues. As Kierkegaard says loud and clear, both *eors* and *philia* are passionate preferences, a form of self-love contrary to the truth of the Christian teaching of charity, love thy neighbor:

> Just as self-love centres exclusively about this *self*—whereby it is self-love, just so does erotic love's passionate preference centre around the one and only beloved and friendship's passionate preference around the friend. The beloved and the friend are therefore called, remarkably and significantly enough, the *other-self*, the *other-I*—for one's neighbor is the *other-you*, or more accurately, the third-man of equality.[43]

For Kierkegaard, the sort of exclusive devotion praised in *eros* and *philia* is essentially self-preferential: It is my beloved and my *philos* who is my second self that I have devoted myself to. In contrast, the Christian virtue of charity is non-self-preferential or what Kierkegaard calls "self-renunciation's love." The long cherished pagan virtues of *eros* and *philia* are really just "glittering vices" with poetic contradictions.[44]

Now with the rise of the Christian theological virtue of charity, *philia* and *eros*, as Kierkegaard puts it, have been thrusted "from the throne."[45] What then is left of friendship? The topic of friendship, as Michael Pakaluk's comprehensive yet rather slim anthology—*Other Selves: Philosophers on Friendship* (1991)—demonstrates, is relatively neglected by philosophers in the post-Aristotelian world. Unlike Aristotle's perfect *philia* that presupposes a civic life with shared values or Plato's erotic *philia* that is integral to the blessed philosophical life, the concept of friendship in the modern world is relegated to the realm of personal affairs, a rare private oasis in the midst of the hostile world of constant deceits and betrayals. For instance, for both Montaigne and Kant, friendship is valued not so much for its virtuosity integral in the shared, good life; rather, friendship is seen as a private place of complete trust, communion, and tranquility away from the turbulence in the everyday dealings. Friendship becomes something extra, segregated from the public realm, and nearly impossible to obtain through one's conscious effort.

True friendship indeed is a rare find, so rare that Montaigne's highest friendship, departing from the civic/social nature of Aristotle's perfect *philia*, now takes on an ineffable, mysterious origin. It is a sort of friendship that cannot be intentionally sought; it is found only with gratuitous serendipity. As Montaigne writes in reflecting on his own friendship with Etienne de la Boetie, "[s]o many coincidences are needed to build up such a friendship that it is a lot if fortune can do it once in three centuries."[46] It is a friendship of perfect blending of two souls beyond rational explanation: "In the friendship I speak of, our souls mingle and blend with each other so completely that they efface the seam that joined them, and cannot find it again. If you press me to tell why I loved him, I feel that this cannot be expressed, except by answering: Because it was he, because it was I."[47] It is as if Montaigne's friendship with Boetie was an actualization of Aquinas's perfect mutual indwelling with a blend of Christian grace that could only be received, but not made through conscious human effort.

The ineffable nature of Montaigne's highest friendship is a clear departure from all previous accounts of true friendship that is thought to be the most precious, but is not something beyond our conscious making. Friendship in the Greek tradition, whether its madness is inspired by the gods or not, is squarely a human phenomenon, an attainable external good. For Aristotle, friendship is the most necessary for living a good life and without which one would not choose to live even when one had all other goods. And for Plato, erotic *philia* offers the gateway into the blessed philosophical life where lovers in their conjoined life help deliver something more precious than physical offspring: Giving birth to beautiful ideas from their pregnant souls. Montaigne's ineffable friendship with a mysterious origin is more than just something extraordinary; true friendship now is fated only for the most fortunate few.

Montaigne's moving description of his true love for Boetie is, however, one without *eros*. Montaigne dismisses Greek's pederastic erotic *philia* as licentious and contrary to morality. Furthermore, he sees erotic love between the sexes as impetuous and fickle in nature. For Montaigne, marriage is essentially a business dealing and its defined obligations are antithetical to the intrinsic good of true friendship, which is a result of free will, not obligation. Curiously, Montaigne does concede that if it were possible to befriend one's spouse, then the friendship would be fuller and most complete, since not just the souls are engaged but also the bodies.[48] Once again, marital friendship that conjoins not just two bodies but also two souls in an everlasting bond would have been the most perfect friendship, if not for the feeble nature of women. As Montaigne concludes in regard to the possibility of friendship, the female sex "in no instance has yet succeeded in attaining it, and by the common agreement of the ancient schools is excluded from it."[49] As a contractual sexual union of two social unequals, marriage is seen as far below the celebrated true friendship of complete trust, communion, and tranquility enjoyed by male peers of equal excellence.

As is well known, the sort of raw, transactional nature of marriage is vividly delineated in Kant's definition of sexual union as "the reciprocal use that one human being makes of the sexual organs and capacities of another" and when the sexual union is in accordance with the law, it is called marriage, "that is, the union of two persons of different sexes for lifelong possession of each other's sexual attributes. The end of begetting and bringing up child may be an end of nature [...]."[50] For Kant, marriage is a legally enforceable contract in which each surrenders one's whole person to the other to use sexually in accordance with "pure reason's laws of right," and should unfaithfulness arises, one has the right to retrieve one's spouse, "just as it is justified in retrieving a thing."[51] This reciprocal equality is essential in ensuring the moral personality of one's own person since the inequality in giving and receiving makes oneself into a thing.

The emphasis on the equal possession of sexual attributes in marital relationship, however, doesn't lend itself to gender equality. As is true for Aquinas, for Kant gender hierarchy is integral to the unity in matrimony. Immediately after his insistence on the equal possession of sexual attributes, Kant makes an exception for spousal domination based on the natural superiority of man:

> [F]or the law to say of the husband's relation to the wife, he is to be your master (he is the party to direct, she to obey): this cannot be regarded as conflicting with the natural equality of a couple if this domination is based only on the natural superiority of the husband to the wife in his capacity to promote the common interest of the household, and the right to direct that is based on this can be derived from the very duty of unity and equality with respect to the *end*.[52]

This is so because the insolubility of a union, as Kant explains, hinges on superiority: "[O]ne partner must *yield* to the other and, in turn, one must be superior to the other in some way, in order to be able to rule over or govern him."[53] In other words, gender hierarchy is integral to the unity of will in marriage.

To Kant, marital unity is built based on husbandly superiority. As he goes on to ask, "[w]ho, then, should have supreme command in the household?— for there certainly can be only one who coordinates all transactions in accordance with one end, which is his." And the answer is simple: "I would say [...] the woman should *dominate* and the man should *govern*; for inclination dominates, and understanding governs."[54] Much like inclination, women cannot be reasoned with and what is irrational obviously cannot govern itself or others. Marriage is the only gateway through which the wife is able to gain rational freedom and civic representation under the husband's guardianship and tutorage. In short, the husband's will is the unity of the will in marriage and he is also the one who governs in the matrimonial life.

Given the disparate characters of the sexes, it is not surprising that for Kant friendship is out of reach of women. Much like Montaigne's ineffable, true friendship, Kant's friendship is one of the sublime and the eternal belonging to the noble sex. But unlike Montaigne's true friendship that with sufficient good fortune one might be bestowed on, Kant's highest friendship—perfect friendship—is an unattainable, transcendent idea; it is a necessary idea in ethics that one should strive for and is commanded by reason as a duty of virtue, but it has no empirical basis. "*Friendship* (considered in its perfection)," as Kant defines it, "is the union of two persons through equal mutual love and respect," but friendship "thought to be attainable in its purity or completeness [...] is the hobby horse of writers of romances," an opinion that Kant holds early on in the opening of his lecture on "Friendship."[55]

The most that one can achieve is what Kant calls "moral friendship," friendship of disposition: "[T]he complete confidence of two persons in revealing their secret judgments and feelings to each other, as far as such disclosures are consistent with mutual respect."[56] In contrast with Aristotle's self-knowledge as the practical end of friendship where the mirroring effect of one's *philos*—the second self—is a necessary aid in self-knowledge, Kant's moral friendship is prized for being an aid in self-disclosure with no other practical ends.[57] The perilous nature of the world, for Kant, in a sense has painted each of us into a corner of social isolation. Friendship is the saving grace that one can count on for a completely unreserved self-disclosure. Unlike perfect friendship which is an unattainable idea, moral friendship, for Kant, is a rare but natural phenomenon like "black swans."[58] Moral friendship offers us that rare oasis to reveal our innermost self. But even in moral friendship, Kant recurrently warns against a complete self-disclosure. In Kant's mind, friendship is a dangerous engagement where deceits and betrayals are always possible, now or in the future.[59]

Kant's skepticism and cynicism toward the possibility of friendship stand in stark contrast with the exaltation of Greek *philia*, erotic or otherwise. Friendship for Kant is not the most necessary external good, nor is it wise to attempt the actualization of mutual indwelling where two souls become transparent to one another. After all, men of principle are hard to find. As Kant laments, "[a]mong men there are but few who behave according to *principles*—which is extremely good" and this is even more so in the case of the fair sex: "I hardly believe that the fair sex is capable of principles, and I hope by this not to offend, for these are also extremely rare in the male."[60]

Nevertheless being a man is much more desirable than being its opposite. As Kant writes, "[w]hen refined luxury has reached a high level, the woman appears demure only by compulsion and makes no secret of wishing that she might rather be a man, so that she could give her inclinations larger and freer latitude; no man, however, would want to be a woman." For being a woman is nothing but folly: "As concerns scholarly women: they use their *books* somewhat like their *watch*, that is, they carry one so that it will be seen that they have one; though it is usually not running or not set by the sun."[61] A woman's charm, as Kant theorizes, lies in her ornamental beauty, not her intellect, which in fact destroys her feminine appeals: "Laborious learning or painful pondering, even if a woman should greatly succeed in it, destroy the merits that are proper to her sex, and because of their rarity they can make of her an object of cold admiration; but at the same time they will weaken the charms with which she exercises her great power over the other sex."[62] It seems that with Kant's palpable cynicism and overt textual misogyny we have arrived at the end of friendship, let alone the possibility of marital friendship.

But in spite of it all, there is a subtle effort to revive both Kantian friendship and marriage. As Lina Papadaki (2010) writes in her defense of Kant, "[t]he account of marriage, I believe, can and should be rescued from Kant's no longer acceptable views on gender. Setting aside Kant's views on the natural differences between men and women, and assuming equality and reciprocity between two spouses can lead to the creation of a true unity of will: one that is represented and controlled equally by both spouses."[63] Citing Charlotte Witt's 1996 lecture on "How Feminism is Re-writing the Philosophical Canon," Papadaki concurs with Witt in saying that we can take those philosophers who are accused of misogyny as holding a mistaken view about women and men, and then safely ignore those views. For "[o]nce we set aside their views on gender, their theories can provide fuel for feminist thought."[64] In other words, it is conceptually possible to separate the philosopher's textual misogyny from his other useful concepts and that separation works to benefit feminist theorizing.

Conclusion

If a philosopher, like Kant, who holds overtly sexist views—not to mention his abhorrent racist views—could be redeemed, then non-Western philosophical traditions such as Confucianism could, in principle, also be revived in a feminist image. However the feminist's re-appropriation oftentimes stops at the door of the Anglo-European textual tradition. Overt textual misogyny in the non-Western canon is regularly cited as the ground for exclusion from feminist theorizing. But as one can see above, Kant's overt textual misogyny did not seem to preclude itself from the feminist possibility of theoretical re-appropriation. After all, Papadaki's (2010) piece in defense of Kant's views on marriage and friendship was published in *Hypatia: A Journal of Feminist Philosophy*, whose journalistic mission as said in the title is to advance feminist philosophy!

As Robin May Schott argues back in 2003, Western feminists by and large have gone through and done with the phase of negative critiques and are now much more engaged in the phase of positive construction of feminist theories emerged out of the ashes of the Western canonical texts.[65] Here I am arguing for the same move for the Confucian texts as well. In the following chapter, we will explore a hybrid account of friendship incorporating Confucian *you* 友 and Greek *philia* as a way to reimagine a feminist marriage and its own internal good.

4

Hybridity of *Philia* and *You* 友: Friendship as Spousal Relationship

In this chapter we are to take a creative journey into the hybridity of Confucian *you* 友 (friendship) with a blend of Greek *philia* as a feminist reconstituted spousal relationship in which spouses are true friends to one another united in both their bodies and souls for the sake of a mutually flourishing, good life. As noted in the previous chapter, the Greek concept of *philia* has a much wider scope than what is conventionally understood in the modern concept of peer friendship, and this is true for the Chinese concept of *you* 友 as well. The ancient Greek's blurring of kinship line, on one end, and civil/political association as well as erotic attachment, on the other, in the discussion of *philia* can also be found in the Chinese concept of *you* 友.

According to the comprehensive *Kangxi Dictionary* (*Kangxi zidan* 康熙字典) of Qing dynasty, there is a cluster of characters that are the ancient variations of the character 友—such as 叒, 拜, 牪, 羿, 㬪, 曷, 卉, 芔, 舜—conveying the same concept of mutually beneficial assistance. The pictograph for *you* 友 first found in the oracle-bone inscriptions of the Shang period (around fifteenth century BCE) is composed of either two left or two right hands facing the same direction: 叒 and 拜 denoting a friendly pair of hands working together.[1] This sort of friendly association as found in the bronze inscriptions from the Western Zhou period (*c.* 1045–771 BCE) signifies kinsfolk. In other words, *you* 友—as friendly association—is first applied to one's kinship.

In the ancient clan-based political system, "*you*" 友 frequently is used to refer to the fraternal bonds between brothers, father-son, and ruler-subject.[2] For instance, in the *Book of Documents* (*Shujing* 書經)—one of the oldest texts documenting the earliest records of dynastic history—the term *you* 友 is consistently used in conjunction with brotherly love and friendly political alliance.[3] In addition to fraternal bonds and friendly political associations, the term *you* 友 in the *Book of Songs* (*Shijing* 詩經) also occurs in the context of courtship and coupling.[4] For instance, as shown in the very first song of *Shijing*, *you* 友 is used to describe the courtship between the lord and the noble lady, a courtship traditionally attributed to King Wen and his royal consort Taisi (i.e., King Wu's mother) who is exalted as "Cultured Mother" 文 母—the most praised maternal model among the three celebrated matriarchs of the house of Zhou in the *Biographies of Exemplary Women* (*Lienu zhuan* 列女傳).[5] Clearly, the concept of friendship in ancient times covers a lot more grounds than the modern concept of voluntary, peer friendship.

Peng 朋 and *You* 友

In addition to the term *you* 友, *peng* 朋 along with the conjoint term *pengyou* 朋友 are frequently used to denote friendly association. The pictograph for *peng* 朋 is represented by two strings of cowries (shell), an ancient currency and ritual item.[6] This ancient meaning of *peng* 朋 can be found in both the *Book of Songs* and the *Book of Changes* (*Yijing*易經).[7] So when *peng* 朋 is used in conjunction with *you* 友 as in *pengyou* 朋友, it denotes "a string or group of friends." In fact, according to the *Kangxi Dictionary* quoting the *Shuowen jiezi* 說文解字 (*Discussing Writings and Explaining Characters*)—the earliest dictionary of the second century CE—the character *peng* 朋 is represented by the loan character *feng*鳳 (phoenix) written in the archaic form 羽, signifying "thousands of birds following the phoenix fly and therefore it is called *peng*" (鳳飛, 羣鳥从以萬數, 故以爲朋).[8] Similarly, as said in the *Shanhai jing* 山海經 (*Classic of Mountains and Seas*)—a possibly fourth-century BCE text— *peng* 朋 is used in the context of birds habituating and flying in group (有 鳥焉, 群居而朋飛).[9] In short, *peng* 朋 denotes band or group. By extension from the conjoint term *pengyou* 朋友, *peng* 朋 also comes to denote friends.

By and large, in pre-Qin texts, *peng* 朋 and *you* 友 have no discernible differences; both denote friendly association. For instance, in the *Book of Songs*, Song 164 "Changdi 常棣," *you* 友 and *peng* 朋 are used interchangeably. Similarly, in the *Book of Changes*, the term *peng* 朋 found in hexagram 2 "Kun 坤," 11 "Tai 泰," 16 "Yu 豫," 24 "Fu 復," 31 "Xian 咸," 39 "Jian 蹇," and 40 "Jie 解," as well as *you* 友 in hexagram 41 "Sun 損," they all donate the same friendly association with no additional qualifications. Although *you* 友, *peng* 朋, and *pengyou* 朋友 all denote friends, *you* 友 is the most commonly used, *pengyou* 朋友 next, and *peng* 朋 the least.[10] The borrowed origin of *peng* 朋 from the conjoint term *pengyou* 朋友 might be the reason for the general textual preference of *you* 友 over *peng* 朋 to denote friendship, and conversely, its less precise meaning denoting not only friendship but also group, band, and strings of cowries might also be the reason that *peng* 朋, instead of *you* 友, is the preferred term in the *Book of Changes*, a book of divination that is intended for a wide range of meanings and applications.

With the exception of the *Book of Changes*, the clear preference of *you* 友 over *peng* 朋 is generally true in pre-Qin texts. For instance, in the opening verse of the *Analects* where Confucius tells the joy of friendship, the character *peng* 朋 is used; however, that is the only instance where *peng* 朋 is found while *you* 友 is used at least nineteen times and *pengyou* 朋友 eight times in the *Analects*. Similarly, in both the *Mencius* and *Xunzi*—two Warring States (*c.* 475–221 BCE) Confucian texts—*peng* 朋 is not used, while *you* 友 is the clear preferred term used at least twenty-seven and twenty-nine times respectively and *pengyou* 朋友 used three and five times respectively.

The lopsided preference of *you* 友 over *peng* 朋 shown in Confucian texts such as the *Analects, Mencius,* and *Xunzi* in part could also be attributed to the Legalist school of thought's association of *peng* 朋 with *dang* 黨 (faction) and its increasing concerns over the danger of clique or faction in state politics as conveyed in the conjoint term *pengdang* 朋黨. Although the concept of *dang* 黨 denoting partiality as in "*wupian wudang* 無偏無黨" (without bias, without partiality) can be found as far back as in the *Book of Documents*, the conjoint term *pengdang* 朋黨 is relatively new and is predominately a Legalist-leaning concept.[11] The term *pengdang* 朋黨 is not found in all *Five Classics* nor in the Confucian *Four Books*; it is found neither in the *Mozi*墨子, nor in the *Daodejing* 道德經or *Zhuangzi*莊子. The earliest occurrence of the term *pengdang* 朋黨 is found in the Legalist-leaning text *Guanzi* 管子, whose authorship is generally attributed to Guanzi—a seventh-century BCE statesman during the early Spring and Autumn period (*c.* 770–476 BCE). The term then achieves its prominence in the emblematic Legalist text, *Hanfeizi* 韓非子—a third-century BCE text of the late Warring States period.

Within the Confucian tradition, the earliest occurrence of *pengdang* 朋黨 is found in the *Xunzi*—also a third-century BCE text of the late Warring States period—where the term is used three times.[12] The term then retains its negative meaning in subsequent post-Qin texts such as *Shiji* 史記 (*Records of the Grand Historian*), *Chunqiu fanlu* 春秋繁露 (*Luxuriant Dew of the Spring and Autumn*), *Xinxu* 新序 (*New Order*), *Yantielun* 鹽鐵論 (*Discourses on Salt and Iron*), and *Yanshi Jiaxun* 顏氏家訓 (*Yan's Family Instructions*). So it is safe to say that the term *pengdang* 朋黨 is a relatively new concept first formulated during the Spring and Autumn period and is firmly established by the time of the Warring States period.

Pengdang 朋黨, as articulated in the *Guanzi* 管子, is a perverted type of friendship, and just like other forms of social perversion, it should be prohibited by the sage. As said in the "Fajin 法禁" chapter of *Guanzi*, "[f]orming factions as friendship (以朋黨為友), concealing evil as goodness, calculating machinations as wisdom, levying exactions as loyalty, and giving away to anger as bravery; those are things sage king prohibits."[13] Furthermore, *pengdang* 朋黨 is equated with the private interest (*si* 私) of the minister who intends to usurp the power of the ruler and to bring chaos to the state. As said in the "Mingfajie 明法解" chapter of *Guanzi*:

> Those use private methods (私術者) are the subordinate who attack the superior and bring chaos to the lord; therefore the law is abandoned and gives way to private conduct. The lord is then isolated by himself and ministers then form factions and groups (人臣群黨而成朋); in this way, the lord is weak and the minister is strong. This is what is called a chaotic state.[14]

In other words, *pengdang* 朋黨 brings calamity to the state by subverting the good with the bad, public with private, and friendship with faction. The same dire warning of the danger of *pengdang* 朋黨 in state politics is then greatly amplified in the *Hanfeizi* 韓非子, where the term *pengdang* 朋黨 appears at least eighteen times while *you* 友 only eight times and *pengyou* 朋友 twice.[15]

The Legalist's obsession over the danger of *pengdang* 朋黨 in state politics must be put in the context of two competing visions of the ruler-minister relationship where Confucians propose a virtue-based mentorship and friendship model, whereas Legalists insist on the strict ordering between the ruler and the minister.[16] As it will become clear later, Confucians see the relationship between the minister and the ruler as a virtuous fellowship where the ruler's duty is to befriend and seek out the virtuous, and the virtuous once recognized, in turn, must be obliged to serve for the common good, so that the ruler is assisted not just by servants or bureaucratic clerks, but by virtuous teachers (*shi* 師) and friends (*you* 友) who provide timely guidance and effective remonstration. This virtue-based model of mentorship and friendship presents a political problem for Legalists who seek a clearly defined power structure in which the order flows from top-down followed by exact compliance and uniformity.

Mentorship and friendship in the political realm, from the Legalist's viewpoint, introduce variables and a potential ground for insurgency and division among the subordinate, as both the Legalist-leaning texts, *Guanzi* and *Hanfeizi*, repeatedly warn the danger of forming factions among the subordinate to benefit their own private interests (*si* 私) in contrast with the common good (*gong* 公) represented by the ruler. For Legalists, the potential equalizing effect of virtuous fellowship upsets the order of power, but for Confucians, the ruler-minister relationship is not just a hierarchical relationship between the master and the servant. Rather, it is an occasion for moral growth in which the ruler and minister are united in a virtuous fellowship.

Along with the competing visions of the ruler-minster relationship, the conceptual demarcation between *you* 友 and *peng* 朋 also begins to emerge during the late Warring States period: *You* 友, by and large, signifies a positive relationship of mentorship or friendship, whereas *peng* 朋 with the danger of *pengdang* 朋黨 lurking in the back primarily denotes a cluster of peers. As defined in the *Baihutong* 白虎通 (*Comprehensive Discussions in the White Tiger Hall*)—a first-century CE text—"*peng* 朋 means *dang* 黨 [i.e., group]; *you* 友 means *you** 有 [i.e., having at hand; assist]." The same text then goes on to quote the *Book of Rites* (*Liji* 禮記) that says "sharing the same mentor is called *peng* 朋; sharing the same aspiration is called *you* 友" (同門曰朋, 同志曰友).[17] In other words, *peng* 朋 is grouped based on similar external factors, while *you* 友 is defined by internal factors of goal sharing. This first-century CE rendition then becomes the standard definition of *you* 友 and *peng* 朋. As pointed out earlier, in pre-Qin texts, this sort of demarcation between *you* 友 and *peng* 朋 is largely absent. Both *you* 友 and *peng* 朋 mean friendly association, and *peng* 朋 only takes on a pejorative tone when it is in the conjoint term *pengdang* 朋黨.

Kinship, *Shi* 士, and *Shi** 師

As pointed out earlier, in ancient times, the term *you* 友, among other things, also signifies fraternal/brotherly love. As said in the Song 241 "Huangyi 皇矣" of *Shijing*, King Ji is praised for filling his heart with *you* 友 toward his brothers and for promoting the prosperity of the country (因心則友, 則友其兄, 則篤其慶). Similarly, as said in the "Kanggao 康誥" chapter of *Book of Documents*:

> The king says, "O Feng, such great criminals are greatly abhorred, and how much more (detestable) are not *xiao* and not *you* (不孝不友)! – as the son who does not reverently discharge his duty to his father, but greatly wounds his father's heart, and the father who can (no longer) love his son, but hates him; as the younger brother who does not think of the manifest will of *tian* 天, and refuses to respect his elder brother, and the elder brother who does not think of the toil of their parents in bringing up their children, and is very not *you* 友 to his younger brother (大不友于弟)."

Clearly, *you* 友 in both above passages from the *Book of Songs* and the *Book of Documents*—two of the five ancient Classics—refers to fraternal love, especially the older brother's love toward the younger brother. And this ancient usage of *you* 友 as fraternal or brotherly love can also be found in later texts, such as the *Analects, Mozi, Guoyu* 國語 (*Discourses of the States*), *Zuozhuan* 左傳 (*Zuo's Commentary*), *Xunzi, Kongzi jiayu* 孔子家語 (*The School Sayings of Confucius*), *Hanshi waizhuan* 韓詩外傳 (*Outer Commentary on the Book of Songs by Master Han*), *Xinxu* 新序 (*New Order*), *Xinshu* 新書 (*New Book*), *Shiji* 史記 (*Records of the Grand Historian*), *Zhonglun* 中論 (*Balanced Discourses*), and *Yanshi Jiaxun* 顏氏家訓 (*Yan's Family Instructions*).

With its ancient fraternal and kinship connection, *you* 友 is also closely related to the foundational excellence of *xiao* 孝. As said in the Song 177 "Liuyue 六月" of *Shijing*, Zhang Zhong is praised for being *xiao* and *you* (張仲孝友). And according to the "Shixun 釋訓" chapter of *Erya* 爾雅 (*Glossary*)—the oldest surviving glossary possibly compiled during the third century BCE to explicate Chinese Classics—this phrase "*xiaoyou* 孝友" in "張仲孝友" means, "being good to one's father and mother is *xiao* 孝 and being good to one's older and younger brothers is *you* 友."[18] Being conjoined with *xiao* 孝, *you* 友 is seen here as an exalted excellence as well.

Furthermore, *xiao* 孝 and *you* 友 are not just familial excellences; they are prerequisites for effective governance. As said in the "Junchen 君陳" chapter of *Book of Documents*, "[b]eing *xiao* and *you* (孝友) with your brothers, you can display these qualities in the exercise of government." In the ancient clan-based political system, it makes sense to conflate familial and political excellences. For one's brother, in all likely account, is also one's political ally, and being filial 孝 (*xiao*) to one's parents and being brotherly 友 (*you*) are qualities required for one's political power. In fact, the term "*tongzhi* 同志" (having the same aspiration)—that is used to define *you* 友 in later post-Qin texts such as *Baihutong*—is actually originated in the sharing of the same surname, according to the *Guoyu* 國語 (*Discourses of the States*), a fifth-century BCE text. As said in the "Jinyu shi 晉語四" chapter of *Guoyu*, "[h]aving the same surname is having the same excellence; having the same excellence is having the same heart-mind; having the same heart-mind is having the same aspiration (同姓則同德, 同德則同心, 同心則同志)."[19] In other words, the concept of *you* 友 is closely connected to one's kinship in ancient times. Much like the Greek *philia*, the Chinese concept of *you* 友 covers a wide range of mutually beneficial associations including kinship.

As the dissolution of the centralized system of the Zhou court gives way to semi-autonomous states during the Spring and Autumn period (*c.* 770–476 BCE), a time when Confucius (*c.* 551–479 BCE) espouses his socio-political philosophy, the excellence of *you* 友 begins to take root beyond kinship. The opportunity to serve at semi-autonomous regional courts begins to widen as states compete with one another for dominance. As is well known, Confucius along with his disciples traveling from state to state for a decade in search of a receptive ruler is a case in point. To partake in state governance is no longer limited to the hereditary clan of a select few. Confucius, the son of a lowly concubine and a minor knight, is also on the move to seek political opportunities. One can imagine that there are many more like Confucius, and the opportunity for friendly association beyond one's kinship also increases, as these wandering scholarly-knights (*youshi* 游士) travel from state to state to advocate for their own ideal political visions.

The term *you* 友 is cognate with *you** 游 (travel; companion), as reflected in the common expression of *jiaoyou* 交游/交友 where traveling and making friends are closely related and at times interchangeable. As said in Chapter 2 "Xiushen 修身" of *Mozi*—a text attributed to Master Mo of the late fifth century BCE—"[o]ne who has wealth but cannot share it with others is not worth befriending (*you* 友). One whose adherence to the Way is not thoroughgoing, whose view of things is partial and not broad […] is not worth having as a companion (*you** 游)."[20] Likewise, as said in the "Quli shang 曲禮上" chapter of *Book of Rites*—one of the Five Confucian Classics— "[t]hose friends who are his fellow-officers will proclaim him respectful; those friends who are his subordinate will proclaim him *ren*; and his peer friends (*jiaoyou*交游) will proclaim him trustworthy." The interchangeability of *you* 友 and *you** 游 signifies that making friends requires social mobility to go beyond one's immediate family and kinship. This certainly is true in the post-Zhou period when wandering scholarly-knights (*youshi* 游士) in search of a suitable ruler becomes increasingly common.

As social mobility increases, to seek mutual help beyond one's kinship becomes an existential necessity. But more importantly, for Confucians, the concept of *you* 友 initiated by trust (*xin* 信) between strangers for mutual assistance has also evolved into a moral imperative of mutual cultivation in pursuit of the same aspiration of moral perfection.[21] The sense of being morally critical and demanding (*zeshan*責善; *qieqie caicai*切切, 偲偲) and the metaphor of "mutual cutting and polishing" (*xiangyu qiecuo*相與切磋) are often remarked by Confucians as the way of friendship.[22] In short, from the Spring and Autumn period onward with the rise of the wandering scholarly-knight (*youshi* 游士), Confucian moral friendship beyond kinship begins to take hold.

Confucius's scholarly-knight (*youshi* 游士) in search of moral fellowship with the ruler is clearly delineated by Mencius (372–289 BCE)—the revered second Confucian master—who repeatedly points out that excellence trumps hereditary positions as well as social factors such as age, rank, or family origin. According to Mencius, the proper way to build friendship between the social superior and the subordinate—as in between emperor and commoner or between aristocrat and his retainer—is to bypass those social determinants.[23] To Mencius deference is not just a prerogative enjoyed by the social superior; as said the *Mencius* 5B3, the way that the social superior defers to his subordinate is called "honoring the virtuous" (*zunxian* 尊賢). Mencius's friendship model is a direct inversion of Aristotle's in that for Mencius the minister/commoner is the one who is conceived of as in possession of virtue and is the one that the ruler/aristocrat should seek to befriend without relying on the advantages of one's nobility. In this way, virtue is seen as a social equalizer where the ruler and minister or the aristocrat and retainer are called friends. Transforming the concept of *you* 友 from mutually beneficial kinship love to moral friendship is a specific contribution of Confucianism to the evolution of the Chinese concept of *you* 友.

As the class of scholarly-knights rises, *you* 友 is also recognized as someone that the scholar-knight (*shi* 士) is especially in need of. For *you* 友 offers the much-needed mutual assistance beyond one's kinship in the socio-political realm. As said in the "Duke Xiang 襄公 the 14th year" chapter of *Zuozhuan* 左傳 (*Zuo's Commentary*), a fifth- to fourth-century BCE text: "The son of heaven has his dukes [...] the hereditary scholar-knight has his friends (宗士有朋友) and the common people have their family and relatives to turn to for mutual assistance."[24] But more importantly, for Confucians, *you* 友 also serves as a moral compass for peer scholarly knights (*shi* 士) in the socio-political realm. As Confucius says in Chapter 15 of *Book of Filiality* (*Xiaojing* 孝經):

> Of old, an Emperor had seven ministers who would remonstrate with him (*zhenchen* 爭臣), even if he had no right method of governing, he did not lose the empire; [...] if the scholarly-knight had friends who would remonstrate with him (*zhenyou* 爭友), a good name would not cease to be connected with him; and if the father had sons who would remonstrate with him (*zhenzi* 爭子), he would not behave reprehensively.

Similarly, in the *Kongzi jiayu*, Confucius is repeatedly quoted as saying that having *zhenyou* 爭友 is a moral imperative for *shi* 士, just as having *zhenchen* 爭臣 for the ruler, and *zhenzi* 爭子 for the father.[25]

To be a *zhenchen* 爭臣 to the ruler, the *shi* 士 must strive to be a mentor (*shi** 師) or friend (*you* 友), not just a functionary vessel. And that is what Confucius and his disciples are aspired to be. As the grand historian, Sima Qian, writes in the "Rulin liezhuan 儒林列傳" (Biographies of Confucians) chapter of *Records of the Grand Historian* (*Shiji* 史記) assessing the various degrees of accomplishment of Confucius's disciples, "[a]fter the death of Confucius, his seventy disciples scattered and wandered among different aristocrats; the great ones become a teacher of the minister, and the lesser ones become a friend of the scholarly-officer (大者為師傅卿相, 小者友教士大夫)."

In fact, during the Han dynasty both teacher (*shi** 師) and friend (*you* 友) are also formalized into the highest two ranks of the official post. As recorded in the "Guanren 官人" (Officials) chapter of *New Book* (*Xinshu* 新書), a Han text, "[t]he Lord's official has six ranks: the first is called teacher (*shi** 師), second friend (*you* 友), third great minister, fourth left-right hand assistant, fifth imperial attendant, sixth servant and laborer." Being the ruler's teacher or friend is obviously a much more exalted rank than being a mere servant, and those rulers who surround themselves with teachers and friends will be much more prosperous as well. As the same text goes on to say, "[t]herefore those with teachers for the state become an emperor (故與師為國者, 帝); those with friends become a lord (與友為國者, 王); [...] those with imperial attendants might survive or might perish (與侍御為國者, 若存若亡); and those with servants and laborers are sure to perish (與廝役為國者, 亡可立待也)." Similar political advice urging the ruler to be assisted by teachers and friends instead of functionary vessels can also be found in the *Outer Commentary on the Book of Songs by Master Han* (*Hanshi waizhuan*韓詩外傳), *New Order* (*Xinxu*新序), and *Lu's Spring and Autumn Annals* (*Lushi chunqiu*呂氏春秋).[26]

In other words, for Confucians, the state is more than just a hierarchical bureaucracy staffed with clerks or servants to execute top-down orders; rather, it is a moral enterprise where the ruler and minister are bound by mentorship/friendship. Dealing with one's friends and teachers is radically different from dealing with one's servants and functionary clerks in both style and substance. In order to avoid the perilous fate of state dissolution as repeatedly warned in various Han texts, the ruler should surround himself with virtuous teachers and good friends (*xiangshi liangyou*賢師良友) who provide the ruler with timely moral guidance and effective remonstration, and to whom the ruler, in turn, must exhibit a sense of deference and mutual regards.

Confucian Friendship

For Confucians, friendship is made for mutual moral perfection, but unlike the Aristotelian perfect friendship between two superior men of equal social status and character, Confucian virtuous fellowship doesn't require a sense of symmetrical equality between friends. As noted earlier, for Mencius, it is a political imperative for the ruler to seek out and befriend the scholarly-knight in virtuous friendship/mentorship, and in making friends, one should not rely on the advantages of one's nobility. Unlike for Aristotle, for the Confucian, virtue and social nobility don't need to go hand in hand, nor does equality in friendship rest on superiority (that is, the proportional equality between two social unequals can only be restored by tilting in favor of the superior). Indeed, there is no such presumption of equality—let it be symmetrical or proportionate—in Confucian moral friendship.

Furthermore, unlike the Kantian perfect friendship, Confucian moral friendship is not built based on the unattainable idea of absolute equality of respect and love between friends. Confucian friendship is made for us mortals, who live among the multitude with different interests and levels of ability. There is no litmus test of equal ability or equal respect and love before friendship can be found. Friendship can come from anyone, if one seeks the path of moral perfection. As Confucius says in the *Analects* 7.22, "[t]hree people strolling together, I am bound to find a teacher (三人行, 必有我師焉); choosing the good to follow and amend my way when encounter the bad." In other words, both the good and the bad found in one's company can serve as a corrective mirror for oneself to either model after or to amend one's shortcoming.

What is essential in sustaining Confucian friendship is the mutual commitment to moral perfection. What friends must share is to stay on the same path to moral perfection, and "those whose paths are different," as Confucius says in the *Analects* 15.40, "cannot lay plan for one another" (道不同, 不相為謀). Or, as said in the *Xunzi* 27.102, "[a] lord must be cautious in selecting a minister and commoner in selecting a friend. Friends are those render mutual support (友者, 所以相有也). If their paths are different, how can they have mutual support (道不同, 何以相有也)?" Friends are those who walk on the same virtuous path, but they need not be already in the possession of prefect virtue or even equal in excellence. As said in the "Ruxing 儒行" chapter of *Book of Rites* in regard to the scholarly conduct of the Confucian:

> The scholarly *Ru* 儒 has those with whom he agrees in aim, and shares the same direction (合志同方), manages the same path, and uses the same methods (營道同術); when they stand on the same level with him, he rejoices in them; if their standing be below his, he does not tire of them; […] if they proceed on the same path with him, he goes forward with them, if not, he withdraws (同而進, 不同而退). This is what making friends is (其交友有如此者).

In short, their continuous commitment to walking on the same path of moral perfection is what sustains Confucian friendship, not their equal possession of ability or excellence.

It is true that in the *Analects* 1.8 and 9.25, Confucius does repeatedly say, "[d]on't befriend those who are unequal to oneself (毋友不如己者)," but this passage is immediately followed by the imperative that "[w]hen one is at fault, don't fear to amend it." The self in these passages is assumed to be morally imperfect and hence in the company of others, the self must be keen on amending one's way. In light of one's moral imperfection, the previous injunction should not be interpreted as saying that one's friends must be as morally perfect as oneself. Instead, what one needs is another pair of eyes and ears to provide critical feedback to oneself in amending one's shortcomings. The duty of friendship is to provide that critical feedback in order to lead one another to moral perfection. As Confucius says precisely in the *Analects* 13.28, "[f]riends are critical and demanding with one another (朋友切切, 偲偲), but amicable with their brothers." Similarly, Mencius says in the *Mencius* 4B30, "[d]emanding goodness is the way of friendship (責善, 朋友之道也); but being so demanding between father and son is the greatest injury to the kindness prevailing between them." Friendship is marked by that critical attitude in comparison to other types of intimate relationship such as parent-child or siblings who are bound to one another first and primarily by mutual affection.

There is a limit as to how far one is able to move friends to the direction of goodness. "Doing one's utmost and lead them to goodness (忠告而善道之)," as Confucius says in the *Analects* 12.23, is the way to treat one's friends, but "if this doesn't work, then stop; don't disgrace oneself." Moral receptivity and mutual support in friendship are essential. As said precisely in the "Guiyan 貴驗" chapter of *Balanced Discourses* (*Zhonglun* 中論), a Han text:

> To speak of the obligations of friendship, it lies in the cutting and making one upright so as to rise in the way of goodness (言朋友之義務, 在切直以升於善道者也); therefore the *junzi* doesn't befriend those who are unequal to oneself (故君子不友不如己者) […] those who are unequal to oneself require oneself to make them upright (不如己者須己而植者也). But then too busy in supporting others, who is going to reciprocate me? (然則扶人不暇, 將誰相我哉).

As pointed out earlier, the metaphor of "mutual cutting and polishing (*xiangyu qiecuo* 相與切磋)" is a mark of friendship, and hence what must be equal between friends for the Confucian is the commitment to mutual support for moral perfection. In other words, mutual support in ascendency to moral goodness is what friendship is for.

It is worth noting that moral goodness or virtue, for the Confucian, unlike for Aristotle, is not something one possesses internally and only secondarily manifests in one's actions toward the other-self. Rather, personal moral growth for the Confucian is a function of, what Roger Ames and Henry Rosemont (2014) call, "associated living."[27] The Confucian self is intractably relational and is co-dependent on one's situated-ness in the existential web of human relationships. And just like the relationally embedded self, virtue also emerges from and is co-dependent on the web of human relationships as well. For the Confucian, there is no virtue as such in and of itself, just as there is no person in and of oneself. Each virtue is situated in and is first emerged out of a specific type of human relationship. We need others not just so that we might exercise our internal moral goodness, but rather only being situated in different relationships, are we able to cultivate the virtue that informs and sustains the relationship.

For instance, to cultivate the excellence of *xiao* 孝, one must cultivate it, first and primarily, in the relationship of parent-child, and the goodness of that parent-child relationship, in turn, is informed by *xiao* 孝. Looking at virtue this way, in friendship, one then must cultivate a sense of being morally critical and morally demanding, and in turn, one's moral goodness is sharpened by such a friendly association. Just as parent-child relationship as the embodiment and the natural site for the cultivation of *xiao* 孝, friendship is the embodiment as well as the natural site for the cultivation of a critical sense of moral goodness. In many ways, one's ability in polishing that critical moral sense is derivative and dependent on one's being situated in friendship. For Aristotle, friendship is one of the greatest external goods as opposed to virtue and contemplation, which are internal goods. But for the Confucian, friendship is indispensable for the cultivation of one's critical moral sense. Friends are not just a reflection of one's second self or those with whom one share things in common, but are those who keep one another on the unwavering path to moral goodness through mutual cutting and polishing their critical moral sense.

Friendship has been long cherished as one among the five essential social relations in canonical Confucian texts: Ruler-minister (*junchen*君臣), father-son (*fuzi*父子), husband-wife (*fu*fu*夫婦), brothers (*kundi*昆弟)/older and younger (*zhangyou*長幼), and friends (*pengyou* 朋友). The doctrine of five social relations first appears in Chapter 20 of *Centrality and Commonality* (*Zhongyong* 中庸) and then in the *Mencius* 3A4 with some minor differences.[28] Placing *pengyou* 朋友 the last on the list of the five social relations doesn't by itself signify the marginality of friendship in Confucian teachings. In fact, as it should be clear by now, there is no textual shortage that exalts the virtue of *you* 友 from early Classics to the later Confucian texts.

Incorporating the early Zhou usage of *you* 友 as kinship love, Confucian *you* 友 is at times used in conjunction with *xiao* 孝 as a bridge connecting the familial and the socio-political realm. As Confucius quotes the *Book of Documents* to explain the fundamentals of governance in the *Analects* 2.21, "[b]eing filial (孝乎惟孝) and friendly to one's brothers (友于兄弟) is also governance." Or, as said in the *Mencius* 4A12, "[i]f one is unable to have the confidence of the superior, one is unable to govern; to have their confidence, one must first have the trust of one's friend (信於友有道); to have the trust of one's friend, one must first be able to please one's parents (悅親有道); to please one's parents, one must first be true to oneself." The same passage with slight variations can also be found in Chapter 20 of *Zhongyong* and in the "Aigong wenzheng 哀公問政" chapter of *Kongzi jiayu*. All in all, friendship is part of the connecting chain of human relationships mediating between the familial and the socio-political realms.

At other times, *you* 友 is conceptualized as part of the foundational excellence of *xiao* 孝. As said in the "Jiyi 祭義" chapter of *Book of Rites*:

> Not being circumspect in residential living is not filial; not being true in serving the ruler is not filial; not being respectful in attending official duties is not filial; not being trustworthy with friends is not filial (朋友 不信, 非孝也); not being courageous in battle is not filial; if one fails in these five things, misfortune will reach one's parents. How can one not be attentive to them?

The same passage can also be found in the *Lu's Spring and Autumn Annals* (*Lushi chunqiu* 呂氏春秋), "Xiaoxing 孝行" chapter—a chapter discusses the various forms of filial conduct—with slight variations: "Not being sincere with friends is not filial (朋友不篤, 非孝也)." Or, as said in the "Jianxia 諫 下" chapter of *Master Yan's Spring and Autumn Annals* (*Yanzi chunqiu* 晏子 春秋): "The way of being a son is to love one's brothers, apply the conduct of one's father, be compassionate to the people, be trustworthy to one's friends (誠信于朋友), and this is what is called *xiao* (謂之孝)." Lastly, in the *Xunzi* 29.4, Confucius is quoted in the context of his response to Zilu's query on *xiao* 孝: "[W]hen the *junzi* comes home, he is sincere in his conduct, and when he goes out, he befriends the worthy (故君子入則篤行, 出則友賢). How then could he not have a reputation for filial conduct (何為而無孝之 名也)."[29] In short, *you* 友 at times is seen as an application of *xiao* 孝 in the socio-political realm and is necessary for both familial harmony and socio-political success.

Contrary to being marginal in Confucius's teaching, being trustworthy in friendship—as said in the *Analects* 1.4 and 1.7—is seen as one of the three things that one should examine oneself on daily and is also one of the three things that one is being judged on as being a learned person.

Confucius himself in the *Analects* 5.26 talks about sharing a relationship of trust with friends, along with bringing peace to the old and protecting the young (老者安之, 朋友信之, 少者懷之), as something that he is aspired to do. Furthermore, having a reciprocal good will in friendship is one of the four things that comprise the way of *junzi* (君子之道四), which Confucius himself confesses—in Chapter 13 of *Zhongyong*—as something he has yet to master.

In the "Deguan situ 地官司徒" chapter of *Rites of Zhou* (*Zhouli* 周禮), *you* 友 is said to be one of the three essential modes of conduct:

> There are three modes of conduct to teach: first it is called filial conduct, that is, be affectionate to one's parents; second is friendly conduct, that is, to honor the virtuous and the good; third is deferential conduct, that is, to serve the teacher and elderly (教三行: 一曰孝行, 以親父母; 二曰友行, 以尊賢良; 三曰順行, 以事師長).

And in the "Wangzhi 王制" chapter of *Book of Rites*, friendship forms part of the seven teachings of the lord: Father-son, brothers, husband-wife, ruler-minister, older-younger, friends, and guests. Far from being a marginal or "dangerous" concept to the family or the state, *you* 友 has a long and strong literary tradition in Confucian teachings, and is regarded as integral to one's moral education in both the familial and the political realms.[30]

Friendship as Spousal Relationship

So how does modern spousal relationship fit into this long conceptual evolution of friendship both in the Anglo-European tradition and in the Confucian tradition? As noted earlier, if marriage is no longer seen as a necessity for women in exchange for male guardianship or financial support, then for what does one marry? And if child-bearing and -rearing is no longer seen as the natural end of marriage ordained by the divine, then what is it that binds marriage together till death do we part? In short, what is a spouse for? Feminists are in dire need of a new conceptual paradigm to replace the old concept of marriage that sees the wife as an auxiliary appendage to the husband, there to raise his children, to manage his household, and to help achieve his dreams and aspirations. We need a feminist marriage that enables women to continue to develop and flourish by becoming something greater than they once were before marriage, instead of being diminished by the sort of sacrifice that is conventionally demanded of them in the roles of wife and mother.

Just as it is true in the Anglo-European tradition, in the Confucian tradition, the spousal relation is, first and primarily, one of functionary distinction. As shown in the doctrine of five social relations, the husband-wife relation is marked by *bie* 別, the differentiated division of labor. Conventionally, women are in charge of the *nei* 內 (inside) and men the *wai* 外 (outside).[31] It is prevalent in many Confucian texts and most obviously stated in the *Book of Rites* that women's education and duties are limited to household management. Men, on the other hand, are provided with a well-rounded educational curriculum and elaborate ritual training in order to enable men to excel in both familial and socio-political realms. A complete person is not just a filial son at home, but also a virtuous leader in the community and beyond. Being limited to an educational and ritual training befitting only for household management, women are essentially functionary vessels, a sort of thing that Confucius says a well-rounded *junzi* should not be.

It is true that in numerous didactic texts such as the *Biographies of Exemplary Women* (*Lienu zhuan* 列女傳) as well as all major dynastic histories from the first unified dynasty of Han to the last dynasty of Qing, women are at times exalted for their virtuous achievements beyond their roles in the household. Nevertheless, domesticity continues to define the proper sphere for women. Take Ban Zhao (*c.* 45–117 CE)—the first and foremost Confucian woman scholar—as an example: Even with all her accomplishments in the dynastic court of Han, Ban Zhao was never granted an official title and her contribution to the completion of the Han dynastic history was also unrecognized.[32] Such an overt omission of women's actual achievements beyond the realm of *nei* 內 can only be understood in the context of *nei/wai* 內外 binary where each gender is defined, first and foremost, by its proper sphere. Women confined to the realm of *nei* 內—the constricted realm of domesticity—are necessarily and invariably auxiliary to men who are aspired to excel in both the familial and the socio-political realms of *wai* 外. This reductive aspect of marriage where the wife becomes functionary and auxiliary to the husband must be overcome.

Within the Confucian tradition, I propose replacing the spousal relationship with friendship, where two people are bound by their mutual commitment to moral perfection in which each is supported by the other in their ascendency to the way of moral goodness. This is neither a transcendent move nor an unachievable ideal. Moral goodness for the Confucian is squarely an earthly one, one that emerges from as well as is an embodiment of the excellence of each existential human relationship.[33] Unlike Plato, for the Confucian, there is no transcendent realm of the form that one ascends to; there is only the earthly harmony in the ever more widened web of human relationships. And unlike Aristotle, the Confucian do not prioritize pure contemplation over practical virtue. The glittering allure of the transcendent ideal is not what the Confucian moral goodness aims at and thereby not what Confucian friendship is there for either.

Confucian *you* 友 is made for us mortals for everyday living, since it is a sort of moral relationship that requires neither an Aristotelian sense of symmetrical equality between friends, nor a Kantian sense of unrealizable absolute equality between love and respect. A good friend for the Confucian is not a mere copy of one's virtuous self, a black swan, or a divine grace, but a necessary component in the making of one's critical moral sense. In the modern spousal relationship, Confucian earth-bound friendship should serve as a model in order to replace the old patriarchal paradigm of marriage as an exchange of functionary, external goods, or as a union for the one-sided glory of men. Spouses should be *you* 友, and their blessed union is a testament of their mutual commitment to walking on the same path of moral perfection in which each cuts and polishes the critical moral sense of the other so that they might both become something greater than they once were, and their ascendency to the way of moral goodness is the result of their everlasting friendship bond. Moral goodness, in sum, is the internal good of friendship and should also be the internal good of modern feminist marriage.

Since moral goodness is what binds Confucian *you* 友 together, selecting a right person is utmost important, but it is not an impossible task. The ability to select a friend, in fact, is seen as part of the necessary progression in one's educational curriculum. As said in the "Xueji 學記" (Records of Education) chapter of *Book of Rites*:

> In the first year, they are being observed regarding their ability to read the texts intelligently and discern each meaning (一年視離經辨志); in the third year, their ability to do their work reverently and to rejoice in companionship (三年視敬業樂群); in the fifth year, their ability to broaden their studies and seek company of their teachers (五年視博習親師); in the seventh year, their ability to discuss the subject of their studies and select their friends (七年視論學取友), this is called small attainment; and in the ninth year, when they know different subjects thoroughly and firmly (九年知類通達, 強立而不反), this is called grand attainment.

The same passage then goes on to say: "When learning alone and without friends, one then becomes solitary and poorly informed (獨學而無友, 則孤陋而寡聞)." Similarly, as said in the *Analects* 12.24: "*Junzi* attracts friends through cultural refinement and friends then assist him in cultivating virtue (君子以文會友, 以友輔仁)." Confucian friendship is an existential phenomenon that is within our humanly ability to acquire and should also be part of one's educational experience in general and moral education in particular. In applying Confucian *you* 友 to modern feminist marriage, one might say that marriage should also be seen as a moral enterprise in which spouses offer each other not only the joy of companionship and informed viewpoints, but also the elation of moral maturity. In short, marriage should be seen as a meeting of two good friends in their mutual ascendancy to the way of moral goodness.

As advised in the *Analects* 16.4, in picking a friend, one should generally associate with people who are true (直), trustworthy (諒), and broadly informed (多聞) and avoid those who are ingratiating (便辟), excessive compliant (善柔), and glib talkers (便佞). And as said in the *Analects* 16.5 and 5.25, one should also cultivate a sense of enjoyment in what is good and proper, and avoid indulging in what is excess or superficial. Lastly, as shown in both *Analects* 15.10 and *Mencius* 5B8, one should strive to befriend and learn from the best, in the past and present, from near and far, so as to hone in one's moral sense. Just as an artisan who wishes to do her job well must first sharpen her tools, one who wishes to cultivate a sense of moral goodness must first learn to serve the worthy and befriend the best. But this doesn't mean that anyone who is less than the best is not worth befriending, since we too are morally imperfect. What really counts is each's willingness to walk on the same path of moral perfection. This is true for spousal selection as well. What each needs is not an exact copy of oneself in virtue and temperament. For us mortals, what we need is a pair of committed hands in supporting each other morally upright.

With whom we choose to associate has a penetrating effect on our moral development. As Confucius says in this well-known passage from the "Zayan 雜言" chapter of *Garden of Persuasions* (*Shuoyuan* 說苑)—a Han text— that to associate with a good person "is like having a fragrant orchid in the room" (與善人居, 如入蘭芷之室) as opposed to having a foul fish when associating with a bad person (與惡人居, 如入鮑魚之肆), but in both cases, once familiarity sets in, one is no longer able to take notice of the fragrance or the foul smell. In a sense, one's environ becomes part of oneself; when the surrounding is red, one becomes red, and when it is black, one becomes black (丹之所藏者赤, 烏之所藏者黑).[34] The permeability of the boundary and the confluence between the self and other is an existential given. Hence as Xunzi sums it up in the *Xunzi* 27.102: "In picking friends and good people, one cannot be callous; this is the foundation of excellence" (取友善人, 不可不慎, 是德之基也).

The mutual molding between friends is also what gives clue to those looking in from outside as to what sort of person is involved in each relationship. As said in the *Xunzi* 23.19, "[i]f one doesn't know one's son, then look at his friends; if one doesn't know one's lord, then look at those surrounding him (不知其子視其友, 不知其君視其左右)."[35] In marriage where spouses are united in both body and soul, the confluence between spouses is even greater than between friends. Hence a heightened moral sense is even more critical in spousal relationship.

In Chinese thought, the first occurrence of the husband-wife relationship explicitly analogized alongside friendship is found in the "Jinshi 禁使" chapter of *Book of Lord Shang* (*Shangjun shu* 商君書)—a fourth- to third-century BCE Legalist-leaning text—that says: "Where the government is perfect, husband, wife, and friends cannot mutually dispose of each other's evil and cover up each other's wrong-doing (故至治, 夫妻交友不能相為棄惡蓋非)," and this is because although their affairs are connected, they don't seek profit together (事合而利異者).[36] That is to say, even in an intimate relationship, spouses and friends should not collude with one another for profit. When a relationship is motivated by profit, moral corruption sets in. As the same text explains, "[w]hen they seek profit together and have the same evil, the father cannot reprimand the son and the lord cannot reprimand the minister (利合而惡同者, 父不能以問子, 君不能以問臣)."[37] For one becomes at risk of moral degradation by being implicated financially. This is true in marriage as well. One of the problems with financial dependency in marriage is that women at times have no other way out but to collude with their spouses and to tolerate moral degradation, such as abuse and infidelity.

In marriage or in friendship, walking on the same path of moral goodness doesn't require sameness in thought or deed. Just as said in the *Analects* 13.23, *junzi* should be affable, but not monolithic with one another (君子和而不同); spouses should also be agreeable with one another without being an echo chamber for the other. Mutual moral rectitude—that characterizes the conduct of a *junzi* as opposed to profit-seeking for a petty person (君子喻於義, 小人喻於利) as said in the *Analects* 4.16—should also be what binds friends together. The *Collection of Cai Zhonglang* (*Caizhonglang ji* 蔡中郎集)—a Han text—in the "Zhengjiao lun 正交論" chapter says perfectly: "In covering the way of friendship, when there is moral rectitude, friends are united and when there is no moral rectitude, friends are apart (蓋朋友之道, 有義則合, 無義則離)." It goes without saying that unlike peer friendship, separation in marriage involves legal wrangling, financial or otherwise. It is a decision of enormous weight, with or without children being involved. But what women should not do is to stay in marriage for financial support, which, as said earlier, tends to put women at risk of moral degradation. Spouses should be *you* 友 that cuts and polishes each other's critical moral sense, not a *dang* 黨 that colludes with one another for advantages, monetary or otherwise.

One's spouse, no less than one's teacher or friend, should also be one's moral guide. As said in chapter 2.12 "Qixiang yuqi 齊相御妻" of *Biographies of Exemplary Women (Lienu zhuan)*—a famed Han text that gives rise to the "lienu" literary genre in dynastic histories from Han to Qing:

> For a worthy to reach perfection, the way must be broadly conceived.
> It is not just a matter of being cut and polished by teachers and friends.
> One's spouse also contributes much to the enterprise (故賢人之所以成者, 其道博矣, 非特師傅朋友相與切磋也, 妃匹亦居多焉).[38]

In many ways, one's spouse is a much more fitting moral guide than one's mentors or peer friends, since spouses have intimate knowledge of each other's strengths and weaknesses, and what each needs to be cut or polished is transparent.

What is more is that the sexual nature of the marital union helps strengthen, not diminish moral rectitude in marriage, since lovers who are first drawn by their passionate love and affection for one another make promises to form an eternal union in which each wishes the other well and loves not just the body but also the soul. Unlike Aristotle's perfect *philia* that neglects the power of *eros* in *philoi*'s shared life, Plato's erotic *philia* has much to teach us. Lovers who are bound in their love of the body should also be bound in their mutual love of the soul, and that erotic madness is what first propels us mere mortals to elevate our temporal bodily love to the sublimity of the eternal love of the soul. The shared life between *philoi* in marriage in which *eros* is a part is ever more complete, since *philoi* share all aspects of life—erotic or intellectual, mundane or spiritual.

Eroticism forms part of a wholesome marriage, and hence the philosophical aversion to eroticism leads to an incomplete understanding of what is possible in forming an even more perfect union in marriage. Sex is not just a contractual, functionary tool for mutual bodily pleasure as Kant infamously characterizes it; nor is it solely for the sake of child-bearing or for the repayment of the marital debt as Augustine and Aquinas have envisioned it. Eroticism, no less than the intellect, also forms part of one's natural self, and marriage is the perfect site for one's erotic expression for the beloved. As Plato teaches us, one's erotic passion for the beloved can also be sublime and soul enriching, since it propels us to seek an ever more completely "mutual indwelling" in one another, not just in the body, but also in the soul through the everlasting loop of love and backlove in the eyes of lovers. In short, propelled by *eros*, lovers long to be part of each other's soul and thereby uplift their souls to moral goodness. Or, what is the same as shown in the *Book of Songs*, the joy of courtship and coupling is also a manifestation of *you* 友.

But of course, in modern feminist marriage, mentorship should not be one-sided from the husband to the wife, nor from the old-skilled hunter to the passive young prey. As said earlier in the Han text of *Lienu zhuan* 2.12, both spouses have much to contribute to the soul-enriching enterprise of moral perfection. It is not a matter of complementary division of labor between spouses as in the Confucian concept of *bie* 別, or even a matter of J. S. Mill's idyllic "reciprocal superiority" in a companionate marriage, since in both cases, women are inevitably, if not exclusively, tasked with the duties of child-rearing and household management to complement the husband's duties in the outside world of commerce and politics. What we need, instead, is a sense of mutual moral vigilance in marriage as well as in friendship.

Spouses, no less than friends, who share a life together, cannot build a shared life with the template of 50/50 equal split as some feminists have advocated. Yes, unduly sacrifice demanded of women in the roles of wife and mother impedes women's ability to live a wholesome life. But the template of absolute equality is unattainable, just as Kant's insistence on the absolute equality between love and respect in friendship, and the result is cynicism or resignation. In a good relationship of any kind, there must be a sense of reciprocity and mutuality, but unlike in a contractual transaction, in a good marriage or friendship, the sort of reciprocity and mutuality involved is not marked by numerical equality in a definitive term. Rather it is a faithful understanding of and a persistent effort in realizing the enduring goodness in one another.

For what is especially appealing about friendship is the penetrating understanding that two good friends have of one another, and that faithful understanding of one another is what enables friends to transcend the temporal needs to repay in kind and in a timely manner that an ordinary dealing in everyday life demands. Friends are faithful to one another, not in a sense of blind obedience, but in a way that insists on the enduring goodness in one another, a sort of goodness that is both actual and potential. By being faithful to one another in this way, friends not only see what is good in one another, but also help realize what else is possible through thick and thin. Looking at marriage in this way, to mandate a 50/50 equal split makes marriage seem not only superficial and contractual, but also contrary to what is required in an enduring friendship, not to mention its unattainability.

In Chinese thought, the two often-cited examples of friendship—the story of Bo Ya 伯牙 and Zhong Ziqi 鍾子期 and the story of Bao Shuya 鮑叔牙 and Guan Zhong 管仲—involve exactly the sort of penetrating understanding and the enduring faith in the goodness of one's friends. For the Chinese, a good friend is the one who listens to one's inner sound (*zhiyin* 知音) and understands one's inner self (*zhiji* 知己). The story of Bo Ya and Zhong Ziqi found in the *Lu's Spring and Autumn Annals* (*Lushi chunqiu* 呂氏春秋) that gives rise to the term "*zhiyin* 知音" is a friendship built based on mutual appreciation of what each does for the other in a way that elevates both. Bo Ya was the lute player and Zhong Ziqi the listener, and when Zhong Ziqi died, Bo Ya destroyed his lute and never played again, since no one would ever be able to appreciate his music as the way Zhong Ziqi did.[39] Zhong Ziqi and Bo Ya in a sense are soul mates, if you will, and they both are made better off in their friendship bond, since Bo Ya's musicality is appreciated the way that it deserves and Zhong Ziqi, in turn, is enriched by Bo Ya's musical talent. One can say that they both become greater than they once were before the friendship bond.

The story of Bao Shuya and Guan Zhong is another example of friendship that demonstrates the enduring faith in what is good and possible in one's friend against all odds. Bao Shuya stood by Guan Zhong's side even in the most unfavorable situations and his enduring faith led Guan Zhong to his eventual political triumph. Bao Shuya's understanding of what is good and possible in Guan Zhong is so penetrating that it surpasses Guan's own parents. As Guan Zhong says later on while being a famed minister of Duke Huan, "[i]t was my parents who born me, but Bao Shuya is the one who understands me."[40] Friends, in a word, see each other not just for who they are, but also what else that is good and possible in them.

Spouses, no less than two good friends, should also see each other for who they are, but also what else that is good and possible in them so that each is able to develop and flourish into a wholesome and worthy partner for life. Yes, at times sacrifice is needed and reciprocity might be delayed. In marriage, no less than in friendship, at times we all do more than our fair share for the sake of the other and our willingness to delay what is due to us is also what makes the bond between friends or spouses faithful and enduring. But in modern feminist marriage what women should not do is to offer a perpetual sacrifice for the one-sided glory of men, nor should the wife derive her self-worth solely from the achievements of her husband. In other words, marriage should not be a one-sided devotion of the wife to the realization of the aspiration of the husband, since she is not made better off, but instead becomes an appendage to him, a functionary vessel that is auxiliary, inessential, and hollow in and of herself.

A complete self-abnegation is never the goal or the function of friendship in the East or the West, and neither should it be for marriage. The marital bond should lift up both spouses through their mutual devotion, enduring faith in, and understanding of one another, and only by doing so, is marriage able to live up to its promise of making two people become something greater than they once were. Women, no less than men, should also be enriched by the marital union in many ways possible—let it be their capacities for passionate love, intellectual pursuit, or parenthood—so that women might also continue to develop and flourish into a wholesome and worthy partner for life.

Conclusion

So in response to the question of "what is the internal good of marriage?" the answer is: Moral friendship. In rethinking spousal relationship as a hybridized Confucian *you* 友 with a blend of Greek *philia*, the functionary and oppressive aspects of marriage are thus made incompatible with this friendship-based marital union. At the same time, by incorporating marital relationship into friendship, the concept of friendship is made ever more perfect. Just as in a good marriage both spouses are uplifted by their marital union, the union between marriage and friendship uplifts both conceptually as well. Spouses, in short, should be best friends who lead one another to moral goodness with penetrating understanding and enduring faith, and the spousal relationship, in turn, is also the best friendship that is everlasting and complete in its form and content by building a truly shared life with all aspects of human capacities—*eros* and all. Or, what is the same, the joy of courtship and coupling is also a manifestation of *you* 友.

A feminist marriage, as I see it, should be a marriage of moral friendship and passionate love, in which the friendly pair of committed hands goes both ways and in which moral goodness is strengthened, not diminished by *eros* or the joy of courtship and coupling. It is, indeed, a new conceptual paradigm of marriage that is made in a Confucian image for feminists; it is also a practical feminist paradigm that we mortals can strive for and realize in our human-all-too-human life. As a mother and wife in a household with two professionals and a school-age child, I, too, feel the strains in navigating the contour of a married life. It is a journey like no other, but it is also a journey that tests the limits of my feminist commitments to gender equity. How far and how much of a sacrifice made on behalf of an equally competent adult is reasonable without being at risk of moral degradation? And when and how should one demand reciprocity without at the same time degrading the marital union into an obligatory business transaction? The liberal feminist model of equal give and take is inadequate. There is no score sheet to keep track of and the calculating nature of an equal split runs counter to the intimate nature of marriage. What we need is not more unrealizable ideals in our flawed life, nor to advocate for a complete evacuation from motherhood and marriage that evades the problem instead of solving it.

By proposing a hybridized Confucian *you* 友 with a blend of Greek *philia* in place of spousal relationship, I intend to provide a practical conceptual tool that enables women to live a feminist life as fully as possible as they embark on their journey of an everlasting marital union. A Confucian *you* 友-based marital union is a union without gender-based division of labor nor gender-based hierarchy, and at the same time, this friendship model offers women the flexibility of charting their own course of what constitutes a faithful and enduring spousal friendship. There is no set formula for the sacrifice and reciprocity in friendship, and neither should it be in marriage. But in both cases, a heightened sense of moral vigilance is required, since that is what friendship is for in the first place, and that should also be the case for marriage as well. Marriage is a friendship with all its perfection—*eros* and all.

5

Democracy and Its Limits

The year 2016 was a challenging time for the institution of democracy where mature democratic states were swept away by the appeals of populist strongmen and policies: The passing of the disastrous Brexit referendum in the UK, the 2016 presidential election with the rise of Trumpism in the political psyche of our nation, and the momentous gains for the far-right movements all across Europe.[1] The United States' internal political turmoil, for better or worse, has a de facto far-reaching impact on the rest of the world and with the shift to the hard-right rhetoric during the 2015–16 election season, the United States thereby led the way for the rest of the world to "mainstream," as it were, the fringe populist, nationalist movements. The rise and the eventual triumph of the Trump candidacy in 2016, in many ways, epitomize not only the breakdown of civility and common decency in political and civil discourse, but more importantly the dangerous limits of democracy.

As Plato prophetically warns in the *Republic*, a democratic system based on capricious individual likes and dislikes will eventually lead to the disastrous road of a tyrannical system where a tyrant emerges out of the chaos of democratic individualism.[2] This seems to ring true in the so-called "anti-establishment" appeal of the Trump candidacy with its unrelenting penchant for a singularly strong man stance to solving the myriad of social and political problems, as Trump proclaimed that "I alone can fix it."[3] Given the historical fact that tyrants such as Hitler, Mussolini, and Putin or even terrorist organizations such as Hamas came to power through democratic means, not to mention the surprisingly strong support for Trump's presidential reelection bid of 2020 gathering over 74 million votes—the largest tally of votes for a losing presidential candidate—despite the daily missteps and controversies throughout his first-term presidency, obviously the promise of a democratic rule is not enough to ensure the continuation of a modern democratic state, let alone a mutually flourishing and inclusive community for all its citizens.[4]

If a modern democratic state is to function well—that is, holding onto its democratic character without at the same time disintegrating into a mob rule where individual angers and resentments trump its civic bonds and obligations to the past, present, and future generations—then the state itself cannot be conceptualized as a mere value-neutral vessel for antagonistic individuals to compete for limited social resources without any regards to the common good. The modern state must be more than an empty container for disparate individuals constrained only by reactive, punitive laws. In facing the rise of national fascism, xenophobia, transphobia, and overt misogyny, not just in the United States but also all across Europe, a shift in the conceptual paradigm of what constitutes a well-functioning state and flourishing, inclusive citizenry is sorely needed.

Confucianism with its sustained emphasis on ritual as a shared social bond and its deep commitment to caring for the vulnerable as the basis of political authority will provide us with a much more wholesome picture of an inclusive, caring state beyond the modern, liberal paradigm that hinges on individual rights and personal autonomy. The so-called "European Enlightenment" project of modernity—where human nature is conceptualized in a negative light conventionally starting with Hobbes onward—theorizes the state authority in a form of social contract with the governed, precisely because without the coercive state authority to constrain each individual no one would be free to pursue and safeguard their own goods in the state of nature.[5] This sort of modern, liberal conception of the state already sets limits on the purpose of the state and the nature of citizenry: The state exists because the inter-subjective relationship among self-centric individuals is one of antagonism. In this increasingly mobile and globalized world, we need something more to hold all of us together in our march to an ever more inclusive future for humanity, than fighting for and safeguarding our own individual goods.

From the feminist standpoint, what is even more troubling about our inherited modern state paradigm in the Anglo-European tradition from Hobbes onward is that the ideal constituent of the state has traditionally been conceptualized as an adult male—free, autonomous, and unencumbered. This political paradigm leaves out all other designated social dependents— the old, the young, the sick, the disabled, and, most of all, women—from its conceptual construction of a fair and just state. For instance, it is indisputable that both Locke and Kant exclude children, women, and laborers, not to mention nonwhites, from the much cherished active citizenship.[6] The commendable liberal inspiration of an equal and just state, nevertheless, is theoretically as well as historically built based on racial hierarchy, economic exclusion, gender subordination, and neglected dependency care. This faulty liberal paradigm is not feminist in its inception; nor is it just, fair, or inclusive in the distribution of labor for dependency care.

Even if the aspects of gender, race, and class could be amended in the contemporary appropriation of these canonical political theories, the issue of dependency will still loom large. Before the rise of care ethics in the early

1980s, the issue of dependency care, for the most part, has been left out of sight, relegating the issue to the private realm (and conventionally women's realm). The willful omission of the issue of dependency care in the liberal political paradigm stands in stark contrast with the issue's rising importance in the contemporary world. In fact, as Leon Kass in the presidential commissioned President's Council on Bioethics reports, "[t]he defining characteristic of our time seems to be that we are both younger longer and older longer."[7] Our prolonged dependency in modern times is exacerbated by the advancement in medical sciences and the complex global economy that requires a much longer period of education and training for the young to be financially viable.

The steady trend of greying the world population most acutely in, but not limited to, wealthy nations has made the issue of dependency care including elder care a central issue of our times.[8] A political theory that fails to address the issue of dependency care inevitably will fail to address the existential demands of human life in general and in our modern times in particular. In contrast, Confucianism with its persistent emphasis on caring for others—especially the old, the young, the sick, and the disabled—stands readily to offer a more compassionate and inclusive political structure that takes into account of the issue of dependency care.

Furthermore, a theory that aims at maximizing individual gains limited only by another individual's claims naturalizes antagonism in one's inter-subjective relationship—let it be with another individual, community, or state. Under this conventional, liberal paradigm, to address collective problems such as income inequality, climate change, environmental conservation, and global health, is often perceived as an unwanted and unlawful intrusion by the state into the lives of the individuals or into the inner workings of a free market on which the livelihood of the individuals depends. Our strong emphases on individual liberty and self-reliance have indeed overshadowed our shared responsibility and our civic duties for the past, present, and future generations. The disastrous fallouts of the Covid-19 pandemic intra- and inter-nationally should have taught us this much: No one is better off, if everyone is not better off.[9]

Confucianism with its sustained emphasis on ritual as a binding thread—that knots oneself to others in the past, present, and future through the outward expansion of one's familial, social, and political roles—makes the sort of self-transformation needed to be compassionate and inclusive of others a seamless progression of life itself. It is widely acknowledged that in Confucianism, the self is conceptualized as two persons in relation; the porous nature of the Confucian self is made to take in others so as to be oneself.[10] As Confucius says precisely in the *Analects* 6.30: "[I]n seeking to establish oneself, one seeks to establish others and in seeking to promote oneself, one promotes others." One can thus infer that, instead of a free and self-reliant man, a ritually bound Confucian self that is constituted by and is inclusive of others stands a much better chance of addressing collective problems—such as income inequality, climate change, environmental conservation, and global health—inter-subjectively.

The classical liberal model of antagonistic individualism is conceptually inadequate. We need a different kind of political paradigm that addresses, first and foremost, the inevitability of dependency by grounding the state authority in its capacity to care for the most vulnerable instead of relegating that caring responsibility to the private realm (and conventionally women's realm); second, we need a political theory that doesn't narrowly focus on defending the negative liberty of the self-reliant man instead of providing an enduring social mechanism to render the self ever more porous to others, so that complex and globalized problems can get addressed and solved. In sum, a modern democratic state infused with Confucian emphasis on ritual to ensure social cohesion and its political imperative to care for the vulnerable is the proper way for us to move forward into the ever more progressive and inclusive future for humanity.

Who Owns the Idea of Democracy?

For some, a hybrid project seeking to infuse the modern democratic institution with Confucian emphases on ritual and dependency care immediately raises the question of compatibility. Much like the issue of compatibility between multiculturalism and feminism or between care ethics and Confucian *ren* as discussed in previous chapters, there is also an ongoing and fierce debate regarding the compatibility between modern democracy—along with its associated concepts and practices—and Confucianism.[11] By now, this pattern of exclusion of Confucianism from contemporary progressive projects—whatever that might be—should seem familiar: Suspicion and rejection abound.

Much like the dispute over what counts as philosophy, democracy is also often said to be Western in nature, in origin, and in essence, and hence, as the argument goes, Confucianism is incompatible with democracy. Any discussion over the incorporation of Confucianism into the modern democratic state is oftentimes met with the charge of willful conceptual confusion accompanied with a blend of outright contempt and hinted ridicule at the very thought of "modernizing" Confucianism. Modernity as it were is also Western in nature, in origin, and in essence, and only Anglo-European intellectual traditions are capable of progressing from their original historical and social contexts to be in sync with and even inform our very modern solutions to our very modern problems—let it be on the issue of gender, race, or contemporary democratic institution.

The familiar dichotomy of Western vs. non-Western, modern vs. traditional, progressive vs. oppressive, or feminist vs. patriarchal repeats itself not only in colonial literatures of the bygone eras, but also in many of the contemporary comparative works, feminist or otherwise. The West represents the paragon of human development and hence is synonymous with progressive modernity, whereas the non-Western world is mired in their oppressive, exploitative, and hierarchical traditions simply incapable of meeting the demands of modernity (aka Western progressive ideas) or responding to Western critiques of their backwater ideologies. Such is the typical response from contemporary scholars whenever they encounter unfamiliar intellectual traditions.

The word "democracy," much like the linguistic root of "philosophy," is Greek, but that does not mean that the conception of democracy can only be Greek in nature, in origin, and in essence. The same applies to the claim that the modern state is and can only be Greek, Lockean, or Kantian in nature, in origin, and in essence. For one thing, the modern democratic state bears no resemblance to the one practiced in the ancient Greek city state of Athens, or as articulated by Anglo-European canonical thinkers such as Locke, Kant, or even Mill. As pointed out earlier, neither Locke nor Kant includes women, children, labor class, nor nonwhites in their conception of active citizenship, not to mention that Locke was intimately involved in and personally profited from the slave trade for decades. Furthermore, as pointed out earlier, Kant was one of the key thinkers in establishing and consolidating the "scientific" account of race theory that in turn helped give rise to an exclusively Western genealogy of philosophy that is still in use in the vast majority of academies in North America today. Even for a self-proclaimed supporter for women's rights and education, Mill was also an avid supporter for and administratively involved in British colonial efforts in India for the entirety of his adult life (from age seventeen in 1823 till his death in 1873)![12]

More often than not, the political theories of these canonical Anglo-European thinkers such as Locke, Kant, and Mill are read through the lens of anachronistic attribution of contemporary progressive ideals as a "natural" progression of their limited or even contrary historical ideas. But by whom are these political rights "naturally" extended to the previously excluded classes of people? Certainly, it was not by those canonical thinkers themselves, since neither Locke, Kant, nor Mill saw any contradictions between their claim of the "rights of men" and their exclusion of an array of people. Hence to see the contemporary rights as a "natural" progression from those canonical theories, one might argue, is also to purposely misread their theoretical intents.

Nevertheless, there is no shortage of contemporary publications attributing the origin of modern democratic state to those Anglo-European canonical thinkers. This sort of generous, theoretical appropriation is rarely extended to non-Western intellectual thinkers who are literally and strictly read within their limited historical and social contexts as artifacts in a time capsule. For instance, Confucianism is often seen as conceptually incompatible with the modern democratic state and its rights-based claims, and is said to be ill-equipped to cope with the demands of modernity.

The shared sense of the modern democratic state as characteristically liberal and Western is not just limited to contemporary scholars of liberalism; by and large, in their encounter with non-Western intellectual traditions, Anglo-European scholars take the stance of classical liberalism as a default referent to distinguish the Western from the rest of the world. For instance, in his brief but forceful comments on Kwong-loi Shun and David Wong's (2004) comprehensive anthology on Confucian ethics, Alasdair MacIntyre—a noted communitarian scholar—uses Lockean political theory as a reference point to contrast the West with the "illiberal" nature of Confucianism. As MacIntyre argues, the Confucian community has failed to adequately debate among themselves in their encounter with modernity, a debate that became inevitable "as a result of Western critiques—including those which invoked conceptions of natural or human rights—of the oppressive and exploitative character of those hierarchal Asian societies in which Confucianism had flourished for so long."[13] Seemingly, in MacIntyre's mind, "Western," "modernity," "human rights" all go hand in hand and, in contrast, the correlation between "Confucianism," "hierarchy," "oppression," and "exploitation" is a proven, unchanging, historical fact.

Furthermore, according to MacIntyre, a traditional Confucian society gives no recognition to the self-governing ability of the labor class or women and hence is profoundly anti-democratic. As he writes, "[y]et the traditional hierarchical structures of Confucian society involved a practical denial of the capacity for self-direction for the vast majority of those whose work sustained them: women, farmers, and fishing crews, more generally those engaged in productive manual labor."[14] In other words, it is historically and empirically proven that Confucianism helps foster a hierarchal, oppressive, and exploitative society to women and laborers in general. MacIntyre's self-righteous contempt toward the so-called "traditional hierarchical structures" of Confucian society and his perceived moral failing of Confucianism in meeting the challenges of "Western" modernity is resoundingly clear.

But unfortunately, MacIntyre's critique of Confucianism is insufficiently self-reflective of the Anglo-European intellectual traditions. The same condemnation that MacIntyre directed at Confucianism should also have been raised against Locke, Kant, or even Mill whose political theories also exclude an array of people. And yet what Anglo-European philosophers have said that is anti-democratic, sexist, or racist is simply whitewashed, ignored, or made irrelevant in the discussion of contemporary issues, while the same textual shortcomings in Confucian philosophy is voluminously amplified. This sort of discrepancy is in line with our common prejudicial attitude toward the Other. As former president George W. Bush—though not known for his rhetorical eloquence—says precisely, "[t]oo often, we judge other groups by their worse examples, while judging ourselves by our best intentions."[15] Sad to say, this holds true in MacIntyre's encounter with Confucianism as well.

It goes without saying that a classical text such as the *Analects, Mencius,* or *Xunzi,* written thousands of years ago, inevitably will fall short of the modern demands of gender parity, racial justice, and democratic equality. The point of studying those classical texts is not to return to the exact historical or social contexts in which they were written, but to draw inspirations and conceptual alternatives to solve our very modern problems in our very modern contexts. Indeed, to invoke Locke, Kant, or Mill in the discussion of the modern democratic state is not the same as to embody every value that Locke, Kant, or Mill had advocated in their own historical and social contexts; that would be impossible nor is it desirable. And MacIntyre obviously understands that, as he writes, "[i]t is not of course my view that modern states embody the values of Locke."[16]

Nevertheless, despite the temporal and value discrepancy between the contemporary and the Lockean one, our very modern state with our very modern values, according to MacIntyre, owe its origin to Locke. As MacIntyre goes on to write, "[i]t is rather that we may need to use a conception of rights that we owe in part to Locke in order to protect ourselves from such states."[17] In other words, our modern concept of equal rights in part is Lockean in character, despite Locke's textual exclusion of an array of people from his discussion of political rights, not to mention Locke's intimate and persistent role in supporting and facilitating the transatlantic slave trade and colonial plantations for decades.[18]

The same willingness to concoct a progressive political conception of the modern liberal, democratic state out of the Anglo-European canonical texts is, however, glaringly absent when it is applied to Confucianism, which is seen as antithetical to even the very idea of modernity. As MacIntyre reflects on the limitations of Confucianism in its encounter with "Western" modernity, "[b]ut my view does involve a denial that any modern state, Asian or Western, could embody the values of a Mencius or Xunzi. The political dimensions of a Confucianism that took either or both of them as its teachers would be those of local community, not of the state."[19] MacIntyre's rejection of Confucianism in the modern political discourse cannot be made more clearly. As far as modernity is concerned, there is no place for Confucianism. A modern, liberal, democratic state, in MacIntyre's view, can only be Western in character and Lockean in particular. That limiting approach to the modern political discourse is Eurocentric, but more importantly, it is an unnecessary self-imposed impoverishment in our imagination of what more and what else is possible and desirable for our shared progressive future for humanity.

The seeming contradiction between Confucianism and modernity as insisted by MacIntyre can be easily overcome, if one extends the same charitable spirit in textual interpretation routinely employed in interpreting Western canonical texts to others. Just as Locke, Kant, and Mill whose political theories are still relevant today in spite of their textual and moral shortcomings in terms of gender, race, and class, Confucianism can also be a rich conceptual wellspring for contemporary readers to draw inspirations from to solve our very modern problems in our very modern world.

Confucianism or Democracy

Since MacIntyre's (2004) resolute rejection to the compatibility between Confucianism and modernity, numerous scholars have endeavored to propose an array of blended systems of Confucian democracy ranging from Roger Ames's (2017) and Sor-hoon Tan's (2004) communitarianism thesis, Daniel Bell's (2015) meritocracy thesis, to Joseph Chan's (2013) service-based perfection thesis. Each offers its unique take on the integration of Confucianism into the modern discourse of democracy, along with its associated concepts such as rights-based claim, personal autonomy, and equality. Criticisms however have been swift focusing mostly on the seeming adulteration of democracy and/or the perceived impossible blend of Confucianism with an array of correlated concepts with democracy. The problem, as most critics see it, is that Confucianism simply is antithetical to democracy, so the proposed blended system of Confucian democracy of any kind—let it be communitarianism, meritocracy, or service-based perfectionism—amounts to a distortion of the concept, the intent, or the proper working of democracy.

Much like the exclusion of non-Western texts from the genealogy of philosophy whose criteria are defined tautologically, a sense of tautology is also at work to exclude Confucianism here. As the argument goes, democracy with all its co-requisite rights and concepts emerged only in the late nineteenth and early twentieth centuries and hence non-Western intellectual traditions that could not possibly have explicitly articulated these co-requisite rights and concepts of democracy are by definition incompatible with democracy. It is true that the language of rights is absent in Confucian texts, but that is also true in the Greek tradition, and yet, contemporary scholars find no greater difficulty in tracing the origin of democracy to the ancient Greek city state of Athens.

The same is true for the concept of equality, self-governance, and autonomy. For instance, neither Locke, Kant, nor Mill championed the modern democratic system that we practice today, nor did they apply all the co-requisite rights and concepts to all constituents of a given state in their political theories, and yet contemporary scholars continue to credit these canonical thinkers with the making of the modern democratic institution, which, as MacIntyre argues, is said to be in part Lockean in character. In order to make these Anglo-European canonical thinkers compatible with modernity, contemporary scholars routinely parse out and focus only on the favorable parts of their political theories, but to do so with Confucianism is immediately flagged as misreading the original intent of the texts.

Those who intend to integrate Confucian philosophy into contemporary progressive projects are, then, left with two impossible choices: Either accepting that Confucian texts are by definition outdated, irrelevant, and antithetical to our modern progressive movements, or devising a tortured conceptual gymnastic to fit the theoretical circle of Confucianism into the modern square of democracy without leaving glaring, gaping holes. Such is the current state of either/or for the field of Asian and Comparative philosophy insofar as our modern progressive projects are concerned. The blended system of Confucian democracy, at best, can only be seen as a deficient imitation of the genuine Western progressive political paradigm. Thus proposed by substandard *philosophants* who confusedly mesh two antithetical conceptual paradigms together in a desperate act of masquerading Confucianism as a semi-progressive system, the blended system of Confucian democracy, of course, can never be as good as the Western model.

Try as it may, Confucianism can only rise up to the primitive stage in the developmental ladder to a genuine democratic system. For instance, in critiquing Joseph Chan's service-based perfection model of Confucian democracy, Yvonne Chiu zeroes in on the lack of genuine moral autonomy in Confucianism which is said to be only capable of rising to the preliminary level with "a voluntary endorsement of morality" and "a reflective engagement in moral life," but is said to fail to achieve the higher level required for genuine moral autonomy, which requires "self-legislation" and "radical free expression of the individual's will."[20] To demonstrate the conceptual incompatibility between Confucian morality and genuine morality required for a truly democratic system, Chiu in part uses a tautological definition of autonomy. As she writes:

> A conception of moral autonomy has to locate the source of the moral law in the moral agent. Autonomy comes from *autos* (self) and *nomos* (laws or convention)—self-legislation, which requires but is also more than voluntary endorsement or reflective engagement with morality. As such, there is no genuine moral autonomy in Chan's reconstruction of Confucianism either.[21]

A hierarchical, developmental logic is clearly implied in this ranking of moral developments: Genuine moral autonomy belongs to the West and clearly, Greek in origin, in nature, and in essence, whereas Confucianism can only rise as far as it goes to the first two preliminary stages that are required but by themselves are insufficient to constitute genuine moral autonomy.

And since the aim of Chan's service-based perfection model is service to the people by ways of moral cultivation, a radical expression of the will for its own sake is not seen as a central, intrinsic value, and that to Chiu is problematic, since as Chiu argues earlier, genuine moral autonomy requires it. To amend this grave Confucian shortcoming, Chiu then provides some possible Anglo-European models, and Mill who advocates for both the intrinsic value of moral and personal autonomy and the importance of virtue in all aspects of life, according to Chiu, is the most obvious choice. As Chiu writes:

> There are some proponents of the importance of virtue in politics who also accept the intrinsic value of personal autonomy, and they might offer some way of accommodating both. The most obvious is Mill, whose advocacy of personal experimentation and authenticity was coupled with the essential importance of knowledge and virtue at every level—in politics, in business, in marriage, and so forth.[22]

In Chiu's view, Mill's liberal political theory offers the best of all possible worlds that on the one hand emphasizes the importance of cultivating virtue in all areas of life including the marital relations not just in the political life, and on the other recognizes the essential and intrinsic value of personal and moral autonomy that is required for the modern democratic state.

But even if Confucian democracy can make the conceptual accommodation within, that may still not be enough. At the end of the day, the proponents of Confucian democracy may still need to choose: Confucianism or democracy. As Chiu concludes the essay with these parting words, "Confucian democracy must come to better terms with both moral and personal autonomy, however; but in doing so, it may need to make even more difficult choices between Confucianism and democracy."[23] The door to a viable blended system of Confucian democracy is practically closed: In order for this blended system to work, proponents will have to either make the theoretical paradigm more democratic and hence less Confucian, or retain its Confucian character and hence non-democratic, if not anti-democratic. This, of course, is an impossible either/or for any serious thinker: To argue for a non-democratic, let alone an anti-democratic, blended system is to belie the name of Confucian *democracy*, but to negate *Confucian* character is also equally preposterous for this blended theoretical paradigm.

The kind of impossible conceptual contortion is not required for Anglo-European canonical thinkers in their contemporary appropriation. Whatever outdated ideas found in their writings are simply glossed over. For instance, in Chiu's invocation of Mill as the ideal model for the blended system of Confucian democracy to amend its perceived shortcoming, Chiu acknowledges that Mill also sets limits to personal autonomy, "namely the Harm Principle," and in addition, Mill "also allows for interference with 'barbarians.'"[24] In other words, Mill's brand of liberalism does not allow for complete neutrality; there are limits to the way in which personal and moral autonomy is exercised. The well-known "Harm Principle" is one, but what about the justified state interference with the "barbarians"? This point was quickly glossed over with no further elaboration. But with a closer reading of Mill's numerous works including his famed *On Liberty* (1859), it is clear that the "barbarians" referenced here belong to the non-white, the colonized. The ultimate aim of colonization for Mill is moral in nature, albeit mired in a racialized developmental logic. It is most curious to note that contemporary scholars, while they are aware of Mill's usage of a racialized developmental logic, remain unperturbed by Mill's own defense over his exclusion of the "barbarians" from the exercise of personal and moral autonomy.

Contemporary scholars in the political discourse continue to discount the elements of race and colonialism in the liberal ideals of Mill's political thought. But without taking these troubling elements into account in the studies of Mill's liberalism, as Anthony Bogues warns, is to overlook the way in which "racial slavery, empire, and colonialism were integral to modernity and to modern political thought."[25] To engage in colonization, as Mill sees it, is good business that makes both moral and economic sense. As Mill writes clearly in the *Principles of Political Economy* (1848), "[t]he question of government intervention in the work of Colonization involves the future and permanent interests of civilization itself and far outstretches the comparatively narrow limits of purely economic considerations."[26] In other words, colonization has a far more encompassing moral value than the narrow scope of economics.

Nevertheless, colonization is the order of the day that every wealthy nation is engaged and can engage in. As Mill in the same text continues to write, "[t]here needs to be no hesitation in affirming that Colonization, in the present state of the world, is the best affairs in which the capital of an old and wealthy country can engage."[27] For Mill, colonization is justified by and is wrapped in a complex web of economic prosperity, civilizing effect, and human development. To colonize other lesser "developed" races and nations is both a moral duty and an economic opportunity for the "civilized" nations to not only alleviate their own internal crowded population and labor problems, but also at the same time to bring the "barbarians" up to speed with the rest of the civilized world, albeit incrementally and imperfectly.

In spite of his liberal cry for personal and moral autonomy, for Mill, despotism is both an acceptable and a necessary form of government in dealing with the "barbarians" whose developmental stage mirrors a nonage infant. As Mill lays out the perimeters for his famed political theory in the "Introduction" of *On Liberty* (1859):

> It is, perhaps, hardly necessary to say that this doctrine is meant to apply only to human beings in the maturity of their faculties. We are not speaking of children, or of young persons below the age which the law may fix as that of manhood or womanhood. Those who are still in a state to require being taken care of by others, must be protected against their own actions as well as against external injury. For the same reason, we may leave out of consideration those backward states of society in which the race itself may be considered as in its nonage.[28]

Race again is destiny; one's rational maturity is not only in part dependent on the progression of one's biological and educational development, but also is predicated on one's race. Those inferior races are stuck in the stage of perpetual infancy regardless of their biological maturity. Only with the tutelage of the civilized can the barbarians possibly be raised up from their nonage so that one day they may be worthy of exercising Mill's liberal principles.

As is clear from Mill's prolonged and intimate involvement in British colonial efforts in India throughout his entire adult life till his death, the day of rational maturity for the barbarians might not come so easily or quickly. Until that day comes, these barbarians should be content with the system of despotism. As Mill continues to write:

> Despotism is a legitimate mode of government in dealing with barbarians, provided the end be their improvement, and the means justified by actually effecting that end. Liberty, as a principle, has no application to any state of things anterior to the time when mankind have become capable of being improved by free and equal discussion. Until then, there is nothing for them but implicit obedience to an Akbar or a Charlemagne, if they are so fortunate as to find one.[29]

It is worth noting that Mill's writings here evidentially reflect his governing principles on the ground. In 1858 before *On Liberty* was published in 1859, Mill resigned from East India Company as its chief examiner only when he failed to defeat proposals granting a modicum of internal self-governing to India that in Mill's view is still in its nonage after decades of his colonial tutelage.[30]

Clearly, Mill's liberal principles require not just the conventional understanding of self-governance, but more importantly a certain type of self-development that apparently has already been achieved by the Anglo-European world leading the way in this racialized, developmental ladder for humanity. In truth, Mill's political theory not only is undemocratic and illiberal; it is racist. But as shown earlier, Mill's racialized developmental logic is brushed aside and uncoupled from Mill's political theory in the contemporary discourse of the modern democratic institution, whereas the undemocratic, oppressive, and hierarchical strains in Confucianism are relentlessly amplified.

The point here is not that Confucianism is or should be compatible with anything and everything; rather, so often this sort of developmental logic as seen in the colonial past repeats itself today when non-Western philosophies are positioned as lesser in comparison with the West wherein genuine morality is to be located. It is true that a strong sense of individualism is not present in Confucianism, but that is true for most of the pre-modern Western thinkers as well—let it be Plato, Aristotle, or Aquinas.[31] Even for Locke, Kant, and Mill, individualism along with its many assorted concepts are only applicable to a certain class of people. But somehow those glaring conceptual gaps between the ancient and the modern or between what is actually said in the Anglo-European canonical texts and the distinctively contemporary ideals are seamlessly bridged without much fanfare whereas deficiency is all what one can find in Confucianism.

To some critics, the deficiencies in Confucianism are just too numerous for a blended system of Confucian democracy to make any sense at all. As basic as granting citizenship in the modern democratic state, Confucianism is said to be incapable of even providing a sensible justification for granting it, since citizenship is a rights-based concept, not a service-based concept. As Sungmoon Kim (2017) writes in his critique of Chan's service-based perfection model of Confucian democracy, "Chan takes for granted that citizenship is a form of political office, but he offers no explanation as to why this is so, nor why we (should) even have citizenship in a modern Confucian society."[32] Admittedly, citizenship is a modern concept, and hence naturally, Confucianism does not offer any explicit justification for granting citizenship as a political office per se, but then again, that is true for the pre-modern Western thinkers as well.

For instance, Plato did not provide an explicit account of granting citizenship, neither did Aristotle, even though both of them wrote extensively on the topic of politics and political institution. Although it is true that in the *Politics,* Aristotle did treat "citizenship" as a political office and did define "citizen" as an active participant in the governing of the *polis* not just a passive recipient subject to its laws and regulations, Aristotle did not provide a clear account as to how exactly one obtains citizenship except being born to both parents who are already citizens.[33] Furthermore, to Aristotle, holding a political office or being excluded from it does not by itself detract from, nor is it an essential part of, one's pursuit of *eudemonia*, not to mention the fact that Aristotle himself is a resident alien holding no rights to participate in the office of citizenship in Athens.[34] Lastly, for both Plato and Aristotle, democracy is definitively not the most favorable political system; ideally, political power should be held by the philosopher-king(s) and men of virtue respectively.

Indeed, the modern sense of citizenship that is granted to all constituents of the state—both born and naturalized—with a wide range of political rights is a modern invention. To invalidate pre-modern textual traditions including Confucianism for their perceived failures to provide an explicit account of citizenship that fits the modern conception is anachronistic. Nevertheless, the historical fact that the modern state didn't happen until the late nineteenth century in China and Korea is then used to further demonstrate the incompatibility between citizenship and Confucianism. As Kim continues to write, "[t]raditional Confucianism is, admittedly, a total stranger to the institution of citizenship. Until the late nineteenth century the term 'citizenship,' let alone its political office, was nonexistent in the pre-republican Confucian societies of both China and Korea."[35] Rarely, if ever, this sort of empirical counter-example is used to invalidate claims made in the Anglo-European canonical texts.

For instance, Locke's *Two Treatises of Government* (1689) is often used as the theoretical basis for contemporary discourse on liberal political theory, and yet his willingness to support, administer, and personally profit from slave trades and colonial plantations has not thus been used to invalidate his political theory. On the contrary, in the latest attempt to "clear" Locke's name, contemporary scholars are willing to go out of their way to uncouple Locke's political theory from his deeds, proclaiming that while Locke's actions might be abhorrent, "his philosophy is not racist—quite the contrary."[36] This is indeed a case of head-spin where Locke, a supporter of new world institutional slavery, should continue to deserve—perhaps even more so— our admiration for his political theory of natural and political rights of man!

It is not just Locke's deeds; there are textual contradictions found in Locke's two *Treatises* and elsewhere that one must also somehow overlook in regard to slavery. Locke, on the one hand, speaks of the horror of slavery and the natural liberty of man. As Locke writes impassionedly in the opening line of the *First Treatise*, "[s]lavery is so vile and miserable an Estate of Man, and so directly opposite to the generous Temper and Courage of our Nation: that its hardly to be conceived that an *Englishman*, much less a *Gentleman*, should plead for it."[37] At the same time, in the *Second Treatise*, Locke legitimizes the practice of slavery when he writes about "the perfect condition of slavery":

> Indeed, having by his fault forfeited his own Life by some Act that deserves Death, he to whom he has forfeited it may (when he has him in his power) delay to take it, and make use of him to his own Service; and he does him no injury by it. For, whenever he finds the hardship of his Slavery outweigh the value of his Life, it is in his Power, by resisting the Will of his Master, to draw on himself the Death he desires. This is the perfect condition of *Slavery*, which *is* nothing else but the *State of War continued between a lawful Conqueror and a Captive*.[38]

Given the fact that Locke invested in a company that had a monopoly on the slave trade in the West African Coast bringing thousands of slaves to plantations each year, and given the fact that Locke was also a governmental administrator overseeing colonial affairs with an intimate knowledge of the conditions of plantations abroad, slavery that Locke wrote in the *Treatises* was definitively not just a historical reference to the ancient past.[39]

Furthermore, Locke advocates for a despotic rule over slaves, since as slaves, they are "by the right of Nature, subjected to the absolute dominion and arbitrary power of their masters" and being properties themselves, slaves "cannot in that state be considered as any part of civil society."[40] Locke had a choice to set a different standard for the treatment of colonial slaves by virtue of his governmental position. But instead, in his writings not just in the two *Treatises*, but more importantly, in *The Fundamental Constitutions of Carolina* (1669/1670/1682), Locke's advocacy for a despotic rule over slaves has become the blueprint for how new world colonies should be organized. As Locke writes in the *Constitutions*, "[e]very freeman of Carolina shall have absolute power and Authority over his Negro slaves, of what opinion or religion soever."[41] Much like Mill's advocacy for despotism over barbarians, Locke's advocacy for despotism over slaves does not seem to damper contemporary scholars' enthusiasm for attributing the modern democratic institution to these canonical thinkers, whereas the blended system of Confucian democracy is said to fail at every turn in its encounter with the modern democratic institution.

The problems for a blended system of Confucian democracy are not just limited to the absence of a clear articulation of modern democratic concepts such as citizenship or equal rights, but also the very mentioning of Confucian ethical value system that prefers the common good and sagely rule, over self-gratification and political egalitarianism. Holding onto these basic Confucian values of virtuous self-cultivation alone is said to be in direct contradiction to the essence as well as the practice of democracy. In particular, it is said that the early Confucians' constant references to *tian* 天 and *dao* 道 as the source of virtues is contrary to democracy which is secular in nature. In a blended system of Confucian democracy, one risks either integrating non-secular concepts of *tian* 天 and *dao* 道 into the secular institution of democracy, or diluting its Confucian character.

For instance, in his critique of Chan's modest proposal of making Confucian perfectionism as a regulative ideal instead of a comprehensive doctrine, Yutang Jin questions whether it is even possible to construct a secular Confucian ideal:

> [F]or early Confucians, Confucian virtues are rarely severed entirely from the metaphysical concepts of Heaven and the Way, the unity of which, according to Mou Zongsan, constitutes the defining nature of Confucian philosophy. The disagreement in the Confucian tradition is not so much about *whether* human virtues derive from Heaven as about *how* they derive from it.[42]

A blended system of Confucian democracy, if it is to "modernize," as it were to decouple itself from these metaphysical beliefs, is to be "deprived of the very core that defines its bearings in the Confucian context."[43] In other words, these metaphysical concepts of *tian* 天 and *dao* 道 are essential to Confucianism and cannot be decoupled from it and thereby making Confucianism incompatible with the secular nature of democracy.

Furthermore, Confucian learning is always encoded with an ethical end, and to model after and to put the virtuous as the ruling exemplar is part of the Confucian learning process, whereas for democracy learning is only a supplemental, not a defining feature of democracy. As Jin continues to write:

> The very point of democracy is that it is not so much about learning as about asserting equal political status. If we learn anything in this process, that is a desideratum rather than its defining feature. Also, the point of Confucian learning is to put the virtuous as the exemplar, and egalitarian tendencies within democracy may well oppose, even nullify, the rather hierarchical structure of Confucian learning.[44]

Simply put, democracy's equal political participation and popular sovereignty are value neutral in content and secular in orientation, and hence cannot have any ethical preferences in its governance, least of all Confucian ones which are metaphysical and hierarchical in nature. This conundrum—the assertion of Confucianism could be democratic or democracy could be justified on Confucian grounds—seems to be an impasse.

But the truth is that, as it should be clear by now, the insolvable conundrum of Confucian democracy is just a verbal dispute. The concept of virtue is essential not only to ethics, but also to the very concept of right that the modern democratic state relies on. For instance, Kant's *The Metaphysics of Morals* (1797) is composed of two doctrines: Doctrine of Right and Doctrine of Virtue, not to mention Kant's reliance on rational theology to construct his moral kingdom of ends on earth as his final end of humanity.[45] More often than not, contemporary scholars decouple Kant's doctrine of virtue from his doctrine of right, his rational theology from his ethics without altering the *core* of Kantian character. So often is the somnambulatory assumption that Anglo-European canonical texts are secular in nature and hence compatible with our contemporary progressive projects, whereas the "traditional" Confucian texts are derivative from and dependent on their dogmatic metaphysics.

In order to move past the seemingly unsolvable conundrums regarding the compatibility between Confucianism and democracy, we will have to start on the same level playing field where both Anglo-European and Confucian classical texts are seen as viable sources for contemporary scholars to draw conceptual alternatives to improve upon the system we have today. A rights-based democratic state undoubtedly is a modern invention. So the question on the compatibility between rights characterizing the system of a liberal, democratic state and rites characterizing the system of a Confucian state is not so much whether Confucian texts written more than two thousand years ago have already had the concept of rights in them. The answer is clearly a no, since the concept of equal rights across gender, race, and class is a modern concoction.

Rather, in studying Confucianism, the question one should ask is whether Confucianism has anything uniquely valuable to contribute to the well-being of the modern life that we now live, by making our modern democratic state a much more caring, progressive, and inclusive one. Given the Confucian political imperative of caring for the vulnerable and its unique emphasis on ritual deference to ensure social cohesion, the answer should also be a resounding yes. In short, it is possible to forge a modern liberal state that is also Confucian in character in our shared good life.

Rights or Rites

Even though the language of rights is absent in Confucianism, the concept of law is not. In fact, it is arguable that the Chinese have one of the earliest bureaucratic systems traced as far back as to the Zhou dynasty (1045–771 BCE) with complex layers of regulations governing the inner workings of the state.[46] Law, by necessity, is impersonal, punitive, and reactive; and due to these characteristics, it has its advantages and drawbacks in state governance. Most notably as Confucius says in the *Analects* 2.3: "Lead the people with administrative injunctions and keep them orderly with penal law, and they will avoid punishments but will be without a sense of shame. Lead them with virtue and keep them orderly through observing ritual and they will develop a sense of shame, and moreover, will order themselves." In other words, laws and regulations can define the outer boundaries of human behavior through enforceable coercion and reactive punishment, but they provide no proactive, positive model and appropriate social mechanism for the actual self-transformation to take place.

Governing by ritual is a much more tenuous proposition than governing by impersonal laws and regulations. But this is not an either/or proposition. The Chinese dynastic state from very early on has already recognized the necessity and efficiency of laws and regulations in statecraft; what is new is that Confucius also recognizes the deficiency of a law-based society. Laws and regulations must be substantiated by ritual. For law functions like a physical fence demarcating the outer boundaries of acceptable human behavior in a civil state, whereas ritual works as the actual knot that binds us to one another personally, socially, politically, and spiritually. Ritual is like a complex set of social rhythms that through positively modeling we have gradually learned to dance to the tune with grace and due measure in our daily encounter with others. In short, to put it in the Kantian idiom, law provides the form while ritual is the actual content of a civil state.

It is possible to integrate the minimally required, enforceable legal requirements of the individual rights to life, liberty, and the pursuit of happiness into the long-standing Confucian political discourse on humane governance. For instance, the subject's natural claim to life can be deduced from the Confucian symmetry of being a humane ruler and being the father and mother of the people (*minzhifumu* 民之父母) who cares for the people like he is attending to a new born babe with utmost sincerity. In caring for the infant, to protect the infant from physical harm is a given (the term *minzhifumu* 民之父母 will be discussed in the following chapter). No Confucian state hence will be able to live up to the political imperative to care for the people, if it also recklessly takes away the subject's very physical existence starting with the vulnerable infant who cannot fend for herself.

Integral to the concept of parenthood is the obligation to not just protect the life of the child, but also provide a nurturing, supportive environment that enables the child to live, grow, and thrive, and that nurturing and supportive environment is antithetical to a tyrannical, oppressive, or exploitative one. Thus, the subject's natural claims to life, liberty, and a share of happiness can be seen as all-inclusive in the Confucian explicit analogy of a humane ruler as the father and mother of the people. In other words, all these three rights claims are implicitly assumed in and are consistent with the Confucian political discourse of what constitutes a legitimate and humane state and ruler.

But, as some would argue, to equate what is ethically required of the Confucian ruler with the legal rights of the individual—rights that the individual can claim against the state—is to misread the Confucian texts.[47] After all, as MacIntyre claims, individual rights are "a Western invention" and are in part Lockean in character.[48] But, by the same token, to attribute equal human rights across gender, race, and class to Locke, Kant, or Mill in modern political discourse is also to misread their political philosophies. It is simply not the case that Locke, Kant, or Mill believes that the sort of individual rights that they champion apply equally to women, the labor class, or the people of color. In other words, we must either modify the so-called "a Western invention" of individual rights to the narrow category of propertied white men or intentionally misread those Western canonical texts.

The point here is not to re-litigate the obvious, double standard. Rather, the point here is that no state can claim itself to be genuinely Confucian—that is, genuinely caring for the subject as if it were tending to a vulnerable new born babe like the nurturing parents would and should—and at the same time be tyrannical, oppressive, or exploitative in its political structure or aim. Raising a healthy child, among other things, requires a stable and nurturing environment for the child to live, grow, and thrive, and a Confucian state that seeks to mimic that ideal parenthood in its approach to political governance conceptually shall also embrace the subject's claim to life, liberty, and a share of happiness as the bare minimum for a civil state. Any state authority acting contrary to that bare minimum falls outside of what makes a civil state possible, Confucian or otherwise.

Conclusion

Indeed, there is no insurmountable difficulty in infusing Confucianism into the modern democratic state with the subject's claim to life, liberty, and the pursuit of happiness. It is hard to see how Confucianism that champions a political system of humane governance would go against these basic conditions for a civil state. But, as noted earlier, law by itself is not the sufficient condition for a caring, progressive, and inclusive state. To take the legal protection of one's autonomy in charting one's own life as the sole aim of the state is to mistake the form for the content. The function of the law is to set the outer boundary for sociality, but law by itself cannot bring about genuine social cohesion. Ritual, on the other hand, whose main function is to bring about social cohesion. As Confucius says in the *Analects* 1.12, "harmony (*he*和) is the most valuable function of ritual." And this is so because, unlike law, ritual offers a positive model for behavioral transformation, as it were, from inside out.

A well-functioning civil state must provide more than just a legal fencing, a value-free zone for disparate individuals that are bound to no one and are bound by nothing other than negative deterrence from unsociability. A cohesive state requires a positive social mechanism to render each individual ever more porous to and inclusive of others in the pursuit of their shared good life. Ritual is the social knot that binds us. Hence one could argue that having the legal form delineating the subject's natural claims of life, liberty, and a share of happiness is only the beginning of a civil state; ritual is what completes a well-functioning, cohesive state. Under this light, not only rights and rites are compatible; the completion of a civil state, in fact, requires rites. And Confucianism as both a political and ethical system with its unique emphasis on rites stands ready to provide viable conceptual tools for us to fine-tune our very modern liberal, democratic state into an ever more cohesive, compassionate, and caring society.

Ritual, Common Good, and Social Cohesion

If there is ever a time when the intractable intertwining nature of the world lays itself bare, it is during the Covid-19 pandemic—a storm that took the world by surprise with its unprecedented speed. The ineffectiveness of using the artifice of national boundaries to fight a pandemic is roundly exposed. The more the wealthier nations hoard and tune out the poor and the needy, the more difficult it is for the world to get a handle on the pandemic, since the viruses are given more time to circulate and to mutate into even more infectious ones which in turn infect more easily and widely. After three years into the Covid pandemic, wealthier nations despite having a 75 percent vaccination rate and giving 60 percent of its population a booster shot continue to be threatened by new Covid variants emerged from lower income nations where less than 1.5 percent of its population have received a booster shot.[1] Truly, it turns out that in order for anyone to be safe, everyone has to be safe first.

And yet instead of coming together to form a united front in order to devise coherent strategies against this novel threat to humanity, the world has descended into chaos with each fighting on and for its own. Mature Western democratic states, in particular—despite having in their possession of superior technologies, resources, and infrastructures—oftentimes have not fared substantially better than other less well-endowed countries. In fact, even during the height of mounting daily infection and death rate, there have been waves of recalcitrant defiance in the name of individual freedom against strict lockdown measures and against vaccine inoculations making safeguarding the vulnerable and achieving a herd immunity ever more difficult to reach without furthering more deaths and sufferings.

The cherished individualism that emphasizes self-sovereignty has, instead, become a rally cry against the health measures of mask wearing and keeping safe physical distancing. The devastation left in the wake of the pandemic however is not shared equally or proportionate to the kind of risky behavior that one exhibits. The older population of age fifty and above, especially those in the nursing care homes, accounts for up to 95 percent of all Covid deaths.[2] The relentlessly high number of deaths among the old and the vulnerable populations exposes the fault line in an individualistic inclined democratic state like ours. There, indeed, cannot come a better time to infuse our modern democratic state with a Confucian sense of political authority that premises on caring for the old, the young, the sick, and the disabled in a mutually enriching ritual harmony.

To build a state that is truly inclusive, caring, and compassionate, the emphasis on liberal individualism or political rights alone will not be able to get us there, as the unusually high number of Covid deaths and infection cases in mature Western democratic states demonstrate, despite all the material advantages that they have at their disposal.[3] A shared sense of social cohesion and common good will need to be our starting point, and ritual is that much-needed binding thread in any society and most of all in an individualistically inclined state like ours.

Origins of Ritual *Li* 禮

The emphasis on ritual in the political discourse is quintessentially Confucian, even though the concept of ritual is a shared one in most human societies. Ritual usually derives its most solemn, sacred importance from religion where ritual is used as a defined means to communicate with the transcendent divine. In most orthodox communities, religious ritual does not change, since ritual is supposed to be a means of transcendence standing outside of time immune to the changing human condition. Religious ritual, in a word, just like the transcendent divine, is supposed to be eternal, contrasting with the temporal nature of humanity in this transient world.[4] In contrast, civil ritual oftentimes carries a profane, pejorative connotation as a formalized social behavior. For instance, in our vernacular expression, being ritualistic and being inauthentic are nearly synonymous. However, neither of these is the case in the Confucian use of *li* 禮. Confucian *li* 禮 covers both religious and civil rites, and both religious and civil rites are sacred in importance and both are also subject to change, albeit conservatively.[5] It is this solemnly spiritual as well as pragmatic feature of Confucian *li* 禮 that makes it a proficient vehicle for social cohesion, and hence it plays a rather prominent role in the Confucian political discourse.

The detailed etymological analysis of *li* 禮 found in the earliest Chinese dictionary, *Shuowen Jiezi,* points to its spiritual origins: *Li* 禮 means "to perform" or "to carry out (according to a certain path) so as to serve the spirit in order to obtain blessings (禮: 履也. 所以事神致福也)." The graph *li* 禮 has two components: *Li** 豊 and *shi* 示. The dictionary explains that the pictograph *li** 豊 is a ritual instrument or vessel (豊: 行禮之器也), and the ideograph *shi* 示 refers to celestial objects such as sun, moon, and stars—signs that we can observe in order to follow the patterns and the seasonal changes to allow us to see the times of fortune and misfortune (示: 天垂象, 見吉凶, 所以示人也, 从二. 三垂, 日月星也. 觀乎天文, 以察時變). In short, *shi* 示 means spiritual matters (示, 神事也).[6] All together, *li* 禮 is defined in part restrictively as referring to the physical requirement of proper ritual items such as vessel, clothing, and food, and in part expansively as referring to the performative and pragmatic aspect of ritual where the ritualist seeks a productive outcome by being in tune with the timing and the surrounding. To be *li* 禮, hence, is to hit the mark through a proficient performance that harmonizes the spiritual, natural, and human world.

Beyond etymology, one can also find various accounts of the origins of *li* 禮 in an array of pre-Han Confucian texts such as the *Analects, Mencius, Xunzi,* and *Book of Rites*: Some attribute the origin of ritual to the Great cosmic force, some to the ancient sage kings, and some to human sentiments. For instance, in the *Book of Rites*—a Confucian Classic devoted entirely to ritual—in its "Liyun 禮運" chapter, *li* 禮 is traced back to the Great one, the cosmic force that divides into heaven and earth (是故夫禮, 必本於大一, 分而為天地), but in its "Yueji 樂記" chapter, the ancient kings also serve as the origin of *li* 禮 (是故先王之制禮樂, 人為之節). Moreover, in its "Wensang 問喪" chapter, human sentiment is said to be the origin of the three-year mourning ritual; as the *Liji* explains, the three-year mourning ritual "is not sent down from *tian* 天, nor sent up from earth, but a matter of human sentiment (孝子喪親, 哭泣無數, 服勤三年 […] 此孝子之志也, 人情之實也, 禮義之經也, 非從天降也, 非從地出也, 人情而已矣)."[7]

The multiple accounts of the origin of *li* 禮 can also be found in other Confucian texts. For instance, in the *Analects* 1.12, *li* 禮 governing all things big and small is said to be prescribed by the ancient kings (先王之道斯為美, 小大由之), and in the *Analects* 3.4, the origin of *li* 禮, as Confucius explains, is about material modesty and proper emotion (林放問禮之本. 子曰: 大哉問！禮, 與其奢也, 寧儉; 喪, 與其易也, 寧戚). In the *Mencius* 2A6, the beginning of *li* 禮 is said to be in the heart of courtesy and modesty (辭讓之心, 禮之端也); similarly, in *Mencius* 6A6, the heart of deference and respect is said to pertain to *li* 禮 (恭敬之心, 禮也). And lastly, in the *Mencius* 7A21, *li* 禮 along with three other cardinal virtues are said to be rooted in the heart-mind (仁義禮智根於心).

Xunzi—in his famed dispute with Mencius on the goodness of human propensity—in the *Xunzi* 23.7 attributes *li* 禮 to the ancient sage kings as a way to curb the excess of human desires that tend to lead to social unrest (凡禮義者, 是生於聖人之偽). But in the *Xunzi* 19.4, *li* 禮 is said to have three roots: "[H]eaven and earth are the root of life, ancestors are the root of kinship, and lords and teachers are the root of governance (禮有三

本: 天地者, 生之本也; 先祖者, 類之本也; 君師者, 治之本也)." In short, Confucian *li* 禮 is by no means exhausted by the religious account; *li* 禮 is as much a spiritual concept as a moral and civic concept essential for a well-ordered state.

Ritual as Means of Governance

Governing by ritual is a hallmark of Confucian political theory; the Confucian emphasis on ritual as a governing mechanism is unique not just within the Chinese intellectual tradition, but also compared to the Anglo-European canonical texts. In particular, from Hobbes onward politics oftentimes is concerned with autonomous adult males in their contractual association with one another. Thus conceptualized, politics is literally a public affair of *men* who are all equal, free, and independent of one another. This background assumption of the political subject naturally generates a different kind of governing mechanism and leads to a different form of political institution. In this adult male-based political paradigm, antagonism constitutes the nature of the political relation between the subject and the state as well as among subjects themselves.

The Hobbesian perpetual state of war in the state of nature is a case in point. Men, as Hobbes puts it, are like wild mushrooms sprung out of nowhere with no intersubjective relationship.[8] The civil state only comes about out of our mutual fear and distrust. While Locke provides a gentler version of the equal, autonomous, and independent individuals in the state of nature, the basic assumption of the political subject continues to be based on a self-centric adult male constrained only through external coercion. This political paradigm naturally gives rise to a limited, value-neutral state whose function is to enforce coercive laws in order to enable a minimally tolerable coexistence of disparate political subjects in their mutual antagonism. A Confucian state governed by ritual however aims at effecting a higher state of being than this sort of bare minimum. Ritual is able to do that because—unlike law whose function is to repel and to coerce—the function of ritual is to harmonize the performing subjects with their surrounding by providing a proper order for each to relate to the other.

Generally speaking, ritual is a public performance with a socially recognizable script, and a ritual script involves various components such as physical objects, postures, sentiments, verbal communications, and timing. In a well-performed ritual, all these elements—the natural, human, and cosmic world—are brought into harmony and hence a productive outcome is effected. In other words, ritual is a purposeful human action to provide order to the world. This ritual-based order is not a transcendent, unchanging order, nor is it structured by coercive laws enforcing only the external behavior of the subject, but leaving the belief, attitude, or mindset of the subject intact. Rather, Confucian *li* 禮 is a conscious human effort to approximate the ideal order of things in which all things are mutually enriching with due measure and grace. This ritual-based order is not just mutually advantageous in the personal realm, but also in the political realm and beyond, since ritual not only provides the concrete content for each individual to relate to the other in the human world, but also requires a proper reflection on the relation between the human world and the natural as well as the spiritual world.

The metaphors of *ji* 紀 (knot), *ju* 矩 (square), *gui* 規 (compass), *sheng* 繩 (chalk-line), *heng* 衡 (scale), *quan* 權 (balance), *biao* 表 (gauge that measures time), and *fang* 坊 (levee/dike) are oftentimes used in conjunction with *li* 禮.[9] As explained in the *Xunzi* 19.8, "[t]hus, just as the marking line (*sheng* 繩) is the perfection of straightness; the balance (*heng* 衡) the perfection of equalness; the compass and square (*guiju* 規矩) the perfection of square and roundness, so too, ritual is the ridgepole of the way of humanity." Or, as said in the "Liqi 禮器" chapter of *Book of Rites*, "[i]n performing ritual, *junzi* must be vigilant. Ritual is the knot (*ji* 紀) of the people. If the knot loosens, the people will be scattered." In other words, ritual—a public, intersubjective performance—is the dramatic script, the symphonic note, and the chorus line that we have learned to speak, play, and dance in synchronic harmony at home and beyond.

The sort of synchronic harmony in a ritual performance, however, is not borne out of external coercion, but is a result of internalized positive social modeling. Guided by reciprocity, ritual also serves specifically to provide a refined, measured, and sustainable outlet for human emotions and to meet human desires. As explained in Xunzi's rather comprehensive discussion on ritual in the "Lilun 禮論" Chapter 19.1, ritual is a work of the sages and it arises to apportion goods and desires so that they may sustain one another over time. Moderating one's material desires in a socially and ecologically sustainable way is one ritual effect among many.

According to the "Liyun 禮運" chapter of *Book of Rites*, we are born with seven dispositions—joy, anger, grief, fear, love, hate, and desire (喜怒哀懼愛惡欲七者)—and the sages use ritual to enhance or moderate these human dispositions in order to govern well (故聖人所以治人七情, 修十義, 講信修睦, 尚辭讓, 去爭奪, 舍禮何以治之). These seven human dispositions are further conceptualized as an uncultivated field in need of ritual as the first facilitating agent that makes a productive and sustainable garden possible. As the same text explains precisely:

Therefore ritual for people is like the yeast is for liquor. [By the use of it] the *junzi* becomes greater and [by the neglect of it] the petty person becomes worse. Therefore the sage kings cultivated the lever of righteousness and the ordering of ritual in order to regulate human dispositions. Those dispositions were the field [to be cultivated by] the sage kings. They fashioned ritual to plough it, set forth righteousness (*yi* 義) with which to plant it, instituted schooling (*xue* 學) to weed it, based in benevolence (*ren* 仁) to gather its fruits, and employed music (*yue* 樂) to give repose.

Without ritual, the field of seven human dispositions—joy, anger, grief, fear, love, hate, and desire—lies uncultivated and hence its productive outcome depends on the mercy of chance. In contrast, with ritual one takes the first step toward the sustainable ownership of the mutually enriching, communal garden. To govern without ritual, as the same passage goes on to explain, is like ploughing the field without a share (故治國不以禮, 猶無耜而耕也). Ritual is essential to governance, just as ploughing is to the field; without the former, nothing productive can come of the latter.

Although ritual by itself, as noted above, is not sufficient to yield a productive field—there are other excellences such as righteousness (*yi* 義), learning (*xue* 學), benevolence (*ren* 仁), and music (*yue* 樂) to work in concert with *li* 禮—ritual for the Confucian is more than just one among many in state governance. Ritual is that by which humanity demarcates itself from bestiality. As said in the *Book of Rites*, "Quli shang 曲禮上" chapter:

The parrot can speak, and yet is nothing more than a bird; the ape can speak, and yet is nothing more than a beast (*qinshou* 禽獸). Now people who observe no ritual propriety are not their heart that of a beast? But if [people are like] beasts without ritual propriety, then father and son might have the same mate. Therefore, when the sages arose, they use ritual in order to teach people, and cause them, by their possession of ritual, to make a distinction between themselves and beasts (使人以有禮, 知自別於禽獸).

Similarly, as in the *Mencius* 3A4, Mencius cautions, without a sagely ritual instruction in the five cardinal social relations—i.e., father-son, ruler-minister, husband-wife, old-young, and friends—even when people are well-fed and warmly clothed, they are still in fact closer to brutes (*qinshou* 禽獸) than humans. Furthermore, as said in the *Book of Rites*, "Jiaotesheng 郊特牲" chapter, in regard to the marriage rites, with such ritual observations there comes universal repose; without such a ritual distinction and righteousness, there is the way of bestiality (禽獸之道也).

Ritual for the Confucian is what elevates humanity above bestiality, and that ritual elevation is attested in our ability to form a cohesive and secured society in spite of our relatively weak physical stamina and agility in comparison with other animals. As Xunzi explains in the following rather lengthy passage detailing the humanity's ritual advantages over other animals in the *Xunzi* 9.19:

> Fire and water possess vital breath but have no life. Plants and trees possess life, but lack awareness. Birds and beasts (*qinshou* 禽獸) have awareness, but lack a sense of righteousness. Humans possess vital breath, life, and awareness, and add to them a sense of righteousness; therefore they are the noblest beings in the world. Their physical strength is not equal to an ox and their walking pace is not equal to a horse, yet they put oxen and horses to their use. Why is that? I say: it is because humans are able to form societies (*qun* 群), and animals cannot. Why can humans form societies? I say: it is due to [ritual] distinction (*fen* 分). How is [ritual] distinction able to work? I say: it is due to righteousness (*yi* 義). Hence, when righteousness is used to mark [ritual] distinction, then there is harmony; when there is harmony, there is unity; when there is unity, there is strength; when there is greater power, there is greater strength; when there is greater strength, objects can be overcome. For this reason, humans can acquire palaces and houses to dwell in safety.

In other words, our collective strength comes from the internal ritual cohesion that binds us together in harmony, and hence ritual enables us to overcome our physical disadvantages compared to other animals to live a materially sufficient and socially cohesive, secured life.

Forming society for Xunzi, as much as it is for Aristotle, is what comes naturally to us as humans. But a society formed without ritual distinction is doomed to chaos, discord, and fragmentation. As Xunzi goes on to say in the *Xunzi* 9.20:

> If a society is formed without [ritual] distinction (*fen* 分), strife is the result. If there is strife, chaos is the result. If there is chaos, fragmentation is the result. If there is fragmentation, weakening is the result. If there is weakening, then it is impossible to overcome objects. For this reason, humans could not acquire palaces and houses to dwell with security. This is why it is unacceptable to neglect ritual (*li* 禮) and righteousness (*yi* 義), even for the shortest moment.

Ritual is able to ensure a sense of societal order and cohesion because ritual provides a remedial effect on various human dispositions. Beyond its pragmatic functions to enhance or moderate human dispositions, ritual also has an aesthetic function. Unlike what is envisioned in Plato's ideal state, the *Republic*, where class-mixing constitutes the greatest evil to the state,[10] the sort of social cohesion under discussion here is not a rigidly ordered class-based society. The ritualized Confucian state is not only socially cohesive and materially secured, but also aesthetically pleasing and culturally refined.

As Xunzi explains precisely in the *Xunzi* 19.13, "[r]ites trim what is too long, stretch out what is too short, eliminate excess, remedy deficiency, and extend cultivated forms that express love and respect, so that they increase and complete the beauty of righteous conduct." In other words, ritual not only provides a public outlet for human emotions, but also embellishes them to heighten the experience of the ritual performance in every important occasion from cradle to grave. As Xunzi goes on to explain in the *Xunzi* 19.16:

> As a general principle, ritual in treating birth provides ornamentation for expressions of joy, and in sending off the dead it provides ornamentation for expressions of grief. In presenting sacrificial offerings ritual embellishes feelings of reverence, and in marshaling troops it embellishes feelings of awe-inspiring majesty.

The corresponding human emotion in each important occasion from birth to death is expressed through ritual so that not only do human sentiments find their proper outlets, but also become increasingly refined. In short, as said precisely in the *Xunzi* 19.7, ritual transforms what is raw and coarse into what is aesthetically pleasing and culturally refined (凡禮, 始乎梲, 成乎文, 終乎悅校).

In performing a ritual script, we not only bring our measured inner emotions and dispositions into synchronicity with our aesthetically refined outer postures and speeches, but also bring the human community into synchronicity with what the natural world is able to sustainably provide with proper timing and material modesty. As Confucius advises in the *Analects* 3.4, "[i]n ritual ceremonies rather than being extravagant, it is better to be modest; in mourning, rather than attending to the minute details, it is better to have deep sorrow." In a well-performed ritual such as mourning ritual, one's inner grief matches one's outer ritual display. Or, as explained in the "Jianzhuan 間 傳" chapter of *Book of Rites*, the reason one wears the headband made with hemp, an unpleasant materials, in the mourning ritual for one's parents is that it serves to show outwardly one's internal distress.[11]

Ritual items serve more than just the outer manifestation of one's inner emotions; proper ritual items must also bridge the human, the natural, and the cosmic world. As said in the "Liqi 禮器" chapter—the chapter explaining the proper usages of ritual items—of *Book of Rites*, ritual items should be "in accord with the heavenly timing, supplied by the earthly material, in agreement with the spiritual beings and human sentiment, patterned after all things in the world."[12] The inner and the outer, the seasonal timing and the earthly supply, the sacred and the mundane—that is, all things in the world—are brought together in synchronicity through a proficient ritual performance. To be ritually proper, as said simply in the *Book of Rites*, "Quli shang 曲禮上" chapter is to follow what is fitting (禮從宜), in timing and circumstances.

Needless to say, a ritual-based state is expansive in function and proactive in nature, and the realm of what counts as "politics" or "governance" permeates into the so-called "personal" and "spiritual." To be proficient in ritual performances requires a lengthy training through positive social modeling, and family is the institution where positive social modeling first takes place. Confucianism's invested interest in raising a healthy family is unparalleled on the world stage of intellectual thought.[13] To fashion a politically expedient subject, for the Confucian, begins with raising a filial child with ritual deference at home, and home is also where ritual learning through positive social modeling begins.

Since positive social modeling is essential in ritual learning, to raise a filial child requires being filial on the part of the parents toward their own parents, in much the same way that to be served well in the civil state, one must first learn to serve others well. As said in the *Xunzi* 30.7:

Junzi has three standards of reciprocity: one who is unable to serve one's superior cannot expect his inferior to serve him; one who is not affectionate toward his own parents cannot expect his own son to be filial; one who is not respectful to his own older brother cannot expect his younger brother to follow his commands. Following these three standards of reciprocity, then one is able to correct oneself.

In short, reciprocity (*shu* 恕), as Confucius says in the *Analects* 15.24, is the enduring guideline in human conduct. This reciprocal imperative begins with the parent-child relationship and then radiates through the wider concentric circles of human relations where the private and the public, the personal and the political, are not seen as a discrete bifurcation, but a graded continuum.

Given that ritual learning requires reciprocal social modeling and a proficient ritual performance requires the synchronicity of various elements including timing, material circumstances, and human sentiment, a ritual-based state by its very nature is harmonious and dynamic at the same time. Or, to put it another way, a ritual-based state is a harmonious state in motion. To perform a ritual that is fitting, among other things, requires the weighing of circumstances which is by definition fluid and particular in nature. As pointed out earlier, unlike ritual in most religious communities that is supposedly eternal and unchanging, Confucian ritual incorporates the necessity of change, albeit conservatively.

Quan 權 and Circumstantial Adaptability

The concept of circumstantial weighing (*quan* 權) is necessary for a proficient ritual performance. As recorded in the famed passage *Mencius* 4A17, Mencius decries the rigidity of following a ritual script without any regards to the fast-moving circumstances such as extending a saving hand to one's drowning sister-in-law in violation of gender separation, and as Mencius goes on to explain, to be able to properly weigh the fast moving circumstances is called *quan* 權. Holding onto one thing without any regards to the changing circumstances amounts to extremity. In the following lengthy passage, Mencius illustrates the danger of doctrinal rigidity by comparing the conduct of Yangzi—the egoist—and Mozi—the altruist—as well as Zimo who follows the middle approach in between these two opposites. As recorded in the *Mencius* 7A26:

> Yangzi chooses egoism. Even if he could benefit the world by pulling out of one hair he would not do it. Mozi advocates love without discrimination. If by shaving his head and showing his heels he could benefit the world, he would do it. Zimo holds onto the middle course of action. Holding onto the middle is closer to being right, but holding onto the middle without weighing the circumstances (*quan* 權) is still like holding onto one extreme. The reason for disliking those who hold onto one extreme is that they cripple the *Dao* by singling out one thing and neglecting a hundred others.

For Mencius, being *quan* 權 is more than simply situating oneself in the middle of two extremes. Being *quan* 權 is to be circumspect to each unique and particular circumstance, instead of rigidly following a doctrinal principle indiscriminately.

The ability to recognize the contingency of circumstances in applying a ritual script is essential to the success of a ritual performance. For instance, altering the ritual script to accommodate physical limitations is recognized in the ritual text, *Book of Rites,* "Sangfu zizhi 喪服四制" chapter: "Women who are bald do not use the coiffure; hunchbacks do not unbare their arms; the lame do not leap; and the old and ill do not give up the use of liquor and meat. All these eight cases are regulated by the consideration of circumstances (*quan* 權)." Ritual hence must be adaptable to different human conditions and abilities such as old age, sickness, or disability, and that ritual adaptability is called *quan* 權.

It is worth noting that weighing human conditions is not the same as making rare exceptions. Changes in ritual are, in fact, normalized as a mirroring effect of the inevitable four seasonal changes in nature. In much the same way, the four cardinal virtues—benevolence (*ren* 仁), righteousness (*yi* 義), ritual propriety (*li* 禮), and wisdom (*zhi* 智)—are also said to have their basis in different human emotions. And among the four cardinal virtues, to be *quan* 權 is what enables genuine knowing (*zhi* 知). As explained in the *Book of Rites*, "Sangfu zizhi 喪服四制" chapter:

> The mourning dress has four definite styles; they change in accordance with what is fitting—this is derived from the changes of the four seasons; [just as the rotation of] affection, distinctions, regulations, and the consideration of circumstances (*quan* 權)—this is derived from the human feelings. In affection, there is benevolence (*ren* 仁); in distinctions, there is righteousness (*yi* 義); in regulations, there is ritual propriety (*li* 禮); and in consideration of circumstances (*quan* 權), there is knowledge (*zhi* 知). Benevolence, righteousness, ritual, and knowledge—these make up the attributes of humanity.

In order to perform a ritual script proficiently, one must know not just what is entailed in that ritual script, but also how to apply the ritual script to each unique circumstance. Learning how to be ritually adaptable is what enables one to truly know how to be ritually proper. Hence not only is change not antithetical to ritual, but to exercise *quan* 權, to be circumspect, is what is required of a proficient ritual performance.

Certainly, changing a ritual script is not a matter to be taken lightly, since ritual, after all, is a public performance. At the same time, change, as argued so far, is not contrary to the Confucian understanding of ritual either. The frequently cited example of two ritual changes in the *Analects* 9.3—one is embraced and the other rejected by Confucius—is a case in point. Confucius embraces the change of a silk cap replaced by a hemp cap as a matter of material frugality while rejecting the change of kowtowing after entering the hall as a matter of immodesty. Confucius's embrace or rejection of a certain ritual change in the *Analects* 9.3 is in line with what Confucius says in the *Analects* 3.4 that explains the root of ritual (禮之本): Material modesty and genuine expression.

A less-discussed example of ritual change in the *Analects* is when Confucius's favorite disciple Yan Hui died; Confucius mourned him as if he were mourning a son, which then seemingly gave rise to a new form of mourning ritual for mentorship and friendship—a newly emerged social relationship that is intimate in nature but not quite a kinship.[14] This invented mourning ritual is then echoed in Confucius's own mourning rites by his surviving disciples. As recorded in the "Tangongshang 檀弓上" chapter of *Book of Rites*:

> At the mourning rites for Confucius, the disciples were in perplexity as to what attire they should wear. Zigong said, 'Formerly, when the Master was mourning for Yan Yuan [i.e., Yan Hui], he acted as if he were mourning for a son, but didn't don the mourning attire [....] Let us mourn for the Master, as if we were mourning for a father, but don no mourning attire.[15]

The sort of perplexity among Confucius's disciples as to how to mourn their mentor hints at the novel nature of this emerging social relationship: Mentorship and friendship beyond kinship. Confucius's own innovation to accommodate this changing social condition demonstrates the elasticity and circumstantial adaptability of *li* 禮.

Beyond the *Analects*, there are ample examples in the *Book of Rites* where Confucius innovates or embraces ritual changes. For instance, in the "Tangongxia 檀弓下" chapter, in responding to Zilu's comment on the poor's inability to meet the ritual requirements of adequately providing for their parents and having a proper burial, Confucius says: "Having only bean soup and water to drink, while the parents are made happy, this may be called filial; only wrapping the body round from head to foot, and interring it immediately, without a coffin, that being all which one's means allow, this may be called *li* 禮."[16] Similarly, in the "Tangongshang 檀弓上" chapter, in regard to Ziyou's query on whether the poor should follow the same ritual requirements as those with means, Confucius responds: "If one has means, don't exceed the prescribed rites. If without means, then covering the body from head to foot and burying it with the coffin being simply let down by ropes. Who in such a case will blame the procedure?"[17] In both cases, the substantial change to the ritual script, in Confucius's view, doesn't distract a bit from what is ritually required of a child to discharge her filial duty to the parents, living and dead. Change—insofar as it is done with one's sincere intention to serve or as long as it is out of material modesty—is not contrary to ritual propriety.

In another passage in the "Tangongxia 檀弓下" chapter of *Book of Rites* where a certain mourning ritual, not originated in antiquity, is attributed to the wailing of Jing Jiang for Mubo (帷殯，非古也，自敬姜之哭穆伯始也). Confucius approves of the change by commending Jing Jiang for her proficiency in knowing the rites. Confucius's high praise of her ritual proficiency is also recorded in the *Biographies of Exemplary Women* where Jing Jiang is one of the two women recorded as receiving such a high praise from Confucius.[18] In the "Tangongshang 檀弓上" of *Book of Rites*, Confucius also praises a man who deviates from the mourning script as a proficient ritual agent to whom Confucius himself is not yet able to measure up.[19] Ritual innovation and ritual proficiency hence are not contrary concepts, nor are women excluded from being proficient ritual agents who innovate and understand the rites.

As evidenced by numerous textual passages, Confucius not only praises those—both men and women—who improvise the rites to fit their unique circumstances, but also himself at times deviates from ritual scripts. As shown in another passage in the "Tangongshang 檀弓上" of *Book of Rites* where Confucius gave a larger gift than what was ritually required to a mere acquaintance in a funerary service, upon being questioned by Zigong for his ritual deviation Confucius responded that the deviation was necessary in order to befit his genuine emotion; to do otherwise would be to invalidate the degree of grief already expressed during the service (予鄉者入而哭之，遇於一哀而出涕. 予惡夫涕之無從也). Depending on one's material circumstances, timings, and one's genuine expressions of human sentiments, proficiency in ritual performances can be decoupled from the conventional ritual scripts. Circumstantial adaptability, hence, is a necessary built-in feature of Confucian ritual.

The most pungent example of Confucius's own ritual deviation is his decision to give his father and mother a joint burial and then to construct a sizeable burial mound totaling four feet tall; both of these ritual practices were not sanctioned in antiquity. As recorded in the *Book of Rites*, "Tangongshang 檀弓上" chapter, the practice of joint burial began in the Zhou period and was credited to the Duke of Zhou (合葬非古也，自周公以來). Furthermore, as explained in another ritual text, *Rites of Zhou* (*Zhouli* 周禮), "Chunguan zongbo 春官宗伯" chapter, the construction of a burial mound where its height should be commensurable to the rank of the deceased was also originated from the Zhou aristocracy (以爵等為丘

封之度與其樹數).[20] Given the fact that Confucius's father was only a minor knight and his mother a lowly concubine, Confucius's decision to give them a joint burial adorned with a sizeable four-foot tall burial mound could be seen as an unprecedented, major ritual infraction.[21]

Confucius understood the gravity of his own ritual deviation; as Confucius remarked in his explanation recorded in the *Book of Rites*, "Tangongshang 檀弓上" chapter: "I have heard that burial in antiquity didn't come with a burial mount (吾聞之: 古也墓而不墳)." But Confucius in the same passage went on to say his ritual deviation was borne out of the need to accommodate the changing time, a time when lengthy travels were not uncommon, and having a joint burial with a much elevated burial mound would make identifying the burial site much easier (今丘也, 東西南北人也, 不可以弗識也). Even though the joint burial mound collapsed spectacularly due to unexpected torrential rain (雨甚 [...] 防墓崩), Confucius's rare ritual failure however didn't detract from his willingness to deviate from the antiquity in order to accommodate the changing time and the changing human condition. In order for ritual to be effective, it must be adaptable to the world. As a result, the sort of harmony that ritual is able to effect is also dynamic in nature.

He 和, Moral Dissention, and Ritual Civility

Harmony is the resultant effect of ritual, but the concept of harmony (*he* 和) is not the same as monotony. In fact, the very concept of *he* 和 itself demands plurality. Etymologically speaking, *he* 和 has to do with harmonization of sounds. According to the earliest dictionary, *Shuowen jiezi*, *he* 和 is defined as "mutual responsiveness [of sounds]" (和: 相應也). Similarly, as defined in the pre-Qin text, *Discourses of the States* (*Guoyu* 國語), "Zhouyuxia 周語下" chapter: "[W]hen sounds correspond and mutually respond to one another it is called *he* 和 (聲應相保曰和)."[22] Likewise, as said in the *Book of Changes*, hexagram "Zhongfu" 中孚, "a crane sings in the woods and its young *he* 和 to it (鳴鶴在陰, 其子和之)." *He* 和, in short, is a purposive response in an effort to harmonize the plurality of sounds.

The musical association of *he* 和 is literally embedded in its early and more complex graph *he** 龢 found on the oracle bones. According to the Qing dynastic comprehensive dictionary, *Kangxi zidan*, the graphic component of *yue* 龠 is a flute-like musical instrument (樂器, 似笛).[23] The metaphor of musical harmony is also textually interwoven into the concept of *he* 和. For instance, in the *Book of Songs*, Song 164 "Changdi 常棣," the metaphor of musical instrument zither and lute is used to denote the joy of domestic harmony (妻子好合, 如鼓瑟琴. 兄弟既翕, 和樂且湛).[24]

He 和 as an aesthetic concept of musical harmonization clearly requires the concept of plurality, since monotony doesn't make music. A *junzi*, as Confucius says in the *Analects* 13.23, seeks harmonization, not monotony (君子和而不同). A harmonized world is a world of productive growth and mutual flourishing as opposed to the infertility of a monolithic world. As said precisely in the *Discourses of the States*, "Zhengyu 鄭語" chapter:

> *He* 和 is indeed productive of things. But sameness does not advance growth. Smoothing one thing with another is called *he* 和. For this reason, things come together and flourish. If one uses the same thing to complement the same thing, it is a dead end and is wasted (夫和實生物, 同則不繼. 以他平他謂之和, 故能豐長而物歸之; 若以同裨同, 盡乃棄矣).[25]

The same passage then goes on to explain the futility of monotony: "A single sound is nothing to hear, a single color doesn't make a pattern, a single taste does not satisfy the stomach (聲一無聽, 物一無文, 味一無果)."

Making a piece of good music requires harmonization of the plurality of sounds, just as making a bowl of hearty soup requires balance in ingredients and tastes. One ingredient soup is as bland as monotone music that feeds neither the body nor the soul. As said in the pre-Qin text, *Zuo's Commentaries*, "Zhaogong 昭公 the 20th year" chapter:

> *He* 和 is like making soup. One needs water, fire, vinegar, sauce, salt, and plum to cook fish and meat. One needs to cook them with firewood, *he* 和 them together in order to balance the taste. One needs to compensate for deficiencies and reduce excessiveness. *Junzi* eat [such balanced food] in order to purify their heart/mind (和如羹焉, 水火醯醢鹽梅, 以烹魚肉, 燀之以薪, 宰夫和之, 齊之以味, 濟其不及, 以洩其過, 君子食之, 以平其心).[26]

He 和 is antithetical to hollow uniformity; rather, *he* 和 is an intentional response to the plurality of things in the world in an effort to harmonize them into a mutually flourishing association. In the same vein, harmony in the political arena cannot be premised on forced uniformity or on silencing dissention.

Dissention is an integral part of the Confucian political and moral discourse. As argued in previous chapters, the concept of *jian* 諫 remonstrance is a frequent concurrent in the discussion of the ruler-minister as well as parent-child relations. As this well quoted passage from the *Book of Filiality*, Ch. 15 demonstrates, when inquired by his disciple Zengzi on whether children can be deemed filial by merely adhering to every parental command, Confucius responds with dismay: "What on earth are you saying? What on earth are you saying? (是何言與, 是何言與)."[27] The presence of moral dissention in fact is the key to the well-being of each relationship from the personal to the social and political, since remonstrance functions like a guard rail against moral lapses. As Confucius in the same passage goes on to say:

> Of old, an Emperor had seven ministers who would remonstrate with him, so even if he had no vision of the *dao*, he still did not lose the empire. The high nobles had five ministers who would remonstrate with them, so even if they had no vision of the *dao*, they still did not lose their states. The high officials had three ministers who would remonstrate with them, so even if they had no vision of the *dao*, they still did not lose their clans. If the lower officials had just one friend who would remonstrate with them, they were still able to preserve their good names; if a father has a son who will remonstrate with him, he will not behave reprehensively. Thus, if confronted by reprehensible behavior on his father's part, a son has no choice but to remonstrate with his father, and if confronted by reprehensible behavior on his ruler's part, a minister has no choice but to remonstrate with his ruler. Hence, remonstrance is the only response to immorality. How could simply obeying the commands of one's father be deemed filial?[28]

Blind obedience and conformity to one's social superior is contrary to what morality demands. As said precisely in the *Xunzi* 29.1, "[t]o follow the dictates of the *dao* instead of those of one's ruler and to follow what is right instead of the wishes of one's father constitute the highest standard of conduct." In short, to be ritually proper requires the exercise of moral dissention in the face of immorality.

The culture of moral dissention in the political discourse goes as far back as the earliest recorded dynastic history, *Book of Documents*, where the ruler's receptivity to remonstration is an indicator of his ability to govern well. As said in the *Book of Documents*, "Shangshu 商書" section, "Shuomingshang 說命上" chapter: "Wood by the use of the line is made straight, and the sovereign who follows remonstration is made sage. (惟木從繩則正, 后從諫則聖.)" In contrast, a cruel king like Shou 受 of Shang—as recorded in the *Book of Documents*, "Zhoushu 周書" section, "Taishizhong 泰誓中" chapter—on the other hand inflicts pain and death on dissenters: "He [i.e., Shou of Shang] has degraded from office the greatly good man; he has behaved with cruel tyranny to his remonstrator 諫 and helper (剝喪元良, 賊虐諫輔)," and as a result the cruel king, Shou 受 of Shang, was overthrown and the Shang dynasty was brought to a ruinous end. As shown in these historical lessons, there is a direct correlation between the king's receptivity to remonstration and effective state governance.

The concept of political remonstration can also be found in another Chinese Classic, *Book of Songs*, that offers glimpses into the life in the early Zhou dynasty.[29] In fact, according to the pre-Qin text, *Rites of Zhou*, "Diguan situ 地官司徒" chapter, *shijie* 司諫 (minister of admonition) in charge of admonition to the ruler was instituted as early as the Zhou dynasty as an official post. This official post was retained even in the dictatorial dynasty of Qin (*c.* 221–206 BCE) famed for its book burning and mass execution of scholars! As recorded in both the Han dynastic history of *Hanshu* 漢書 and the Tang comprehensive encyclopedia, *Tongdian* 通典, a slight variation of the ministry of admonition as in *Jianyi Dafu* 諫議大夫/*jiandafu* 諫大夫 was instituted during the Qin dynasty and continued on during the Han dynasty (秦置諫議大夫, 掌論議, 無常員, 多至數十人, 屬郎中令. 至漢武帝元狩五年, 始更置之. 劉輔以美才, 擢為諫大夫).

To remonstrate with one's superior is entailed in the duty of those who serve. As explained in the Han text, *Comprehensive Discussions in the White Tiger Hall*, the "Jianzheng 諫諍" chapter, "[w]hy is it that the minister has the duty to remonstrate with the ruler? It is for the sake of utmost loyalty (*zhong* 忠) and sincerity (*cheng* 誠). For how can one love without exertion and how can one be loyal without remonstration?" And as shown earlier in the *Book of Documents*, to be receptive to moral dissention is what keeps the ruler from descending into tyranny and the state from the peril of a political ruin.

To remonstrate is not the same as laying bare of the faults of others. As Confucius explains in the *Book of Rites*, "Biaoji 表記" chapter: "In the service of a ruler there should be the wish to remonstrate, but no wish to set forth [his faults] (事君欲諫不欲陳)." Likewise, as explained in the *Book of Rites*, "Shaoyi 少儀" chapter: "One in the position of a minister and inferior might remonstrate [with his ruler], but not speak ill of him (為人臣下者, 有諫而無訕)." The aim of remonstration is not to publically confront or humiliate, since direct confrontation and public humiliation, more often than not, tend to widen the rift and deepen the strife. Instead of aiming to antagonize, remonstration is always done with the intent to mend the relationship of which one is a part so that mutual flourishing is possible.

Having the opportunity to remonstrate with one's parents is part of the three joys a *junzi* treasures. As recorded in the Han text, *Outer*

Commentary on the Book of Songs by Master Han, Ch. 9, Zhengzi who is famed for his filial conduct in his response to Zixia's query on the three joys of a *junzi* says:

> Having parents that one respects, having a ruler that one can serve and having offspring one can pass on to constitute the first joy; having parents that one can remonstrate with, having a ruler that one can to go to and having a child that one can guide constitute the second joy; having a ruler that one can explain things to and having a friend that one can assist with constitute the third joy (有親可畏, 有君可事, 有子可遺, 此一樂也. 有親可諫, 有君可去, 有子可怒, 此二樂也. 有君可喻, 有友可助, 此三樂也).

To remonstrate with one's parents is a joyful occasion for a *junzi* because it presents an opportunity for relationship growth and mutual flourishing. In short, instead of having the me-against-the world or us-vs.-them mindset, a ritually bound Confucian *junzi* takes the we-are-all-in-this-together approach in addressing personal, social, and political discord.

A Confucian *junzi* takes social cooperation as the default position, because ritual, as an indispensable means for effective governance, has a remedial effect on the self. Ritual moderation and embellishment is not just a process of self-focused character training. Rather, in performing a ritual script, the self is always other-regarding; ritual, just as the Confucian self, is fundamentally relational. The other, regardless of their social status, is the focused center of one's reverence in a ritual performance, and through that reverential ritual engagement one's dispositions are thus enriched. As explained in the *Book of Rites*, "Quli shang 曲禮上" chapter:

> Ritual is seen in humbling one's self and giving honor to others. Even porters and peddlers are sure to display this giving honor; how much more should the wealthy and noble do so! When the wealthy and noble know to love ritual, they do not become proud nor dissolute. When the destitute and lowly know to love ritual, their minds do not become cowardly (夫禮者, 自卑而尊人. 雖負販者, 必有尊也, 而況富貴乎? 富貴而知好禮, 則不驕不淫; 貧賤而知好禮, 則志不懾).

The remedial effect of ritual benefits all regardless of their stations in life. Ritual guides all aspects of life—in serving or receiving, in birth or death, in joy or grief—and in each case, as said in the *Book of Rites*, "Quli shang 曲禮上" chapter, "one is to be respectful, reverent, measured and yielding; that is how a *junzi* illustrates ritual (是以君子恭敬撙節退讓以明禮)." Through ritual, the self is rendered ever more porous and receptive to other's needs as the range of one's ritual proficiency expands with one's life experiences.

A society that is structured by ritual is one in which political subjects are reverential to one another with respect to not just their contemporary, but also what came before and what is yet to come. Ritual, after all, is steeped in tradition; it is a social script made sacred through its intentional, cultural transmission from one generation to the next and beyond. In preforming a ritual, one is not just responding to the immediate other as one's contemporary; one is also carrying the weight of the ancestral past and is co-responsible for transmitting the past to the next generation and beyond. To know ritual, as said in the *Analects* 8.8, 16.13, and 20.3, is to know where to stand. And where one stands is as much of a reflection of one's current social standing as one's standing in the intergenerational transmission of this culture of ours.

Needless to say, not all ritual scripts are worth keeping and as shown earlier, there are ample examples of ritual modifications and innovations in the Confucian tradition. Unlike religious rites where change is seen as accidental or as an incidence of human fallibility, Confucian rites incorporate the element of circumstantial adaptability, albeit conservatively. The ability to adapt to the shifting living conditions is the built-in element of and is also the tensile strength of Confucian ritual, which is meant to flow with life itself. With ritual, the life one lives is more than a life of one's own, but a life that is made significant by anchoring one's stance in the perpetual continuum of the past, present, and future that is yet to come. One's mindfulness of this perpetual continuum of the past, present, and future knotted together by ritual is the shared social mechanism that provides coherence and cohesiveness to the Confucian state.

In the modern liberal state, political constituents are conceptualized as disparate individuals whose separateness is aggravated by the emphasis on the uniformity of equality, freedom, and independence; each political subject is entitled to focusing strictly on one's narrowest possible range of self-interests. The resultant effect is an adversarial model inter-subjectively at home and beyond, a model that makes the other an object to be tolerated or managed as a lesser evil in the face of mutual distrust and mutual destruction, but not a subject to be deferred to and honored with one's utmost sincerity. Although Kant does talk about treating others as an end in themselves and never as a means to one's own end, there are substantial differences between the Kantian respect for persons and the Confucian ritual civility. In the Confucian world of ritual, the other is always a concrete person, and to have ritual reverence for others requires a substantiated response to the needs and dispositions of the concrete person.

For the Confucian, seeing the other having a concrete presence is a necessary condition for a successful ritual performance. For instance, even in mourning or ancestor worship, seeing the departed as if they were present is the key to expressing one's genuine grief and respect. As said in the *Zhongyong*, Ch. 19, "to serve the dead as if they were alive, to serve the departed as if they were still present is filiality at its utmost (事死如事生, 事亡如事存, 孝之至也)." Ritual, in other words, not only is other-regarding, but also necessarily makes the other a concrete presence to whom one defers with utmost sincerity.

Conclusion

Ritual civility in our own liberal democratic state is now needed more than ever. Looking at our ever-deepening state of political strife that culminated in the failed insurrection to overturn the 2020 presidential election outcome—a time when the level of incivility and institutional distrust has been unprecedented in recent memories—a bit of ritual civility and mutual respect would have been most welcome.[30] The antagonistic drive to divide our country into two irreconcilable "red" states and "blue" states has led some to even contemplate the possibility of a "national divorce,"[31] unraveling the united front of this country of ours reminiscent of the turbulent times of the nation's civil war's past. Certainly, to hold this country of ours together, we need more than just the rights to pursue our own individual life, liberty, and happiness framed in mutual antagonism. After serving in the field of foreign affairs for decades, Ambassador Richard Hass contends that the emphasis on rights alone does not make a good citizenry; rights must be balanced by civic obligations. His *The Bill of Obligations: The Ten Habits of Good Citizens* (2023) urges the incorporation of ten obligations into our concept of rights, beginning with the obligation of civility as the utmost important one. Ritual civility, in other words, is indispensable for a functioning democracy, especially for a country like ours.

Certainly, a democratic state requires the plurality of opinions and the rights to dissent from the majority. But to be critical and to be civil are not contrary concepts. Furthermore, harmonization and plurality are not antithetical to one another either; in fact, the former requires the latter. A Confucian state that is bound by ritual hence is conceptually compatible with the sort of plurality demanded in a liberal state. But more importantly, the Confucian ritual-based state is able to go beyond the Hobbesian model of mutual antagonism inter-subjectively. In a ritually bound Confucian state, the plurality of opinions and political dissention must be expressed in a way that is civil and respectful of the receiving other, since dissention is always done with the aim to strengthen, not to diminish, the relationship in question.[32]

The Confucian cooperative approach would be much more effective in addressing larger scales of social, political, environmental, or health issues intra- and inter-nationally. An aggregate of disparate individuals doesn't by itself make a secured and cohesive state, just as the emphasis on the natural rights of man doesn't by itself make a progressive, inclusive society. Much to the contrary, an individualistically inclined state like the United States has fared much worse than other mature democratic countries on a myriad of social issues. It is no secret that the United States has been ranked at or near the bottom compared to other comparable wealthy nations on dealing with all of these larger social problems: The United States has no paid parental leave, has the most expensive health care system and the lowest life expectancy, has the most expensive child care cost and lags far behind in equal access to early childhood education, has the largest wealth and income gap, and produces far less in renewable energy to account for its immense energy usage, not to mention having the highest number of Covid deaths in the world during the height of the Covid-19 pandemic.[33]

Setting aside complex contributing factors, the celebrated American myth of a self-made man in the land of liberty certainly doesn't help foster a sense of shared responsibility inter-subjectively and inter-generationally. Indeed, to build a more inclusive and compassionate modern state, we will need to go beyond the individual rights-based model. A modern democratic state infused with Confucian care-based political authority, ritual, and civility will help heal our entrenched political divide and more importantly help build a more inclusive, compassionate world where the needs of the dependent— the young, the old, the sick, and the disabled—are no long consigned to the womanly sphere, but instead the first consideration of a *ren*-based state.

A Practical Ethic for Life

How a political constituent is conceptualized has a far-reaching impact on what sort of civil society is desirable, what the limit of the state is, and where its authority lies. A rights-based state provides an individualistic model of mutual antagonism where the issue of dependency is seen as the second order of things or is merely brushed aside into the realm of the personal, oftentimes falling into the so-called "woman's domain"—a domain of the non-political, the non-rational, and the non-ethical. Given the fact that Anglo-European canonical philosophers such as Plato, Augustine, Aquinas, Descartes, Leibniz, Spinoza, Locke, Berkeley, Hume, Kant, Bentham, Schopenhauer, Nietzsche, and Sartre were bachelors and had no experience of family life beyond their own childhood, it is not surprising that the issue of dependency care rarely surfaces in their writings.[1] In the vast amount of philosophical writings in the West, there is very little attention paid to the topic of family.[2] This is especially true in the discussion of politics and ethics where the basic political or moral subject is invariably conceptualized as an adult male whose political or moral duty arises only through contract or voluntary rational deliberation. Involuntary familial relationships and their associated obligations stand outside of our ethical and political concerns.

As O'Neill and Ruddick, in their reflection on the lack of attention to family in Western philosophy, explain precisely:

> Family arrangements are regarded as below the level of attention of political theory, familial decisions as involving no ethical problems distinct from those which may arise between any two individuals. A territorial division of normative questions into political theory and ethics has left questions about the family in no man's land, which, perhaps significantly, is often regarded as woman's sphere.[3]

Indeed, ethical and political concerns regarding the family conventionally fall in "no-man's land" where the issue of dependency care is deemed politically and ethically irrelevant to the rational mind of the patriarch. As a point of contrast, Confucianism has long taken the topic of family as its focal point and hence is able to provide a much more wholesome vision of a care-based political state. In particular, the Confucian *datong* 大同 (great community) as its highest political aspiration is able to articulate a much more inclusive and compassionate future for humanity.

Dependency Care and Political Authority

As argued earlier, the faithful political subject in a Confucian state literally grows out of a ritualized filial child in the family. It is well known that *xiao* 孝 (filiality) governs the duty of the child to the parent, but what constitutes proper parental care to the child receives much less attention. It is true that most of the Confucian writings focus on the nature and the extent of the filial duty that the child must strive to perform in service of the parents in life and beyond. As discussed in the earlier chapter, many of the contemporary scholars have pointed out the disparity, with some seeing the emphasis on filial duty as a major deficiency in Confucian ethics. However, this need not be the case. To care for one's parents with utmost sincerity is not only a natural response derived from gratitude for the prior care that one had received but an ethically sound response to human interdependency and vulnerability as well.

Although the appropriate parental care to the child doesn't draw the same amount of attention, the discussion on the importance of providing proper parental care, especially in the early childhood, is distinctively Confucian compared to the vast majority of Anglo-European philosophical traditions including contemporary feminist philosophy. As Erin Cline (2015) in her rather comprehensive study on the Western and Confucian views on childhood development concludes:

> Even when compared with the work of contemporary feminist philosophers, some of who do emphasize the unique value of parent-child relationships, the work of Confucian philosophers stands out for its insistence on the importance of the earliest stages of our development, during the prenatal period and the early infancy, and its contention that filial piety—which stems from the right kinds of parent-child relationships—serves as the foundation for nearly every other virtue and moral capacity.[4]

The emphasis on proper parental care in the early childhood, seeing it as ethically and politically consequential, is uniquely Confucian compared to the vast majority of Anglo-European writings—feminist or otherwise.

In the Anglo-European philosophical tradition, Plato's proposal of the dissolution of family in his famed *Republic* indeed sets the tone for the perceived incompatibility between the family and the state where one's loyalty to the family distracts one from the loyalty owed to the state.[5] Although Plato's dissolution of family is rejected by Aristotle as unworkable, in comparing Plato's proposal as diluting wine with water Aristotle in fact affirms the Platonic concept of family as rooted in self-love.[6] Hence for both Plato and Aristotle, the state, instead of the family, plays an essential role in transforming a child into a proper citizen. The importance of parental care and childhood education then falls by the wayside insofar as citizenship is concerned. All in all, from ancient to modern, from Plato to Hegel, childhood in the history of Western philosophy represents a sort of dark stage in one's development, a stage of the irrational, the pre-civil, and the pre-moral. Adulthood is then seen as a radical break from the dependency and the irrational nature of childhood, instead of a building up from it.

In contrast, childhood development in Confucianism is seen as an indispensable stage for one's moral and civic development, and hence providing appropriate parental care to the child is paramount not only in formulating the child's moral character, but also in fashioning a faithful civic subject. For the Confucian, there is no dichotomy between the family and the state, nor is there a contrasting disjunction between the irrational nature of childhood and the purported rational nature of adulthood. Moral development begins in the earliest possible stage of childhood and continues on till death. A faithful civic subject, in this Confucian paradigm of co-dependency, literally grows out of a filial child at home. Hence providing appropriate parental care at home is not just a personal affair, but a matter meriting sustained political attention.

Unlike in Plato's *Republic*, in a Confucian state the function of the family is not superseded by the civic unity. And unlike Kantian ethics, Confucian ethics does not discard the relevance of intimate attachments in one's ethical life. Appropriate parenting and familial attachment are frequently used as a metaphor for a benevolent ruler in Confucianism. The analogical metaphor of a benevolent ruler as the father and the mother of the people (*minzhifumu* 民之父母) can be traced back to the ancient Classics, *Shujing* and *Shijing*, and is widely used in later texts such as the *Mencius, Xunzi, Liji, Daxue, Xiaojing, Shuoyuan, Hanshi waizhuan, Baihutong, Kongzi jiayu, Xinshu,* and *Lienu zhuan*.[7] The prevalence of this metaphor clearly demonstrates its normative reference in the Confucian political discourse. Furthermore, to analogize a benevolent ruler as the father and the mother of the people can also be seen as an intentional intermingling of the family and the state as a radial continuum and at the same time an elevation of the importance of family in state governance where a harmonious and cohesive state depends on a harmonious and cohesive family.

It is worth noting that the Confucian metaphor of the ruler as the father and the mother of the people is not the same as the conventional Western reference of the divine right of King as a natural right of the patriarch embodied by Adam, the first patriarch. Parenthood, in the Confucian political discourse, is an ethical attainment. By merely occupying the position of the sovereign doesn't make one a rightful king. As stated clearly in the *Xunzi* 18.2 contrasting the benevolent rule of Tang and Wu with the tyrannical rule of Jie and Zhou Xin:

> Tang and Wu did not seize the whole world. Rather, they cultivated the *dao*, carried out their moral duty, caused whatever benefited the whole world in common to flourish, and removed whatever did harm to the whole world, so that the whole world offered allegiance to them. Jie and Zhou Xin did not abandon the world. Rather, they turned against the inner power of [their forebears] Yu and Tang, brought chaos to the division of social functions inherent in ritual and moral principles, behaved like wild beasts (*qinshou* 禽獸), gathered up their own ultimate catastrophe, completed their own evil, so that the whole world abandoned them [….] Tang and Wu were considered as the father and the mother of the people (*minzhifumu* 民之父母). Jie and Zhou Xin were hated as predators of the people [….] Therefore whether a person is a son of heaven depends entirely on what kind of person one is.

One's conduct must befit one's political position. To love and to care for the people makes one the father and the mother of the people, whereas to terrorize the people with one's beastly conduct makes one a thief of the people and is despised as such, leading to one's eventual political demise. Whether the king befits the title of being the father and the mother of the people entirely depends on the king's conduct; there is no natural right of king bestowed by the divine. Political authority for the Confucian is an achieved ethical accolade.

Furthermore, unlike in the West where the father is oftentimes used as the sole reference of authority—let it be in the context of family, state, or religion—in the Confucian political discourse, the father and the mother always occur as a pair in the political reference of a benevolent ruler. Despite many gender disparities, as far as the excellence of parenthood is concerned, reverence to the mother is on par with the father. For instance, Confucius's decision to have a joint burial for his mother and father in spite of being contrary to the custom of the antiquity can be seen as a sign of parental parity in Confucian teachings.[8] Some might even argue that mother holds a special place of reverence in the Chinese cultural narrative. The quintessential image of Mengmu—the mother of Mencius—as the celebrated embodiment of maternal wisdom along with many maternal icons such as Tairen (sage King Wen's mother) and Wenmu (sage King Wu's mother) immortalized in the Han text of *Lienu zhuan* (*Biographies of Exemplary Women*) is indicative of maternal reverence.[9]

The Confucian reverence for exemplary women, especially mothers, is unparalleled in the intellectual history of the world. The *Lienu zhuan* is probably the earliest existant text devoted solely to women's records, not just in the Chinese tradition but also in human written records.[10] This popular text lays the foundation for the inclusion of exemplary women in all major dynastic histories from Han onward till the last dynasty of Qing.[11] From very early on, for the Confucian, the mother's contribution to the family is neither subsumed under the father's, nor is it brushed aside, as it is commonly the case in the Western intellectual history. For the Confucian, mother has a distinctive role to play and her work is essential to the success of the family. Hence, the highest accolade can be bestowed on the beloved ruler, who embodies the excellence of parenthood, is always "the father and the mother of the people (*minzhifumu* 民之父母)."

What characterizes the excellence of parenthood, among other things, is affection and generosity. As said in the *Mencius* 3A4, in the father-son relationship, there is affection (父子有親), and as recorded in the *Xunzi* 12.3, in response to what makes a person a father, Xunzi says: "It is to be generous, kind, and ritually proper (寬惠而有禮)." Likewise, as said in the *Book of Rites*, "Liyun 禮運" chapter: "When there is generous affection between father and son, friendly relation between brothers, and harmony between husband and wife, the family is in good condition (父子篤, 兄弟睦, 夫婦和, 家之肥也)." To embody that genuine affection and generosity that parents have for their child in the civic relation between the ruler and subject is seen as the benchmark for a benevolent ruler—the ground for political authority.

Just like a good parent, a benevolent ruler must be responsive to what delights or causes strife for the people. As said in the *Great Learning*—one of the canonical Confucian Four Books—"[i]n the *Book of Songs*, it is said, 'How much to be rejoiced in are these rulers, the father and the mother of the people!' When a ruler loves what the people love, and hates what the people hate, then is he what is called the father and the mother of the people (詩云: 樂只君子, 民之父母. 民之所好好之, 民之所惡惡之, 此之謂民之父母)." And just like a good parent, the ruler must also provide for the people. As recorded in the *Mencius* 1A4, Mencius admonishes the King Hui of Liang for his disregard for the well-being of his people:

> In your kitchen there is fat meat and in your stables, there are well-fed horses, and yet your people look hungry and in the outskirts of cities, people are dying from starvation. This is to show beasts (*shou* 獸) the way to devour people. Beasts devour one another and people find that repugnant. If in being the father and the mother of the people, one rules without the avoidance of leading beasts to devour people, then wherein is he the father and the mother of the people?

Likewise, in the *Mencius* 3A3, it is said that much like a negligent parent, a cruel ruler unconcerned with the people's well-being burdening them with heavy taxation and then hoarding all the goods for himself causing the vulnerable— the old and the young—dying in the ditches is undeserving of the accolade of being the father and the mother of the people (使老稚轉乎溝壑, 惡在其為民父母也). In addition, a good parent must ensure the safety of the child. A ruler being the father and the mother of the people, as Confucius says in the *Book of Rites*, "Kongzi xianju 孔子閒居" chapter, must have the foresight to ensure the safe perimeter of the state (四方有敗, 必先知之. 此之謂民之父母矣).

Lastly, a benevolent ruler, just like a good parent, must also instruct the people through positive social modeling beginning with the ruler. As Confucius says in the *Book of Rites*, "Biaoji 表記" chapter:

> Difficult is it to attain to what is called the perfect humanity of *junzi*! It is said in the *Book of Songs*, "The happy and courteous ruler is the father and the mother of the people." Happy, he [yet] vigorously teaches them; courteous, he makes them pleased and restful. With all their happiness, there is no wild extravagance; with all their observance of ritual propriety (*li*禮), there is the feeling of affection (*qin* 親). Notwithstanding his awing gravity, they are restful; notwithstanding his filial kindness (*xiaoci*孝慈), they are respectful. Thus he causes them to revere him as their father, and love him as their mother. There must be all this before he is the father and the mother of the people.

In other words, to be the father and mother of the people, the ruler will first need to embody various virtues including filiality and ritual propriety so as to set a positive social model for the people, like a good parent does for the child. Just as demanding as parenthood, rulership demands work from the ruler on behalf of the people by providing proper instructions through her positive personal conduct.

The ruler is the excellence-in-chief, and her conduct radiates and functions as a measuring yardstick, soliciting corresponding conduct in the people. As said in the *Great Learning*:

What is meant by "The making the whole kingdom peaceful and happy depends on the state governance," is this: When the ruler behaves to the aged, as the aged should be behaved to, the people become filial (*xiao* 孝); when the sovereign behaves to the elders, as the elders should be behaved to, the people learn deference (*di* 弟); when the ruler treats compassionately the young and helpless (*xugu* 恤孤), the people do the same. Thus the ruler has a principle with which, as with a measuring square, to regulate one's conduct (絜矩之道). What one dislikes in one's superior, let one not display in the treatment of one's inferior; what one dislikes in one's inferior, let one not display in the service of one's superior [....]—this is what is called "The principle with which, as with a measuring square, to regulate one's conduct".

In short, just like a good parent, a benevolent ruler leads by example and is guided by the generous principle of reciprocity where one's authority is premised, first and foremost, on one's sincerity in serving and caring for others at home and beyond.

In fact, caring for the vulnerable is how the way of the Confucian is characterized by their competing contemporary school of thought, the Mohist. As recorded in the *Mencius* 3A5, the Mohist characterize the way of the Confucian as one that follows the ancient in caring for the people as if they were caring for a new born infant (儒者之道, 古之人 "若保赤子"). The metaphor of caring for a new-born infant, as noted by the Mohist, has its ancient roots; its first occurrence is found in the earliest dynastic records, *Book of Documents*, "Kangzhao 康誥" chapter: If the king tended to the people as if he were tending to his own new born infant, then the people would be tranquil and orderly (若保赤子, 惟民其康乂). And the way the parents should tend to the new-born infant is to be responsive and sincere. As the same passage from the *Book of Documents* is further elaborated in the *Great Learning*:

In the "Kangzhao" [of *Book of Documents*] it is said, "Act as if you were tending an infant." If one is really sincere about it, though one may not hit exactly the wants of the infant, one will not be far from doing so (康誥 曰: "如保赤子." 心誠求之, 雖不中不遠矣).

Remarkably, the discussion of caring for a new-born infant with utmost sincerity and responsiveness occurs not in the context of the so-called "womanly sphere," but instead in the context of state governance and rulership. As the same passage in the *Great Learning* goes on to say, "[f]rom the benevolent (*ren* 仁) example of one family a whole state becomes benevolent, and from its courtesies (*rang* 讓) the whole state becomes courteous, whereas from the greed and perverseness (*tanli*貪戾) of one person, the whole state may be led to rebellious disorder—such is the nature of the influence." Caring for one's family has a radial effect on the whole state and the caring example starts with the ruler. In the Confucian tradition, not only is caring not seen as a predominately feminine characteristic, but more importantly, providing good care for the vulnerable is an integral part of the Confucian political discourse.

For instance, in response to what constitutes a kingly government, Mencius cites the example of the sage king Wen's *ren*-based governance where caring for the four categories of the most vulnerable people—widower, widow, childless, and orphan—was King Wen's first political priority to illustrate the point. As recorded in the *Mencius* 1B5:

> Old men without wives (*guan*鰥), old women without husbands (*gua*寡), old people without children (*du*獨), young children without fathers (*gu* 孤)—these are the four types of people that are the most destitute and have no one to turn to for help. Whenever king Wen put benevolent (*ren* 仁) governance into effect, he always gave these four first consideration.

Sage king Wen's prioritization of caring for these four categories of vulnerable population is taken as paradigmatic of a kingly, benevolent approach to governance.

Adding to the list of the above-mentioned protected categories of people that a benevolent *ren*-based state should care for is the disabled. Xunzi in his discussion on what constitutes the regulation of a king specifically addresses the needs of the disabled as part of the essential function of the state. As recorded in the *Xunzi* 9.1:

> Those who have one of the Five Defects (*wuji*五疾) should be raised up and gathered in so that they can be cared for. They should be given official duties commensurable with their abilities and employment adequate to feed and clothe themselves so that all are included and not even one of them is overlooked.

The so-called "five defects," according to the later commentary, refer to those who have mental and physical disabilities.[12] In sum, caring for those social dependents—the young, the old, the sick, and the disabled—is the defining feature of the Confucian benevolent state whose political authority is, first and foremost, premised on its caring capacity.

In the long history of canonical Anglo-European political philosophy—from Plato, Aristotle, Hobbes, Locke, Hume, Rousseau, Kant, Hegel, to Mill—rarely is the need to care for the social dependent mentioned as the essential function of the state. Political governance is, by and large, defined by masculine rationality, a realm where rationality is exercised among free, equal, and independent adult males, literally and exclusively. And since social dependents are unable or are perceived as lacking the natural endowment to exercise the requisite rationality, they are excluded from the consideration of citizenry and their needs are seen as outside the purview of what sort of essential functions that the state should provide. If caring for the dependent is not perceived as an essential function of the state by virtue of the fact that those who envision what a state is supposed to do are by the requirement of citizenry to be without the burden of caring for others or to be cared for, then the sort of state that is envisioned consequently also excludes those who need care and those who do the actual caring work. In this sort of political paradigm, caring for others—that is conventionally viewed as belonging to the womanly sphere—doesn't even arise to the level of political discourse, let alone a shared responsibility that a kingly government must give its first consideration.

Dependency is an existential given, as Eva Kittay (1999) and other care ethicists have pronounced that we are all some mother's child. For each of us to be a thriving, flourishing adult, someone must have performed attentive and responsive care on our behalf, especially during our most vulnerable stages of growth—infancy and childhood—and for any political theory to overlook the importance of family and appropriate parental care at the earliest possible stage is to overlook what makes life possible in the first place. To care for others and to be cared for is not just a personal matter. To dismiss the political importance of caring for others is to dismiss the merits and the plights of those (oftentimes they are women) who are chronically tasked with caring for the young, the old, the sick, and the disabled. But more importantly, to dismiss dependency care is to dismiss the shared responsibility to care for the social dependent who are, nevertheless, also the constituents of the modern civil society. Those who cannot care for themselves, too, are democratic constituents and their caring needs must be addressed socially and politically. As noted earlier, a prolonged dependent life for the young and the old is what characterizes our modern times. Now more than ever a different political paradigm that takes into account of our existential dependency is urgently needed for us to continue to move toward a more progressive, inclusive, and caring future.

Datong 大同 and Inclusive Community

Contrary to the liberal aspirations of equality and dignity of personhood, the toxic rhetoric of the Trump candidacy in the 2016 presidential election, his 2020 failed reelection bid, and his 2024 comeback campaign have been mired in racial resentment, xenophobia, and misogyny, as Trump proposed to create a special registry for Muslims, to build a southern border wall having Mexico paid for it, and to incite rioters to storm the US Capitol in an attempt to disrupt a peaceful transition of presidential power, not to mention his infamous Access Hollywood tape where sexual assault against women is seen as a powerful man's prerogative.[13] But in spite of all these, Trump not only triumphed with a surprising win in 2016, managed to gather over 74 million votes in his 2020 reelection bid, secured more than enough Senate votes to ensure acquittals for his two House impeachments, and his overwhelmingly dominant position within the Republican Party for the 2024 presidential nomination among primary voters.[14]

Many voters were drawn by Trump's economic appeals to the working class whose factory jobs have been decimated by the shifts in global economy and the increase in automation, but Trump's promises of jobs and economic prosperity have been thinly veiled in populist nationalism, as his campaign slogan for 2016, 2020, and 2024 presidential election says it all: "Make America Great Again." Indeed, the call for an inclusive community and cultural hybridity is more than just an academic exercise; it is needed now more than ever to ensure our open and democratic future for this country of ours.

Instead of a nationalistic exclusion, the Confucian utopia of *datong* 大同 where all are cared for and none is left behind should be a shared political vision for any modern democratic state. As recorded in the *Book of Rites*, "Liyun 禮運" chapter, Confucius recounted a time when the great *dao* prevailed and the world was a harmonious unity:

When the great *dao* prevailed, the world belonged to the general public (*gong*公). They chose the worthy and capable, were trustworthy in what they said, and cultivated harmony. Therefore people did not love only their own parents and did not rear only their own children. Thus, the old could live out their lives, the strong had their employment, the young had their growth, and the widower (*jin* 矜), the widow (*gua* 寡), the orphan (*gu* 孤), the childless (*du* 獨), the disabled (*fei* 廢), and the sick (*ji* 疾) all had their care. Men had their proper occupations (*fen*分) and women had their domestic belongings (*gui* 歸). They hated casting away goods, but not necessarily to keep them for themselves. They hated leaving their strength unemployed, but not necessarily to employ it for themselves. Therefore, scheming had no outlet, and theft, chaos, and robbery did not arise, so that the outer doors were left unlocked. This is called the Great Community (*datong*大同).

Its gender-based roles and division of labor notwithstanding, this idyllic community represents the highest political aspiration for the Confucian. Its realization, as shown in the passage, is premised on our willingness to go beyond the narrow concerns of our own selves or our immediate families to also care for others, especially the vulnerable, so that the old, the young, the sick, and the disabled are not left to their own devices without proper care.

An inclusive, caring political community is quintessentially Confucian whose political theory doesn't hinge on rational self-centric concerns. In order to build this idyllic Confucian Great Community (*datong*大同), we will need a different conception of the self, a self that is at its core porous to others so that each is constitutive of the other from the start of each's personhood. When the well-being of the self at its very outset is not just an individual concern of self-happiness, but a larger relational issue where the self and the other must be addressed simultaneously, the resultant is Great Community (*datong*大同) for all.

An individualistic self who is presumed to be free, equal, and independent of others as the proper political constituent in modern Anglo-European political theories from Hobbes onward, in many respects, stands in the way of an expanded political care for all, since one's self-concern—enlightened or otherwise—is the first and the only referent in all his rational, contractual deliberations. To care for others can only fall under a private act of mercy, but no such political obligation is proposed as an essential function of the state. Coupling the deep-rooted political individualism with the free market practice, what we have in this modern world is a sort of individualism mostly expressed in a secular form of consumerism.

To be an individual is to be free to consume materially, socially, or politically depending the likings of one's own. In this paradigm, shared values and the common good invariably must yield to the immediate and shifting concerns of the individual in question. After all, the free, equal, and independent individual is the very constituent of this modern state whose existence is justified solely based on the individual's needs to protect his individual rights to life, liberty, and the pursuit of happiness from any unwanted encroachment of other individuals or the state. To lay claim of any sort of shared values or the common good is, from the outset, an unduly violation on the rights of the individual in question. It is, indeed, an impasse between the absolute claim of the individual and the political obligation to care for others. As argued earlier, this seems to be the case in this country of ours, the land of the free, where capitalistic individualism remains a political orthodoxy and where social welfare policies lag significantly behind all other mature democratic nations.

Socio-political inclusivity requires a different conception of the self, going beyond a talk of tolerance where the inclusion of others in the civil society is seen as a necessary rational concession in fear of mutual destruction and chaos. In the survey of world philosophies, Confucianism offers a viable conceptual paradigm that is much more amicable to building a genuine inclusive community where the self is porous and other-regarding. As George Rupp (2015), a former dean of Harvard Divinity School, writes in regard to the human centric propensity of the Confucian spiritual sensibility: "For the Confucian, there is no access to the ultimate except through social relationships."[15] This is the case because inclusive community building for the Confucian is not just an external manifestation of one's inner moral excellence; instead, for the Confucian, spirituality can only be expressed through community building, and hence social relationships are that through which one comes to be oneself.

The Socratic imperative of "know thyself" or the Cartesian "I" if put in the Confucian context will not lead to a discussion on the quality of the individual soul, nor on the discrete functions of the mind. Instead, the question of self-knowing for the Confucian begins with navigating the complex web of human relationships that sustains oneself. The Confucian ritual self, in a word, is made viable by taking root in the garden of human ecology in which one is first sustained through the conscious care by others, and then through one's growth, one in turn sustains others intra- and inter-generationally. It is a world of cooperative living bound by ritual civility and mutual obligations. This Eden of Great Community is premised on the porous nature of the self where the self and the other are mutually dependent and mutually enriching.

Ontologically speaking, an essential self unchanging throughout one's life time is a useful political fiction, but a fiction nevertheless. By all accounts, it is impossible for us to articulate clearly what an essential self that underpins the concept of individual political rights constitutes. The emblematic illusiveness of the essential self famously raised by Hume is a clear reminder.[16] Nonetheless, we continue to cling onto it for political expediency or merely for psychological comfort. As Henry Rosemont Jr. in his audacious project entitled *Against Individualism* (2015) points out:

> [I]t appears that it is very difficult to describe what it is to be an individual self—for ourselves or for others—and yet we are inclined to continue to believe that every human being can know themselves, and

can be uniquely identifiable in isolation from all other human beings, and therefore there must always be a clear answer to the question "Who am I?" and "Who are you?" and "Who is she?" for each of us.[17]

This habit of the modern mind naturally gives rise to an individualistic inclined society, despite all its inadequacies in dealing with and in describing our everyday intertwining existence.

In order to build a truly inclusive community not just for ourselves here at home but also globally, the first step we need to take is to go beyond our entrenched liberal individualism. As Rupp indicates simply in his book title *Beyond Individualism* (2015), it is to go beyond the limits of individualism by opening itself up to allow for "both contributions and critical perspectives from multiple traditions."[18] To acknowledge the limitation and the provincial nature of liberal individualism is conceptually necessary for other viable alternatives to arise at all. To do otherwise, as Rupp writes, is to presume that "the world is more or less like us—or, at least in its heart of hearts, wants to be like us […]."[19] After decades of humanitarian works often in war-torn communities worldwide, Rupp urges us to do the hard work to learn about and from other cultures. Liberal individualism doesn't have the last word on the subject of political governance; it doesn't foreclose all possibilities for future progressive humanity.

There is much the Confucian tradition can contribute to the enrichment of our modern state and to the enrichment of this hybridized world where social, political, or ecological problems oftentimes traverse multiple boundaries. In truth, regional issues do not always remain regional. For instance, the civil war in Syria has led to the continuous flow of refugees to Europe and beyond, and the agricultural practices of slash-and-burn in the forests of Indonesia are a major source of health problems in all of Southeast Asia, not to mention the Covid-19 pandemic that has brought the world down to its knees.[20] Seeking greater inclusion, hence as Rupp concludes, "cannot only be an aspiration that idealists cherish"; instead, it is "a worthy ideal and also a practical requirement."[21] Globalization is an irreversible historical fact; building an inclusive community is the proper way for all of us to move forward into an ever more progressive future. This union of ours by the inclusion of Confucianism is thus made ever more prefect.

Contemporary Applications

The aim of constructing a hybrid account of feminist theory with characteristic Confucian terms, methods, and concerns is to provide all with a set of alternative conceptual tools to think through their own lives so that the range of possible solutions to gender oppression is no longer confined to what the Anglo-European intellectual traditions can provide. Like liberal feminism, Marxist feminism, or radical feminism, this newly constructed Confucian feminism also belongs to the pantheon of feminist theories. As a feminist theory, each offers its distinct way of looking at the root of gender oppression and offers its best approach to address the assorted issues of gender oppression. For instance, a Marxist approach to gender oppression offers a material-based and a class-based analysis and its solution focuses on addressing the capitalistic monopoly over the means of production. This Marxist approach to women's oppression has its critics, but its distinct approach is widely recognizable whenever this feminist theoretical paradigm is invoked. By the same token, a liberal approach to gender oppression offers a rights-based and individual-based analysis and its solution focuses on addressing equal rights and equal opportunity. This liberal approach has its faults but we all recognize its distinctiveness in addressing the issue of gender oppression. So it is fair to ask: What is Confucian feminism's distinctive approach to the issue of gender oppression and what is its distinct vision of a liberating future?

In this hybrid blend of Confucianism and feminism, a family-based and a care-based approach is what characterizes the paradigm of Confucian feminism. This dual lens of family and care will be what guides our understanding of both the root of gender oppression and liberation. From the theoretical vantage point of Confucian feminism, women are oppressed historically and presently because women are excluded from a patrilineal familial structure that prioritizes man—his family, his lineage, his accomplishment, and his legacy—by making woman into an auxiliary, functionary, and replaceable component to the marital union that they share. In this patrilineal family structure, not only is woman not cared for; she is destined to care for all others living a life of servitude. Not until she reaches seniority, is she entitled to be cared for by her adult sons and daughters-in-law. It is true that seniority is a mitigating factor for women propelled by the Confucian respect for the elders, but all things being equal, women are the first in line to serve and the last in line to be served by others. In short, women are oppressed because they are auxiliary to the patrilineal family that demands women's constant care but cares for them little.

With the dual lens of family and care as the distinctive approach of Confucian feminism to women's oppression, it is also fair to ask: How is this paradigmatic approach applicable to specific women's issues, concerns, and experiences so that it merits the name "a practical ethic for life"? For instance, how does Confucian feminism respond to elder care which is one of the most pressing issues today, especially in wealthier countries like ours? Or, how does Confucian feminism respond to the issues faced by the LGBTQIA+ communities where the public acceptance of their sexual preference and gender expression is still not where it needs to be for them to be fully integrated into the public/civic life? The steadily decline in birth and marriage rate has not only exacerbated the problem of elder care but also put increasing pressure on women to retreat from their share of the public life in order to prioritize their domestic roles of wife and mother as women everywhere have been molded to be for eons. The so-called "left-over women" *shengnu* 剩女 (the Chinese equivalent of a spinster) or the commercialized notion of "light-mature women" *qingshounu* 輕熟女 (the Taiwanese equivalent of a financially independent woman delaying marriage) are cases in point.[22]

It is well accepted among scholars that Confucianism bases both its ethical and political ideal on the institution of family. Unlike the vast majority of the Anglo-European intellectual traditions—both ancient and modern—that either neglect the importance of family or make family as merely one among many essential components for living a good life, Confucianism sees family as a fundamental site in which the sprouts of goodness are cultivated into an array of robust virtues that guide a life well-lived domestically, communally, politically, and beyond. More importantly, a radical bifurcation of family/state and private/public is not present in Confucianism that maps the ever-expanding web of familial, communal, and political relations in a continuous, concentric fashion where the political builds and depends on the communal, which in turns builds and depends on the familial. This series of overlapping dependencies is understood not just in a temporal, chronological order, but also in a normative, ethical order where the family is the wellspring of virtues that sustain the myriad of personal, communal, and political relations.

Given the importance of family in the Confucian ethos, how the family institution is conceptualized has a profound impact on its constituents and each's positionality. Among the Confucian five core social relations (*wulun* 五倫), three are familial: Father-son, husband-wife, and siblings. And among these three essential familial relations, the spousal relation is what enables all other human relations to emerge. As said in the *Book of Rites*, "Jiaotesheng 郊特牲" chapter, "the union of *tian* and *di* (heaven and earth) gives rise to a myriad of things in the world, just as the marriage rite is the beginning of a myriad of generations (天地合而後萬物興焉. 夫昏禮, 萬世之始也)." The marriage rite that binds two people into a marital union, in other words, is the wellspring of all human relations just as the union between *tian* and *di* is the wellspring of all things in the world.

The spousal relation is the cornerstone of family that makes the father-son and siblings relations possible, and the proliferation of which in turn makes the ruler-minister political relation and friendship possible. As said precisely in the *Book of Changes*, "Xu 序卦" hexagram:

> Have *tian* 天 and *di* 地 existing, then there comes a myriad of things. Have a myriad of things existing, then there comes man and woman (*nannu* 男女). Have man and woman existing, then there comes husband and wife (*fu*fu* 夫婦). Have husband and wife existing, then there comes father and son. Have father and son existing, then there comes ruler and minister. Have ruler and minster existing, then there comes high and low. Have high and low existing, then there comes the intricacies of ritual propriety and righteousness.

Or, as said simply in the *Mencius* 5A2, "[t]hat man and woman (*nannu* 男女) dwell together is the greatest of human relations." Spousal relation is premised on gender differentiation, which, in turn, is marked by the binary concept of *nei/wai* 內外 (inside/outside) where the correct place of man is in the *wai* 外 and woman the *nei* 內. As said in the *Book of Changes*, "Jiaren 家人" hexagram, "Tuanzhuan 彖傳" commentary, "in the hexagram *Jiaren* 家人 (family), woman's correct place is in the *nei* 內, man's correct place is in the *wai* 外. That man and woman occupy their correct places is the great righteousness of *tian* 天 and *di* 地." Differing from the binary concept of *yin/yang* 陰陽, the *nei/wai* 內外 binary when applied to gender is meant to differentiate and to separate.[23]

Gender differentiation, as noted earlier, according to the *Xunzi* 5.9, is what elevates humanity above bestiality: "Even though beasts (*qinshou* 禽獸) have fathers and sons, there is no affection between them, and even though they have males and females (*pinmu* 牝牡), there is no distinction between man and woman (*nannu* 男女)." Without such gender differentiation, as Xunzi warns in the *Xunzi* 17.19, licentiousness would ensue and familial relations would come undone: "[W]hen the *nei* 內 and *wai* 外 are not differentiated, man and woman (*nannu* 男女) are licentious, then father and son are suspicious of each other." Hence, the primary function of *nei/wai* 內外, when it applies to gender, is to differentiate and to separate between genders so as to mark proper ritual as well as physical boundaries. This *nei/wai* 內外 gender demarcation has a profound impact on woman, since by virtue of her gender positionality in the *nei* 內 she has no legitimate claim beyond the domestic.

Women are consigned to the *nei* 內 with no direct access to the *wai* 外—the realm of culture, political authority, and remembrance—and hence, in practical terms, women are auxiliary, functionary, and replaceable components to the patrilineal family structure. Women's relation to the realm of *wai* 外 must be mediated by their father, husband, or son. And that male meditation consequently creates conundrums for those women whose talents and aspirations go beyond what is needed for them to perform domestic duties as wives and mothers. To undo the *nei/wai* 內外 gender differentiation, hence, is the first in order in Confucian feminism in order to confront the problem of gender oppression. Women, much like men, in their quest for Confucian moral perfection not only should be able to, but more importantly morally compelled to traverse the limiting boundary of domesticity so as to extend their spheres of influence from the self, family, community, state to the world at large in a continuous, concentric fashion. After all, a man of virtue—much like Confucius himself spending a decade of his life traversing different states in search for a receptive ruler—strives to lead and benefit the world, not just his own family.

In order to begin to address the problem of gender oppression, Confucian feminism, first and foremost, advocates for the dissolution of the *nei/wai* 內外 gender distinction so that women of talents and virtues can also strive to serve the world beyond the confine of domesticity. But to undo the *nei/wai* 內外 gender distinction does not need to entail the end for the institution of family or the institution of marriage. For sure, no one should be compelled to enter the marriage institution, nor is marriage the only form of enduring, intimate relationship available to mutually consenting adults in our modern world. But as far as the institutions of marriage and family are concerned, what needs to change is the patrilineal structure of family and the one-sided demands for women's servicing care that renders women into a functionary vessel, a sort of thing that is contra to Confucius's teaching on what a well-rounded *junzi* should be.

Gender-based division of labor in the family will have to give way to a capacity developmental model where the young are raised not with a view of their eventuality of assuming the *nei/wai* 內外 positionality, but with a view of their becoming a person of magnanimity (*daren* 大人) going from the self to the world in the greatest possible sense, instead of being small and petty (*xiaoren* 小人) in whatever they do or with whomever they love. In other words, without the *nei/wai* 內外 gender distinction in Confucian feminism, women—both born and trans, queer and straight—are no longer raised with the sole purpose of one day becoming a wife or mother in the *nei* 內. Much like men, women should be raised to bring forth the four sprouts of goodness into their virtuous manifestations, leading and benefiting the world in the largest possible sense and to the largest extent possible.

The effect of consigning women to the positionality of *nei* 內 is clearly reflected in the contemporary sociological terms of the so-called "left-over women" *shengnu* (剩女) in China or the commercialized notion of "light-mature women" *qingshounu* (輕熟女) in Taiwan where professional women are publically shamed, ridiculed, or at best ambivalently tolerated for their seemingly prioritizing their selfish desires to stay single instead of entering the time-honored institution of marriage for the sake of assuming their domestic roles of wife and mother. The derogatory categorization of women who opt out of the marriage institution as a social surplus, a wasted "left-over" bit and the characterization of being an unmarried adult woman as a temporary state through which a truly mature woman (*shounu* 熟女) will eventually pass as she moves toward assuming the roles of wife and mother are not just limiting to women per se by creating social *cachets* for these gender roles. These conceptual categorizations of women as *shengnu* 剩女and *qingshounu* 輕熟女present yet another perilous situation for the LGBTQIA+ communities by virtue of their sexual preference and gender expression that are already contra the heteronormative way of life.

In the contemporary world, those in the LGBTQIA+ communities are often demonized and exoticized for their contra-heteronormative way of life. However during the pre-modern times, the degree of normalization of what now falls under the queer identity vary from culture to culture. The Greek male homosexual practice as evidenced in Plato's various dialogues—such as *Lysis* and *Symposium*—comes to mind. There is also a long tolerated tradition of homosexuality/bisexuality, especially among men of status, in pre-modern China. Various pre-Qin and Han texts—both Confucian and non-Confucian—contain records alluding to or documenting those non-binary sexual expressions without explicitly condemning them. Hence, some scholars have gone even further to suggest that there are possible grounds for the compatibility between Confucianism and queer rights/expressions.[24] This important topic deserves a full and thorough investigation which however is beyond the scope of this current project.

Suffice to say that, within the paradigm of Confucian feminism, one way to enable these marginalized communities to live a fully integrated public life is to undo the *nei/wai* 內外based normative demarcation for gender expressions. Once the concept of gender is uncoupled from the *nei/wai*-based gender expressions, one is free to be oneself—let one be lesbian, gay, bi-, trans-, queer, intersex, asexual, and more. One is free to engage in any form of enduring and intimate relationship with another consenting adult insofar as the relationship is anchored in mutual moral perfection as its internal good. In other words, in Confucian feminism, gender is never a mere function of one's sexed body, nor is it derivative from hierarchal gender roles; rather one's gender expression—let one be a woman, man, or they—forms part of one's relational cultivation to moral perfection inter-subjectively.

In Confucian feminism that is without the *nei/wai* 內外 gender distinctions and positionalities, no unmarried persons are ever social surpluses, "left-over" bits, neither should singlehood be a mere transitory phase in one's life. Furthermore, those in the LGBTQIA+ communities living a contra-heteronormative way of life will no longer be forced to consign themselves to an impossible either/or choice according to the binary of *nei/wai* 內外 gender demarcations. The worth of a woman (or a man)—both born and trans, queer and straight—doesn't need to be defined by their marital status or sexual expression. Confucian moral perfection belongs to all, not just to any particular gender expression, sexual preference, or marital status.

Certainly, marriage is not the only enduring, intimate relationship that one can seek, but if one so chooses to enter the marriage institution, the spousal relation, as argued in the earlier chapters, will have to be replaced by friendship so that the sort of one-sided demands for women's servicing care will no longer be justified by the gender-based division of labor. The institution of marriage in the modern era is no longer defined by its purported economic benefits for women in exchange for their sexual and domestic servitude for men, nor is the sexual nature of the marital union in need of a religious or a moral sanction to make sex itself "legitimate" or "purposeful." As opinioned by the US Supreme Court in its landmark ruling on the same-sex marriage right (2015), marriage is an institution in which both parties in their marital union become greater than they once were. Spouses—both in hetero- and same-sex marriages—should be best friends who share all aspects of life, *eros* and all, in an effort to realize what is good and whatever else is possible in one another. Marriage, an intimate, enduring union, in a word, is the perfect vehicle for nurturing and sustaining the kind of perfect moral friendship that has been dreamed of by philosophers of both the East and the West, and hence friendship should also be the defining feature of our modern feminist marriage.

Family, as it is well-known, is an important component in Confucian ethos, and it is also the case in Confucian feminism. Family is the moral foundation for our relational personhood and informs us the nature of our mutual dependency in our civic life. In Confucian feminism, the solution to gender oppression will not be one of voluntary abandonment of our familial relationships. Learning to care for others is an essential part of our moral personality; it is not just only that to be a good person, we must care for the needy starting with one's family, but more importantly, in the process of learning to care for others, we *become* a better person that is both good for ourselves and good for others. In other words, we become better as a person in the process of learning to be one. This is so because caring for others takes us out of our natural gravitation toward our own self-wants and needs. Instead, we become receptive to the needs of others and to be moved by their vulnerability. This moral component of care is well articulated by contemporary care ethicists; this is also a recurring theme in Confucian teachings. Hence it is also an important component in formulating a liberating future from the vantage point of Confucian feminism.

It might sound counter-intuitive that caring for others starting with one's family should be part of a feminist liberating future, since so much of what is wrong with any oppressive relationship, marital or otherwise, is the insatiable demands for women's servicing care for others. And as argued in previous chapters, this is also one of the critiques against care ethics by its early critics. Needless to say, one-sided demands for women's servicing care are not the aim for care ethics nor for Confucianism, even though in practice, women have been and are still on the receiving end of that one-sided demands for servicing care. But the liberating future for women, as argued passionately by many, cannot be hinged on making women themselves *less* caring. To walk away from our vulnerable loved ones cannot lead to a more compassionate and inclusive future that feminists long for.

In an individualistic inclined society like ours, voluntary abandonment of our loved ones, especially vulnerable seniors, to understaffed and underserved nursing care facilities is already endemic. More abandonments cannot be the solution to gender oppression. The severity of the problem of elder care, although it is never hidden, has come to the clear forefront in the early stages of the Covid-19 pandemic where the abhorrently high mortality rate among seniors in the nursing care facilities is indicative of the structural problem of the modern state where our shared vulnerability and dependency are treated as exceptions to the normative life of independency, autonomy, and detachment. Those who need care are then pushed outside the domain of ethics as well as politics to be reliant on an array of disparate individual responses in the form of either unpaid domestic care or paid private care and both of which, more often than not, are performed by women. So given that, advocating more care seems counter-intuitive. However, I would argue that it is precisely because of that, advocating for more care—but in a form of structural and moral reform—is necessary to solving some of the problems faced by women.

Learning from Confucianism, to care for the vulnerable should be the first consideration of a compassionate and inclusive *ren*-based state. State-run or -subsidized assisted living and nursing facilities are not the be-all and end-all answer to the growing problem of elder care in today's world, as it is clearly shown in the high death rate in both state-run and private nursing facilities for seniors all across Europe and the United States. For sure, a *ren*-based state, as Confucianism teaches us, should care for the vulnerable due to age, sickness, disability, or the force of circumstances, but all levels of society need to partake in the culture and practice of care starting with one's family.

Elders, for instance, should be given a dignified way of living out of their remaining lives in their own family, in their own neighborhood, and in their own community to the greatest extent possible. Policies should gear toward making that a workable reality, for instance, by giving financial support to the care-giver, by providing free community day-care centers for seniors, by encouraging multi-generational dwelling, and most of all by instilling a care-centered value in the moral character of a people. Men, no less than women, should also partake in this Confucian moral endeavor by first learning how to care for vulnerable others with sincerity, since to be Confucian, as said many times over, is characterized by their sincere endeavors to care for the most vulnerable of all—the new-born babe—who cannot yet verbalize their needs or to indicate their willingness to reciprocate later on. Nevertheless, a good Confucian cares and cares with utmost sincerity to ensure the most vulnerable among us not only survive but continue to thrive to the greatest extent possible.

All of us should strive to care like Confucian in one's own person and in a *ren*-based state. Without this sort of moral and structural reform, women will continue to shoulder the vast majority of the caring activities at home and beyond. The work of caring for the dependent will then not only continue to fall on women who are oftentimes characterized as dependent themselves, but also continue to be stigmatized as the lesser, the undesirable, or the unfortunate exception to an otherwise independent, autonomous, and detached life that everyone should have lived. Feminists in their search for an end to gender-based oppression should not be indifferent to the vile indifference—prevalent especially in an individualistic inclined society like ours—to the suffering of the vulnerable starting with one's family. Learning to care for others is the starting point of actualizing a much more compassionate, inclusive world for all where caring for others and to be cared for are not seen as some unfortunate exceptions, but instead it forms the foundation of one's moral personhood and a well-functioning state. In short, the path to a feminist liberating future in Confucian feminism must first travel through caring for the needy starting in one's family.

In Confucianism the life-long journey of self-cultivation to moral perfection must begin with sustaining and nurturing familial relations, and for most of us family refers to one's biological or marital relations. But having none of that due to the force of circumstances does not diminish one's ability to partake in self-cultivation. Keep in mind, family in Confucianism does not necessarily need to be defined by blood relations or one's marital status.

As said in the *Analects* 12.5, for an exemplar person, *junzi,* who extends the same deferential respect and care that one has for one's family to everyone she encounters, within four seas all are one's siblings (四海之內, 皆兄弟也). In the event where one's blood or marital relations are absent, family can still be constructed with strangers. Certainly, no one should be obliged to stay in abusive relationships, familial or otherwise. But it is worth noting that Confucius does advocate for mending one's familial relations whenever and for however long one is able to. The road to moral perfection in Confucianism simply cannot bypass the family. Familial relations are fundamental human experiences and hence should also be the starting point of one's journey to moral perfection as well as feminist liberation.

From the vantage point of the Confucian feminist paradigm, first and foremost, we understand that to end gender-based oppression, we must first eradicate the *nei/wai*-based gender distinction and subsequently the gender-based division of labor in the spousal relation; friendship would then replace spousal relationship in marriage. Second, we understand that once women—both queer and straight, born and trans—are no longer confined by their positionality of *nei* 內, their marital status, singlehood, or sexual expression will neither define nor detract from their moral personhood. Confucian moral personhood is defined by one's constant striving for moral perfection, concentrically expanding from family to the world at large. Lastly, in order to build a truly compassionate, inclusive world—as feminists and as Confucians—we must care for the vulnerable in our own person and in our political leadership. And in so doing, all are counted for in our feminist liberating future.

Conclusion

In the end, the question of what sort of life is ethically more satisfying cannot be answered by focusing solely on the self, which, after all, is elusive ontologically. A richer and fuller account of the self, from the very start, must take into account of others with whom one is intractably bound to and dependent on. A self that is in the midst of the continuous stream of human ecology captures not just the descriptive aspect of the existential self much more fully, but also its normative aspect that should guide us in our everyday living. Caring for others is an existential given that makes life possible to begin with, and our self-conscious understanding of these existential webs of relationships that sustain and nourish life should also give rise to a greater appreciation of our sociality and mutual dependency. A self that is ritually knotted to others with sincerity and reciprocity is by its nature porous and other-regarding, and hence it is much more in sync with the vision of a progressive, inclusive, and caring future that is both Confucian and feminist.

What sort of self that we choose to embrace is not only ethically, but also socially and politically consequential. Each of us after all, as both Aristotle and Xunzi have remarked, is social in nature and forming society is concomitant with our humanity. To live ethically and to live socially and politically cannot be separated; what sort of political vision that we choose to embrace has a direct impact on our ethical life. And a much more ethically satisfying life where others are reciprocated with utmost sincerity obviously lies in the embrace of an inclusive community. To be inclusive and to reciprocate is more than a gesture of altruism; it is where each of our vitality lies. Take Rupp's (2015) metaphor of the Sea of Galilee and the Dead Sea as an example: The Sea of Galilee is a sea of vitality compared to the Dead Sea which is toxic and barren, and the difference is that the former takes in fresh water but also feeds downward streams as well, whereas the latter only takes.[25]

It is a choice that we all must make: Is it the Sea of Galilee or the Dead Sea? Are we each an island onto ourselves taking what we need but reciprocating no one, or are we co-dependent beings who are ritually bound to one another in a continuous stream of intra- and inter-general reciprocal care? Each of us must decide what sort of self we are. Confucian feminism advocates for a much more porous, relational self that is receptive to our existential interdependency and vulnerability starting with one's family and concentrically extending to the world at large. Its promised feminist future thereby is truly ethically satisfying and inclusive.

Epilogue

It is true that sexism plagues much of Chinese history and continues to permeate a plentitude of social and cultural practices today, and it is also true that Confucianism for the most part of Chinese history has been held as the moral backbone of the state and the emblem of Chinse high culture. There is no escaping that Confucianism bears some blame for gender oppression both past and present. But patriarchy and misogyny are not an exclusive invention of the Confucian tradition and nor is overt textual misogyny limited to non-Western canonical texts. If feminist inspirations could be drawn from Anglo-European philosophers such as Plato, Aristotle, Locke, Hume, Kant, Nietzsche, or Heidegger despite their overt textual misogyny, then it should present no more challenges to charitably re-appropriate Confucianism for all sorts of modern progressive projects including feminism. It is my take that it is possible to refashion Confucianism in a feminist image so as to provide viable conceptual tools for all to navigate the existential contour of our human-all-too-human lives and to envision a progressive, inclusive, and feminist future for humanity.

It need not be the case that our shared, inclusive future can only be plausibly charted by the Western, if not strictly liberal, tradition. Modernity and non-Western are not contrary terms, nor is the West synonymous with all that is good and possible for humanity. A progressive future for humanity can also be Confucian and feminist at the same time. Much like other feminist theoretical paradigms, this newly constructed theoretical paradigm of Confucian feminism also aims at providing women with its own distinctive theoretical tools to articulate women's issues, concerns, and experiences. This project however is not a cultural recovery project for "Chinese" women per se, however that cultural boundary of "Chinese-ness" is defined. Nor is this a descriptive project reflecting the actual feminist movements on the ground, since there are as many "Chinese feminisms" as there are women.[1] Rather, this is a philosophical project that charts a hybrid feminist theory based on characteristic Confucian terms, methods, and concerns.

This Confucian feminism is an inventive project that creatively imagines an inclusive, ethically satisfying future that is Confucian and feminist at the same time. But of course, one might argue that the impact of a comparative feminist project like this one on the so-called "real" world is minuscule. It is all an academic exercise that matters to no one, other than a narrow circle of specialists who quibble among themselves to score academic points. Yes, the relevance of academic works is an often-raised question, especially to the discipline of Humanities in general, not just to the discipline of philosophy, although the conventional image of philosophy as a discipline for the absurd and the exoteric certainly doesn't help the case here.[2] I will not try to enlist all the benefits of studying philosophy here, as there is enough ink spilled on the subject already illustrated in various introductory texts and in essays on the value of philosophy.[3]

Broadly speaking, how we conceptualize ourselves has a direct impact on what course of action we deem as valuable and on what we see as the proper role of the other, including the state, plays in our lives. And the prevalent norm in this culture of ours is indisputably individualistically inclined, perhaps more so than any other wealthy nation in Europe.[4] The resultant of this radical individualism in our social policies, as shown previously, is also startling: The United States ranks at or near the bottom on matters such as paid parental leave, income inequality, access to early childhood education, and Covid-19 death prevention, despite all the material advantages at our disposal. How we think of ourselves and what sort of social policies are deemed as legitimate are intimately connected. To remedy that—if that is something that we want to do—we will first need to imagine a different conceptual paradigm for the self and the political institution that is much more inclusive and compassionate.

Yes, this is an academic project that is feminist in character and Confucian in content, but how we think of ourselves and what sort of life that we live are not two disjunctive propositions. In our individualistically inclined society, we are imagined as in control of our own destiny that we are free to pull ourselves up by our own bootstraps and are only accountable to ourselves alone. Equality can only be measured in terms of our freedom to rise or fall on our own, not in terms of our mutual obligations to one another in ensuring a dignified existence for all. After all, as Senator Ted Cruz—an avid proponent of the Tea Party movement and the Freedom caucus—once says: "Give me a horse and a gun and an open plain, and we can conquer the world."[5] What more does a man need? To roam free in an open land of opportunity is the quintessential image of a self-reliant man, a man who is autonomous, independent, and, most of all, unencumbered by the dependent. Our existential experiences of ourselves and the lives that we actually live, however, say otherwise. This American myth of a self-reliant man nevertheless has a powerful grip on our cultural psyche. To loosen that chock-hold, first, we will need to imagine other possibilities, and what this Confucian-feminist project provides essentially is that imagined possibility in hopes of a different future for humanity, a future where all are counted for.

As feminists, we all must decide what sort of life is truly ethically satisfying and truly inclusive of the historically oppressed others living on the margins of society. The search for happiness, as Aristotle teaches us, is a pursuit common to us all, the final end of all our actions. But the search for happiness cannot be achieved with a self-centric approach. The answer to the question of "what is happiness?" cannot be reduced to "what do I want to do to make me happy?" Our individual happiness paradoxically cannot be achieved through merely focusing on our narrow self-interests. As Rupp writes precisely in *Beyond Individualism*:

> All of us wrestle with the question of what is the good life, I therefore urge us to focus not only on individual happiness and accomplishment [...] but also to recognize that such goals can be attained only as we engage larger issues, participate in ever more inclusive communities, and commit ourselves to causes that in the end embrace all of humanity, indeed the whole cosmos.[6]

This is so because interdependency and inclusivity are what makes life like ours possible and are also what sustains its vitality. Living a life of a self-reliant man that cares for no one is an ethically impoverished life of solitude.

Life like ours is essentially a life of interdependency. Hence in wanting to establish oneself, as Confucius teaches us, one also establishes others intersubjectively. The extended circle of one's radial influence is the true measure of one's lived personhood that is ever more expansive and inclusive. This sense of Confucian personhood is ever more fitting for this world of ours where social, political, economic, environmental, and global health issues are oftentimes trans-national, trans-gender, and trans-class as well. To insist on building a walled life for oneself is not only unattainable empirically, but also ethically deficient.

Feminists' search for liberation for women should not and could not just be a narrow focus on self-liberation. For sure, woman should have a sense of self-worth and no one should be pressed into accepting a role of unlimited self-giving in a patrilineal family structure that demands her care but cares for her little. In the search for a liberating future, woman however should not lose sight of what sustains life in the first place and what makes life truly worth living. The natural lure of focusing on the "I" might bring a temporary relief but no long-lasting respite to the self that is left wanting. To live an ethically sound life, we need to care for one another. Caring for others is not just a good thing to do; it is also good for us by taking ourselves out of the perpetual loop of self-centrism that walls ourselves in our own wants, needs, pains, or joys. Caring for others offers an ethical way out of the tyranny of the "I." And we need to start our caring inclusivity with our own family that first sustains and nourishes us.

Human relationality is the bond that binds us and the anchor that gives weight to our temporal existence. To overlook that is to set ourselves adrift into the abyss of the absurd. The meaning of our lives in the present depends on what has been made available to us not only historically, but also equally, if not more so, depends on what we hope will continue to survive us in the future. An infertile, dying world deprives us not just the future generation; it makes our continuing survival at the present time superfluous.[7] What all these add up to is that in our search for liberation, we must take into account of this human ecology where the self is enmeshed with others and where the past, present, and future form a bidirectional continuum.

Caring for others doesn't need to be an impediment to living a truly liberated, ethically satisfying life. Instead, when done right, caring for others is, and perhaps, the only thing that can save us from ourselves, the tyranny of the "I." Speaking from my own experience of caring for my late mother-in-law during the last few months of her life, although it was not without its own practical challenges, it was a truly liberating experience for me. In encountering her vulnerability and frailty while not being expected to care for her, I was confronted by the cruelty of being allowed, and to a certain extent being expected, to be indifferent to the plights of one's family. That expected indifference haunted me. In spite of all the demands befallen on me, I was unable to turn my gaze away from her vulnerability and frailty.

By committing myself to care, I was liberated from that angst of hypocrisy of being a feminist and a Confucian and at the same time not being moved by the plights of human vulnerability. Through caring for my late mother-in-law, I came face to face with my feminist self. To be a feminist has to mean more than just being able to realize one's goals and being able to tally one's achievements; there has to be more in a truly liberated, ethically satisfying life. By reimagining Confucianism in a feminist fashion, I can genuinely say that I care because I am a Confucian and I care because I am a feminist.

Notes

Prologue

1   For the moral failings of the Western canonical thinkers, see Bernasconi and Lott (2000b), Valls (2005), Duncan Bell (2010), Oltermann (2014), Kirkpatrick (2019), *The Guardian* (2019), and Rosenlee (2020).
2   Schott (2003, 46).

Chapter 1

1   Woo (1999, 110).
2   For a discussion of footbinding in feminist literatures, see for instance, Dworkin (1974), Greenhalgh (1977), Daly (1978/1990), Grimshaw (1986), Jaggar (1995), Card (1996, 2000, & 2002), Callahan (2009), and Stewart (2014).
3   See for instance, Okin (1994) & (1995).
4   For the intercultural exchange between the West and China from the sixteenth to the eighteenth century, see Mackerras (1989), Clarke (1997), Mungello (1999), and Perkins (2007).
5   For the systematic exclusion of non-Western philosophical thoughts from the history of philosophy, see Bernasconi (1995), Park (2013), Wimmer, Bernasconi, Hountondji, and Norton-Smith (2015), Norden (2017), and Rosenlee (2020).
6   Garfield and Norden (2016) and Norden (2017).
7   Knox and Miller (1985, 9–10). For Hegel's criticism of Chinese Philosophy, see Young Kun Kim (1978).
8   Knox and Miller (1985, 15).
9   Ibid., 166–7.
10   Park (2013).
11   Eze (1997, 109–49) and Bernasconi (2000a).
12   Moellendorf (1992, 246 & 253), and Knox and Miller (1985, 51 & 173).
13   For an extended list of courses and their frequency taught by Kant, see Louden (2000, 4–5).
14   Kant, *Opus postumum* (21:213–14); trans. Forster (1993, 66).
15   Kant, "Of Different Human Races" (2:438); eds. Zoller and Louden (2007, 92–3).
16   Ibid., 2:441; 95.

17 Kant, "Idea for a Universal History" (8:29–30); eds. Zoller and Louden (2007, 119).

18 Kant, *Religion within the Boundaries of Mere Reason* (6:51–2 & 6:101–2); eds. Wood and Giovanni (1996, 95 & 135–6).

19 Kant, *Critique of Judgment* (170); for translation, see Pluhar (1987, 7). For more on the connection between Kant's teleology and race, see Larrimore (2008).

20 See for instance, Hill and Boxill (2001), Kleingeld (2007), Flikschuh and Ypi (2014), and Steve Fuller (2018).

21 Hume, "Of National Characters" (emphasis original); ed. Miller (1985, 208).

22 For more details, see Louden (2011) and Rosenlee (2020).

23 See for instance, Valls (2005).

24 Okin (1999, 16).

25 Ibid., 22–3 (emphasis original).

26 See Sullivan (1983), Parekh (1999), Bogues (2005), and Duncan Bell (2010).

27 Mohanty (2003, 17).

28 Margalit and Raz (1995, 86).

29 Okin (1999) & (2002). Also see Phillips (2007).

30 Phillips (2007, 150).

31 Okin (2002, 220).

32 Narayan (1997, 16).

33 Beauvoir (1949 [1989], 81).

34 Taylor Mill (1852 [1994], 177–8).

35 Taylor (1995, 256).

36 See for instance, Held (2006).

37 For care ethics' early critics and defenders, see for instance, Card (1990), Hoagland (1991), Tronto (1993), and Jaggar (1995).

38 See Lai Tao (2000), Star (2002), Yuan (2002), (2005), & (2019), Chenyang Li (2002) & (2015), Herr (2003), Held (2006), Luo (2007), Dalmiya (2009), Noddings (2010), Rosenlee (2012) & (2014), Epley (2015), and Foust and Tan (2016).

39 Chenyang Li (1994, 86).

40 See for instance, Jaggar (1995, 199–201), Tronto (2013, 24), and Collins (2015, 2 & 6). For a rare lengthier engagement with Confucianism outside the Asian and Comparative philosophical community, see Groenhout (2014, 494–5, & 499–501).

41 Held (2006, 22).

42 Noddings (2010, 140).

43 Held (2006, 64).

44 Dalmiya (2009, 206).

45 Ibid., 207 (emphasis original).

46 Ibid., 208.

47 Ibid., 192.

48 Ibid.

49 Baier (2000, 20).
50 For translation of the *Analects*, see Ames and Rosemont (1998b).
51 Held (2006, 60).
52 Ibid.

Chapter 2

1   Chenyang Li (1994, 81 & 85).
2   Ibid., 86.
3   Yuan (2002, 125).
4   Star (2002, 93); emphasis original.
5   Chenyang Li (2002, 130–40).
6   Held (2006, 66 & 73).
7   Friedman (1993, 151).
8   Held (2006, 158).
9   Sommers (1989, 730); emphasis original.
10 Ibid., 729.
11 English (1979 [1989], 687).
12 Ibid., 683.
13 Dixon (1995, 83).
14 Keller (2006, 269).
15 Ibid.
16 Ibid., 269–70.
17 For the translation of the *Xiaojing*, see Ames and Rosemont (2009).
18 Russell (1922, 40).
19 Ibid.
20 Slote (1998, 46).
21 Holzman (1998, 185 & 190).
22 Ibid., 198.
23 Herr (2003, 481); emphasis original.
24 Raphals (2004, 216–17).
25 Ibid., 222.
26 Ames and Rosemont (2009, xiii).
27 See for instance, Knapp (1995) and Holzman (1998).
28 See Alan Chan and Tan (2004).
29 See Knapp (1995, 197) and Alan Chan and Tan (2004, 1).
30 For a short philosophical explanation of the term "*xiao*," see Shun (2003, 793).
31 For the translation of the *Mencius*, see Lau (1970).
32 See for instance, *Analects* 4.18, *Mencius* 6B3, *Xiaojing* Ch. 15, and *Xunzi* 29.1 & 29.2.
33 For more details on the story, see Holzman (1998, 186–8).
34 Williams (1981, 18).

35 Ibid.
36 Ibid.
37 As qtd in Langton (2000, 206).
38 As qtd. in Ibid., 204.
39 For the translation of *Zhongyong*, see Ames and Hall (2001).
40 See for instance, Tu (1985, 84) and Ames and Hall (1987, 114).
41 Kittay (1999, 107).
42 Ames and Rosemont (2009, xi).
43 Held (2006, 66) and Kittay (1999, 19).
44 Kittay (2002, 238).
45 Ibid., 245.
46 For the trans. of *Liji*, see Legge (1885).

Chapter 3

1   Mill (1869 [2003], 348).
2   Yalom (2001, xvi).
3   For more details, see *USA Today* (2015).
4   As qtd. in Mahoney and Williams (1998, 4). For more on the legal loopholes for marital rape, see *NPR* (2019).
5   Mill (1869 [2003], 347).
6   Yalom (2001, xviii).
7   *Ga Code Ann.* (1935, 53–501); as qtd. in *Obergefell v. Hodges* (2015).
8   See *Time* (2009), *The New York Times* (2012), *CNN* (2015), *American Bar Association* (2022), and *Forbes* (2023).
9   For the 2004 report, see *60 Minutes* (2004). For the 2014 survey, see *Harvard Business Review* (2014).
10 *NPR* (2020).
11 Deresiewicz (2007, 57).
12 Wollstonecraft (1792 [2003], 268).
13 Mill (1869 [1994], 169).
14 Ibid., 160.
15 Deresiewicz (2007, 57).
16 See for instance, Aristotle's *Nicomachean Ethics* (*NE*) Book 8, *Eudemian Ethics* (*EE*) Book 7, *Rhetoric* Book 2, *Politics* Book 2 & 3, and *Magna Moralia* Book 2; for translation, see Barnes (1984/1995). For contemporary scholarships on Aristotle's concept of friendship, see Nussbaum (1986, 354), Sherman (1997, 199), Sim (2007, 195), Salkever (2008, 75–6), and Connolly (2012, 72).
17 See for instance, Plato's *Lysis, Phaedrus, Symposium, Alcibiades*, and *Law* Book 8; for translation, see Cooper (1997). For contemporary scholarships on Plato's concept of friendship, see Timothy Fuller (2008, 201), Nichols (2009, Ch. 4), and Murr (2014, 3).

18 Plato, *Phaedrus* 256a7ff.
19 Kant, *The Metaphysics of Morals*, "The Doctrine of Virtue" (*MM*/DV) 6:469–73; for translation, see Gregor (1996).
20 Aristotle, *NE* 1157b32ff, 1158b26-32, & 1159b3 and *EE* 1238b15-25 & 1240b1-2.
21 Ibid., *NE* 1166a1-31 & 1171b32-33, and *EE* 1240b1ff.
22 Ibid., *NE* 1167b5-6.
23 For Aristotle's writings on female inferiority, see *Generation of Animals* (*GA*) and *Politics*. For excerpts, see Mahowald (1978/1994, 22–31).
24 Aristotle, *NE* 1162a25-26.
25 Ibid., *EE* 1238b15-25 & 1241b29-32, and *NE* 1160b33-35.
26 Ibid., *EE*1238b26-29 and *NE* 1158b24-28.
27 Nussbaum (1986, 358).
28 Aristotle, *EE* 1240b2.
29 For a discussion on Aristotle's omission of *eros*, see Nussbaum (1986, 370–1).
30 For a discussion on the differences between Plato and Aristotle's take on friendship, see Salkever (2008, 73).
31 Plato, *Phaedrus* 256b7-c6 and *Law* 836c3-6. Also see Murr (2014, 3–34).
32 For a discussion on medieval church fathers' attitude toward sex, see Ruether (2000) and McLaughlin (2000).
33 Fullam (2012, 682).
34 See Bible, see *King James Bible Online*.
35 For a discussion on Aquinas's view of friendship, see Quinn (1996), Schwartz (2007), and Schindler (2008).
36 Aquinas, *Summa Theologiae* (*ST*) II-II.23-6; for translation, see Pakaluk (1991, 171–84).
37 Ibid., *ST* I-II.28.1-2; ibid., 161–5.
38 Ibid., *ST* I-II.28.4; ibid., 168.
39 For Aquinas's discussion on marital relationship, see *ST* I-II.26.1-4, 27.1-4, 28.1-6 & *ST* II-II.23.1-5, 25.1-7, 26.4-6; also see Pakaluk (1991, xiii).
40 Fullam (2012, 680–1).
41 Aquinas, *Summa Contra Gentiles* (*SCG*) III:123; for translation, see Bourke (1956/1975, 148).
42 Aquinas, *ST* II-II.23.1; Pakaluk (1991, 172).
43 Kierkegaard, *Works of Love*; for translation, see Pakaluk (1991, 241); emphasis original.
44 Ibid., *Works of Love*; ibid., 240–41.
45 Ibid., *Works of Love*; ibid., 235.
46 Montaigne, *Of Friendship*; for translation, see Pakaluk (1991, 188).
47 Ibid., *Of Friendship*; ibid., 192.
48 Ibid., *Of Friendship*; ibid., 190–91.
49 Ibid, 191.
50 Kant, *The Metaphysics of Morals*, "Doctrine of Right" (*MM*/DR) 6:277; for translation, see Gregor (1996).
51 Ibid., *MM*/DR 6:277-8.

52   Ibid., *MM*/DR 6:279; emphasis original.

53   Kant, *Anthropology* (*Anth.*) 7:303; emphasis original. For translation, see Zoller and Louden (2007).

54   Ibid., *Anth.* 7:309; emphasis original.

55   Kant, *MM*/DV 6:469–70; emphasis original. Also see *Lectures on Ethics* (*LE*); for translation, see Infield (1930/1963, 200).

56   Ibid., *MM*/DV 6:471.

57   For Aristotle, see *Magna Moralia* 1213a10-26; also see Nussbaum (1986, 364), Sherman (1997, 211), and Aubenque (1998, 26). For a comparison on Kant and Aristotle's view of friendship, see Veltman (2014, 281).

58   Kant, *MM*/DV 6:472.

59   Ibid., *LE*; Infield (1930/1963, 208). Also see *MM*/DV 6:472.

60   Ibid., *Observations on the Feeling of the Beautiful and Sublime (Obs.)*; Goldthwait (1960, 74 & 81); emphasis original.

61   Ibid., *Anth.* 7:307; emphasis original.

62   Ibid., *Obs.*; Goldthwait (1960, 78).

63   Papadaki (2010, 288). For a revival of both Kant's concept of friendship and marriage, also see Denis (2001).

64   Papadaki (2010, 294).

65   Schott (2003, 46).

Chapter 4

1   See Vervoorn (2004, 6), He (2007, 293), and Ames (2011, 118).

2   See Vervoorn (2004, 4), He (2007, 292–3), and Huang (2007, 4).

3   See for instance, *Shujing*, "Dagao大誥" chapter: "肆予大化誘我友邦君"; "Shaogao 召誥" chapter: "予小臣敢以王之仇民百君子越友民"; "Mushi 牧誓" chapter: "嗟! 我友邦冢君"; "Kanggao 康誥" chapter: "封, 元惡大憝, 矧惟不孝不友" and "兄亦不念鞠子哀, 大不友于弟"; "Junchen 君陳" chapter: "惟孝友于兄弟, 克施有政"; for translation, see Legge (1879). Also see Vervoorn (2004, 8–9).

4   See *Shijing*, Song 1 "關雎": 參差荇菜, 左右采之. 窈窕淑女, 琴瑟友之; Song 165 "伐木": 伐木丁丁, 鳥鳴嚶嚶. 出自幽谷, 遷于喬木. 嚶其鳴矣, 求其友聲. 相彼鳥矣, 猶求友聲; for translation, see Waley (1996). Also see Vervoorn (2004, 9–12).

5   *Lienu zhuan* 1.6; for translation, see Kinney (2014).

6   Vervoorn (2004, 7) and Ames (2011, 117).

7   *Shijing*, Song 176 "菁菁者莪" and Song 300 "閟宮." *Yijing*, hexagram 41 "損" and 42 "益"; for translation, see Legge (1882).

8   For more details, see He (2007, 292).

9   *Shanhai jing*, "Beishan jing 北山經" chapter; for the inclusiveness of the publication date, see Fracasso (1993).

10   He (2007, 292).

11 For the term "*wupian wutang* 無偏無黨" in the *Shujing*, see "Hongfan 洪範" chapter.

12 See *Xunzi*, Ch. 13 "臣道" (The Way of the Minister), Ch. 14 "致士" (Attracting Scholars) and Ch. 16 "彊國" (Strengthening the State); for translation, see Knoblock and Zhang (1999) 2 vols.

13 For the translation of *Guanzi*, see Rickett (1998).

14 For more, see *Guanzi*, "Canhuan 參患" chapter: "道正者不安, 則才能之人去亡; 行邪者不變, 則群臣朋黨; 才能之人去亡, 則宜有外難, 群臣朋黨, 則宜有內亂"; "Junchen I 君臣上" chapter: "治國無法, 則民朋黨而下比, 飾巧以成其私. 法制有常, 則民不散而上合, 竭情以納其忠"; "Junchen II 君臣下" chapter: "群官朋黨以懷其私, 則失族矣"; "Mingfa 明法" chapter: "外內朋黨, 雖有大姦, 其蔽主多矣; 是以忠臣死於非罪, 而邪臣起於非功, 所死者非罪, 所起者非功也, 然則為人臣者重私而輕公矣"; "Lizheng jiubaijie 立政九敗解" chapter: "人君唯毋聽群徒比周, 則群臣朋黨, 蔽美揚惡, 然則國之情偽不見於上, 如是, 則朋黨者處前, 寡黨者處後; 夫朋黨者處前, 賢不肖不分, 則爭奪之亂起, 而君在危殆之中矣."

15 For instance, see *Hanfeizi*, "二柄 (Two Handles)" chapter: "越官則死, 不當則罪, 守業其官所言者貞也, 則群臣不得朋黨相為矣"; "孤憤 (Solidary Indignation)" chapter: "官爵貴重, 朋黨又眾, 而一國為之訟" and "主利在豪傑使能, 臣利在朋黨用私"; "外儲說左下 (Outer Congeries of Sayings, the Lower Half Series)" chapter: "朋黨相和, 臣下得欲, 則人主孤; 群臣公舉, 下不相和, 則人主明"; for translation, see Watson (2003).

16 Vervoorn (2004, 28) and Huang (2007, 5).

17 *Baihutong*, "Sankang liuji 三綱六紀" chapter; for translation, see Tjan 1949/1952. For more on the discussion, see Lai (1996, 219), Ames and Hall (1998a, 261), and He (2007, 292). However, I was unable to locate this quoted passage "同門曰朋, 同志曰友" in the received version of the *Liji*. And the *Baihutong* is the only pre-Qin text that I can find that has this quote from the *Liji*.

18 For the probable dating of the text *Erya*, see Coblin (1993).

19 For more, see He (2007, 293). For the publication date of *Guoyu*, see I-Jen Chang et al. (1993).

20 For the translation of *Mozi*, see Johnston (2010).

21 See for instance, *Analects* 1.4, 1.7, & 5.26 and *Mencius* 3A4 & 4A12.

22 See for instance, *Analects* 13.28; *Mencius* 4B30; *Guanzi*, "Dizizhi 弟子職" chapter; *Erya*, "Shixun 釋訓" chapter; *Shuoyuan*, "Jianben 建本" chapter; *Lienu zhuan 2.12*, "Qixiang yuqi 齊相御妻"; *Zhonglun*, "Guiyan 貴驗" chapter; *Hanshi waizhuan*, Ch. 5; *Yangzi fanyan* 揚子法言, Ch. 1; and *Yanshi jiaxun* 顏氏家訓, "Mianxue 勉學" chapter.

23 See *Mencius* 2B2, 5A4, 5B3, 5B7, and 7A43.

24 For the publication date of *Zuozhuan*, see Cheng (1993).

25 See *Kongzi jiayu*, "三恕 (Three Reciprocity)" chapter: "父有爭子, 不陷無禮; 士有爭友, 不行不義"; "六本 (Six Bases)" chapter: "君無爭臣, 父無爭子, 兄無爭弟, 士無爭友, 無其過者, 未之有也"; "子路初見 (Zilu's First Encounter)" chapter: "夫人君而無諫臣則失正, 士而無教友則失聽".

26 For more, see *Hanshi waizhuan* 韓詩外傳, Ch. 5: "故上主以師為佐, 中主以友為佐, 下主以吏為佐, 危亡之主以隸為佐"; and Ch. 6: "吾聞諸侯之德, 能自取師者王, 能自取友者霸, 而與居不若其身者亡." Also see *Lushi chunqiu* 呂氏春秋, "Jiaozi 驕恣" chapter: "諸侯之德, 能自為取師者王, 能自取友者存, 其所擇而莫如己者亡"; and "Sande 上德" chapter: "吾於陽城君也, 非師則友也, 非友則臣也." Lastly, see *Xinxu* 新序, "Zashiyi 雜事一" (Miscellaneous I) chapter: "諸侯自擇師者王, 自擇友者霸, 足己而群臣莫之若者亡."

27 Ames and Rosemont (2014, 118–20 & 134).

28 For more discussion of the differences, see Vervoorn (2004, 3).

29 For more on the connection between *xiao* and friendship, see *Kongzi jiayu*, "Kunshi 困誓" chapter: "故君子入則篤行, 出則交賢, 何為無孝名乎" And *Hanshi waizhuan*, Ch. 9: "是以君子入則篤孝, 出則友賢, 何為其無孝子之名." Lastly, see *Yantielun* 鹽鐵論, "Xiaoyang 孝養" chapter: "閨門之內盡孝焉, 閨門之外盡悌焉, 朋友之道盡信焉, 三者, 孝之至也."

30 For the claim that friendship in Confucianism is marginal or "dangerous," see Kutcher (2000) and Huang (2007).

31 For more details on the concept of *nei/wai*, see Rosenlee (2006, Ch. 4–5) and (2023b).

32 For more details on Ban Zhao, see Rosenlee (2006, Ch.6) & (2023a, 2023b) Also see Swann (1932) and Pang-White (2018).

33 For the earth-bound character of Confucianism, see Ames (2011).

34 For a similar passage, also see *Yanshi jiaxun*, "慕賢 (Admiring the virtuous)" chapter: "是以與善人居, 如入芝蘭之室, 久而自芳也; 與惡人居, 如入鮑魚之肆, 久而自臭也. 墨子悲於染絲, 是之謂矣."

35 For similar passages, also see *Shuoyuan*, "Zayan 雜言" chapter: "孔子曰: 不知其子, 視其所友; 不知其君, 視其所使," and "Fengshi 奉使" chapter: "故曰: 欲知其子, 視其友; 欲知其君, 視其所使." Also *Kongzi jiayu*, "Liuben 六本" chapter: "子曰: 商也好與賢己者處, 賜也好說不若己者. 不知其子, 視其父; 不知其人, 視其友; 不知其君, 視其所使; 不知其地, 視其草木." Lastly, *Lunheng* 論衡, "問孔 (Asking Confucius)" chapter: "夫欲知其子, 視其友; 欲知其君, 視其所使."

36 For the publication date of *Shangjun shu*, see Levi (1993).

37 For more discussion on the passage, see Vervoorn (2004, 32): footnote 126.

38 For the trans. of *Lienu zhuan*, see Kinney (2014).

39 For more, see Vervoorn (2004, 24), Henry (1987, 10–12), Huang (2007, 21), and Lu (2007, 238).

40 *Liezi* 列子, Ch. 6; for translation, see Graham (1960/1990).

Chapter 5

1 For the rise of the far-right movements in Europe, see *BBC News* (2019b) & (2022b).

2 Plato, *Republic* Book VIII; for translation, see Cooper (1997).

3   As qtd. in *The Atlantic* (2016).
4   For the 2020 presidential election vote tally, see *NBC News* (2021).
5   For more on "European Enlightenment," see Bristow (2010/2017).
6   See Clark (2003), Mendus (2003), Bernasconi and Mann (2005), Bernasconi (2002, 2011), Louden (2011), Boxill (2017), and Rosenlee (2020).
7   As qtd. in Brooks (2005).
8   For the greying world, see *Politico* (2017). For the problem of elder care in China, see Yuan (2019, Ch. 7).
9   For the Covid-19 death toll worldwide as of April 4, 2023, see *WHO* (2023).
10   For the porous nature of the Confucian self, see Tu (1985), Ames and Hall (1987), and Rosemont (2015).
11   See Tu and De Bary (1998), Ames and Hall (1999), Bell and Chaibong (2003), Tan (2004), Shun and Wong (2004), Chang and Kalmanson (2010), Angle (2012), Joseph Chan (2013), Sungmoon Kim (2014, 2017), Daniel Bell (2015), Ames (2017), Chiu (2017), and Jin (2020).
12   For Mill's colonial involvement, see Sullivan (1983), Goldberg (2002), Bogues (2005), and Duncan Bell (2010).
13   MacIntyre (2004, 210).
14   Ibid.
15   As qtd. in *Time* (2016).
16   MacIntyre (2004, 217).
17   Ibid.
18   See Bernasconi and Mann (2005), Farr (2008), and Uzgalis (2002 & 2017).
19   MacIntyre (2004, 217).
20   Chiu (2017, 47).
21   Ibid., 48.
22   Ibid., 58.
23   Ibid.
24   Ibid., 57.
25   Bogues (2005, 218).
26   Mill, *Principles of Political Economy,* Book V, Ch. 11, Sec. 14 "Colonization."
27   Ibid.
28   Mill, *On Liberty*, "Introduction," (1859 [1995], 13).
29   Ibid.
30   See Bogues (2005, 230).
31   For the making of the modern self, see Taylor (1992).
32   Sungmoon Kim (2017, 8).
33   Aristotle, *Politics* III, 1275b18-21.
34   See Mulgan (1990, 204–5).
35   Sungmoon Kim (2017, 9).
36   Uzgalis (2017, 29).
37   Locke, *First Treatise*, Ch. I "Introduction;" emphasis original.
38   Ibid., *Second Treatise*, Ch. IV, Sec. 22–3; emphasis original.
39   For more details, see Bernasconi and Mann (2005, 89), Farr (2008, 496–500), and Uzgalis (2017, 29).

40	Locke, *Second Treatise*, Chapter VII: Of Political or Civil Society, Sec. 85.
41	As qtd. in Bernasconi and Mann (2005, 92). Also see Farr (2008, 499).
42	Jin (2020, 382), emphasis original.
43	Ibid.
44	Ibid., 383.
45	Kant, *The Metaphysics of Morals*; for translation, see Gregor (1996). *Religion within the Boundaries of Mere Reason* 6:94–5; for translation, see Wood and Giovanni (1996).
46	For more details on bureaucracy in early China, see Feng Li (2012).
47	See for instance, Angle (2012, 81).
48	MacIntyre (2004, 217).

Chapter 6

1	*US News* (2022).
2	*AARP* (2020) and *The New York Times* (2021b).
3	*WHO* (2023).
4	For an in-depth study on ritual, see Ing (2012).
5	For a short introduction to the sacred nature of Confucian secular ritual, see Fingarette (1972).
6	For more, see Ames (2011, 173) and Ing (2012, 24).
7	For more, see Ing (2012, 24–6).
8	For a feminist critique of Hobbes, see Pateman (2003, 168).
9	Ing (2012, 20).
10	Plato, *Republic* (434c): "Meddling and exchange between these three classes, then, is the greatest harm that can happen to the city and would rightly be called the worst thing someone could do to it."
11	For more, see Ing (2012, 34).
12	For more, see Ing (2012, 95–6).
13	For a detailed study of childhood and family in early China, see Kinney (2004) and Cline (2015).
14	For Yan Hui's death, see *Analects* 11.8, 11.9, 11.10, & 11.11. Also see Olberding (2004).
15	For more, see Ing (2012, 96–7).
16	Ibid., 49–50.
17	Ibid., 93–4.
18	*Lienu zhuan* 1.9 & 6.6; for translation, see Kinney (2014). For an extended discussion on Jing Jiang, see Raphals (2002, 275).
19	For more, see Ing (2012, 133–34).
20	Ibid., 163.
21	Ibid., Ch. 7.
22	For more, see Chenyang Li (2006, 583).
23	For more, see Ames (2011, 169).

24 *Shijing*, Song 164 "Changdi 常棣" is then quoted in the *Zhongyong* 中庸, Ch. 15 (子曰:「射有似乎君子, 失諸正鵠, 反求諸其身. 君子之道, 辟如行遠必自邇, 辟如登高必自卑.《詩》曰:『妻子好合, 如鼓瑟琴; 兄弟既翕, 和樂且耽. 宜爾室家, 樂爾妻帑.』」子曰:「父母其順矣乎!」) to emphasize the importance of caring for one's family before venturing out into the world; for translation of *Zhongyong*, see Ames and Hall (2001).

25 For more, see Chenyang Li (2006, 584).

26 Ibid., 585.

27 For translation, see Ames and Rosemont (2009).

28 A similar passage can also be found in the *Xunzi* 29.3: 魯哀公問於孔子曰:「子從父命, 孝乎?臣從君命, 貞乎?」三問, 孔子不對. 孔子趨出以語子貢曰:「鄉者, 君問丘也, 曰:『子從父命, 孝乎?臣從君命, 貞乎?』三問而丘不對, 賜以為何如?」子貢曰:「子從父命, 孝矣. 臣從君命, 貞矣, 夫子有奚對焉?」孔子曰:「小人哉!賜不識也!昔萬乘之國, 有爭臣四人, 則封疆不削; 千乘之國, 有爭臣三人, 則社稷不危; 百乘之家, 有爭臣二人, 則宗廟不毀. 父有爭子, 不行無禮; 士有爭友, 不為不義. 故子從父, 奚子孝?臣從君, 奚臣貞?審其所以從之之謂孝, 之謂貞也。」; for translation, see Knoblock and Zhang (1999).

29 See for instance, *Shijing*, Song 240 "Sizhai 思齊," Song 253 "Minlu 民勞," and Song 254 "Ban 板"; for translation, see Waley (1996).

30 For the US Capitol insurrection on January 6, 2021, see *The New York Times* (2021a).

31 For the public support for a "national divorce," see *National Review* (2023).

32 For a Confucian-inspired take on civility and rudeness, see Olberding (2019).

33 See *The New York Times* (2021c & 2021d), *The Guardian* (2017), *US News* (2016), *Fortune* (2015), and *EIA* (2016).

Chapter 7

1 See Rosemont (2015). Also see Wolff (2016).

2 See Blustein (1982) and Cline (2015).

3 As qtd. in Cline (2015, 98).

4 Cline (2015, 287).

5 Plato, *Republic* Book V, 457c ff; for translation, see Cooper (1997).

6 Aristotle, *Politics* Book II, 1262b; for translation, see Barnes (1984/1995).

7 For the *Shujing*, see "Taishishang 泰誓上" chapter (惟天地萬物父母, 惟人萬物之靈. 但聰明, 作元后, 元后作民父母) and "Hongfang 洪範" chapter (天子作民父母, 以為天下王). For the *Shijing*, see Song 172 (樂只君子, 民之父母) and Song 251 (豈弟君子, 民之父母). For the *Liji*, see "Jitong 祭統" chapter (祭而不敬, 何以為民父母矣), "Kongzi xianju 孔子閒居" chapter (孔子閒居, 子夏侍。子夏曰:「敢問《詩》云:『凱弟君子, 民之父母』, 何如斯可謂民之父母矣?」孔子曰:「夫民之父母乎, 必達於禮樂之原, 以致五至, 而行三無, 以橫於天下. 四方有敗, 必先知之. 此之謂民之父母矣.」), and "Biaoji 表記" chapter (子言之:「君子之所謂仁者其難乎!《詩》云:『凱弟君子, 民之父母.』凱以強教之; 弟以說安之. 樂而毋荒, 有禮而親, 威莊而安, 孝慈而敬. 使民有父之尊, 有母之親. 如此而後可以為民父母矣, 非至德其孰能如此乎?). For the *Daxue*, see (《詩》云:「樂只君子, 民之父母。」民之所好好之, 民之所惡惡之, 此之謂民之父母). For the *Mencius*, see 1A4 (曰:「庖有肥肉, 廄有肥馬, 民有飢色, 野有餓莩, 此率獸而食人也. 獸相食, 且人惡之. 為民父母, 行政不免於率獸而食人. 惡在其為民父母也?), 1B7 (故曰, 國人殺之也. 如此, 然後可以為民父母.」), 2A5 (則鄰國之民仰之若父母矣. 率其子弟, 攻其父母, 自生民以來, 未有能濟者也), and 3A3 (為民父母, 使民盻盻然, 將終歲勤動, 不得以養其父母, 又稱貸而益之. 使老稚轉乎溝壑, 惡在其為民父母也?」). For the *Xunzi*, see 9.18 (故天地生君子, 君子理天地; 君子者, 天地之參也, 萬物之摠也, 民之父母也。), 18.2 (湯武者, 民之父母也; 桀紂者, 民之怨賊也。), and 19.20 (《詩》曰:「愷悌君子, 民之父母。」彼君子者, 固有為民父母之說焉. 父能生之, 不能養之; 母能食之, 不能教誨之; 君者, 已能食之矣, 又善教誨之者也.). For the *Xiaojing*, see Ch. 13 (《詩》云:『愷悌君子, 民之父母。』非至德, 其孰能順民如此其大者乎!」). For the *Shuoyuan*, see "Zhengli 政理" chapter (孔子曰:「《詩》云:『凱悌君子, 民之父母』, 未見其子富而父母貧者也。」). For the *Hanshi waizhuan*, see Ch. 1 (吾聞聖人仁士之於天地之間也, 民之父母也), Ch. 6 (《詩》曰:「愷悌君子, 民之父母。」君子為民父母何如?曰:「君子者, 貌恭而行肆, 身儉而施博, 故不肖者不能逮也. 殖盡於己, 而區略於人, 故可盡身而事也. 篤愛而不奪, 厚施而不伐; 見人有善, 欣然樂之; 見人不善, 惕然掩之; 有其過而兼包之; 授衣以最, 授食以多; 法下易由, 事寡易為; 是以中立而為人父母也.), and Ch. 8 (《詩》曰:「愷悌君子, 民之父母。」子賤其似之矣.). For the *Baihutong*, see "Hao 號" chapter (或稱君子何? 道德之稱也. 君之為言群也; 子者, 丈夫之通稱也. 故《孝經》曰:「君子之教以孝也, 下言敬天下之為人父者也。」何以言知其通稱也, 以天子至於民. 故《詩》云:「凱弟君子, 民之父母。」) and "Jue 爵" chapter.... (天子者, 爵稱也. 爵所以稱天子者何? 王者父天母地, 為天之子也 [...]《尚書》曰:「天子作民父母, 以為天下王。」何以知帝亦稱天子也, 以法天下也?). For the *Kongzi jiayu*, see "Wudide 五帝德" chapter (宰我曰:「請問禹。」孔子曰:「高陽之孫, 鯀之子也, 曰夏后. 敏給克齊, 其德不爽, 其仁可親, 其言可信. 聲為律, 身為度. 亹亹穆穆, 為紀為綱. 其功為百神主, 其惠為民父母.). For the *Xinshu*, see "Chunqiu 春秋" chapter (夫君者, 民之父母也) and "Jundao 君道" chapter (《詩》曰:「愷悌君子, 民之父母。」言聖王之德也). For the *Lienu zhuan*, see 6.15 (《詩》云:『愷悌君子, 民之父母。』今人有過, 教未施, 而刑已加焉. 或欲改行為善, 而其道無繇. 朕甚憐之. 夫刑者至斷支體, 刻肌膚, 終身不息, 何其痛而不德也! 豈稱為民父母之意哉! 其除肉刑.」).

8   See *Liji*, "Tangongshang 檀弓上."

9   See *Lienu zhuan*, Ch. 1 "Maternal Rectitude"; there are fourteen entries with sixteen maternal models included in the chapter. For translation, see Kinney (2014).

10 See Kinney (2014, xv) and Cline (2015, 68).

11 For a list of dynastic histories containing the *lienu* entries, see Judge and Hu (2011, 292–93), Appendix B.

12 For the later commentary on the "five defects," see Watson (1963, 34).

13 See *The New York Times* (2015 & 2021a), and *The Washington Post* (2016a & 2016b).

14 See *NPR* (2021) and *FiveThirtyEight* (2023).

15 Rupp (2015, 77).

16 Hume, *A Treatise of Human Nature*, Book I; see Mossner (1984).

17 Rosemont (2015, 47).

18 Rupp (2015, 180).

19 Ibid., 31.

20 See *BBC News* (2019a & 2022a) and *The New York Times* (2021c).

21 Rupp (2015, 182).

22 See To (2015), Martin (2016), and Shlam and Medalia (2020).

23 For more on *yin/yang*, see Rosenlee (2006, Ch. 3 & 2023b).

24 For more, see Sin-Yee Chan (2016 & 2023). Also see Baek (2023).

25 Rupp (2015, 82–4).

Epilogue

1   See Chen (2011), Dai (2019), and Yuan (2019).

2   See Wielenberg (2006).

3   See Deutsch (1997), Blackburn (1999), Craig (2002), Rosenlee (2009), and Solomon, Higgins, and Martin (2012).

4   See *Pew Research Center* (2016).

5   As qtd. in *NPR* (2014).

6   Rupp (2015, 84).

7   Nagel (1979, Ch. 1 & 2).

Bibliography

60 Minutes. 2004. "Staying at Home," by Rebecca Leung, October 8. http://www. cbsnews.com/news/staying-at-home-08-10-2004/ (accessed 10 April 2024).

AARP. 2020. "95 Percent of Americans Killed by COVID-19 Were 50 or Older: Chronic Conditions, Aging Immune Systems Increase Vulnerability," by Rachel Nania, October 30. https://www.aarp.org/health/conditions-treatments/info-2020/coronavirus-deaths-older-adults.html (accessed 22 April 2024).

Allen, Jeffner. 1984/1993. "Motherhood: The Annihilation of Women." In *Feminist Frameworks: Alternative Theoretical Accounts of the Relations between Women and Men*, ed. Alison M. Jaggar and Paula S. Rothenberg, 380–5. New York: McGraw-Hill.

American Bar Association (ABA). 2022. "New Report on Profession Focuses on Judicial Demographics." August 1. https://www.americanbar.org/news/abanews/aba-news-archives/2022/08/new-report-on-profession/ (accessed 22 April 2024).

Ames, Roger T. and David L. Hall. 1987. *Thinking through Confucius*. Albany: State University of New York Press.

Ames, Roger T. and David L. Hall. 1998a. *Thinking from the Han: Self, Truth and Transcendence in Chinese and Western Culture*. Albany: SUNY.

Ames, Roger T. and Henry Rosemont Jr., intro. & trans. 1998b. *The Analects of Confucius: A Philosophical Translation*. New York: Ballantine.

Ames, Roger T. and David L. Hall. 1999. *The Democracy of the Dead: Dewey, Confucius, and the Hope for Democracy in China*. Chicago: Open Court.

Ames, Roger T. and David L. Hall, intro. & trans. 2001. *Focusing the Familiar: A Translation and Philosophical Interpretation of the Zhongyong*. Honolulu: University of Hawaii Press.

Ames, Roger T. and David L. Hall, intro. & trans. 2003. *Daodejing: A Philosophical Translation*. New York: Ballantine Books.

Ames, Roger T. and Henry Rosemont Jr., intro. & trans. 2009. *The Chinese Classic of Family Reverence: A Philosophical Translation of the Xiaojing*. Honolulu: University of Hawaii Press.

Ames, Roger T. 2011. *Confucian Role Ethics: A Vocabulary*. Honolulu: University of Hawaii Press.

Ames, Roger T. and Henry Rosemont Jr. 2014. "Family Reverence (*Xiao*) in the *Analects*: Confucian Role Ethics and the Dynamics of Intergenerational Transmission." In *Dao Companion to the Analects*, ed. Amy Olberding, 117–36. New York: Springer.

Ames, Roger T. 2017. "On How to Construct a Confucian Democracy for Modern Times (or Why Democratic Practices Must Not Lose Sight of the Ideal)." *Philosophy East & West* 67.1 (January): 61–81.

Analects 論語. *Chinese Text Project*. http://ctext.org/analects; for trans., see Ames and Rosemont, 1998b (accessed 22 April 2024).

Angle, Stephen C. 2012. *Contemporary Confucian Political Philosophy*. Malden: Polity.

Aquinas, Thomas. 1259–65 [1956/1975]. *Summa Contra Gentiles*. In *Saint Thomas Aquinas, Summa Contra Gentiles, Book Three: Providence Part II*, trans. Vernon J. Bourke. Notre Dame: University of Notre Dame Press.

Aquinas, Thomas. 1269–72 [1991]. *Summa Theologiae*. In *Other Selves: Philosophers on Friendship*, ed. Michael Pakaluk, 146–84. Indianapolis: Hackett.

Aristotle. 1984/1995. *The Complete Works of Aristotle*, ed. Jonathan Barnes, 2 vols. Princeton: Princeton University Press.

Aubenque, Pierre. 1998. "On Friendship in Aristotle." *The South Atlantic Quarterly* 97.1: 23–8.

Baek, Hyeon. 2023. "Confucianism and Queers: Confucian Defense of LGBTQ Rights." Conference presentation at the 23rd *International Society for Chinese Philosophy* (ISCP) conference, at the University of California, Riverside, June 20–23.

Baier, Annette C. 2000. "Hume: The Reflective Women's Epistemologist?" In *Feminist Interpretations of David Hume*, ed. Anne Jaap Jacobson, 19–38. University Park: Penn State University Press.

Baihutong 白虎通 (*Comprehensive Discussions in the White Tiger Hall*). *Chinese Text Project*. https://ctext.org/bai-hu-tong; for trans., see Tjan 1949/1952 (accessed 22 April 2024).

Barnes, Jonathan, ed. 1984/1995. *The Complete Works of Aristotle*, 2 vols. Princeton: Princeton University Press.

BBC News. 2019a. "Indonesia Haze: Why Do Forests Keep Burning?" September 16. https://www.bbc.com/news/world-asia-34265922 (accessed 22 April 2024).

BBC News. 2019b. "Europe and Right-wing Nationalism: A Country-by-country Guide." November 13. https://www.bbc.com/news/world-europe-36130006 (accessed 22 April 2024).

BBC News. 2022a. "Why Has the Syrian War Lasted 11 Years?" March 15. https://www.bbc.com/news/world-middle-east-35806229 (accessed 22 April 2024).

BBC News. 2022b. "Who Is Giorgia Meloni? The Rise to Power of Italy's New Far-right PM," by Paul Kirby. October 21. https://www.bbc.com/news/world-europe-63351655 (accessed 22 April 2024).

Beauvoir, Simone De. 1949 [1989]. *The Second Sex*, trans. & ed. H. M. Parshley. New York: Vintage Books.

Bell, Daniel A. and Hahm Chaibong, eds. 2003. *Confucianism for the Modern World*. New York: Cambridge University Press.

Bell, Daniel A. 2015. *The China Model: Political Meritocracy and the Limits of Democracy*. Princeton: Princeton University Press.

Bell, Duncan. 2010. "John Stuart Mill on Colonies." *Political Theory* 38.1: 34–64.

Bernasconi, Robert. 1995. "Heidegger and the Invention of the Western Philosophical Tradition." *Journal of the British Society for Phenomenology* 26.3 (October): 240–54.

Bernasconi, Robert. 2000a. "With What Must the Philosophy of World History Begin? On the Racial Basis of Hegel's Eurocentrism." *Nineteenth-Century Contexts* 22: 171–201.

Bernasconi, Robert and Tommy L. Lott, eds. 2000b. *The Idea of Race*. Indianapolis: Hackett.

Bernasconi, Robert. 2002. "Kant as an Unfamiliar Source of Racism." In *Philosophers on Race: Critical Essays*, ed. Julie K. Ward and Tommy L. Lott, 145–66. Malden: Blackwell.

Bernasconi, Robert and Anika Maaza Mann. 2005. "The Contradictions of Racism: Locke, Slavery, and the *Two Treatises*." In *Race and Racism in Modern Philosophy*, ed. Andrew Valls, 89–107. Ithaca: Cornell University Press.

Bernasconi, Robert. 2011. "Kant's Third thoughts on Race." In *Reading Kant's Geography*, ed. Stuart Elden and Eduardo Mendieta, 291–318. Albany: SUNY.

Bible. King James Bible Online. https://www.kingjamesbibleonline.org/ (accessed 22 April 2024).

Blackburn, Simon. 1999. *Think: A Compelling Introduction to Philosophy*. New York: Oxford University Press.

Blustein, Jeffrey. 1982. *Parents and Children: The Ethics of the Family*. New York: Oxford University Press.

Bogues, Anthony. 2005. "John Stuart Mill and 'the Negro Question': Race, Colonialism, and the Ladder of Civilization." In *Race and Racism in Modern Philosophy*, ed. Andrew Valls, 217–34. Ithaca: Cornell University Press.

Bourke, Vernon J., trans. 1956/1975. *Saint Thomas Aquinas, Summa Contra Gentiles, Book Three: Providence Part II*. Notre Dame: University of Notre Dame Press.

Boxill, Bernard. 2017. "Kantian Racism and Kantian Teleology." In *The Oxford Handbook of Philosophy and Race*, ed. Naomi Zack, 44–53. New York: Oxford University Press.

Bristow, William. 2010/2017. "Enlightenment." *Stanford Encyclopedia of Philosophy*, August 29. https://plato.stanford.edu/entries/enlightenment/ (accessed 22 April 2024).

Brooks, David. 2005. "Longer Lives Reveal the Ties That Bind Us." *The New York Times*, Oct. 2. http://www.nytimes.com/2005/10/02/opinion/longer-lives-reveal-the-ties-that-bind-us.html?_r=0 (accessed 22 April 2024).

Cai Zhonglang ji 蔡中郎集 (*Collection of Cai Zhonglang*). *Chinese Text Project*. http://ctext.org/caizhong-langji (accessed 22 April 2024).

Callahan, Joan. 2009. "Same-Sex Marriage: Why It Matters—At Least for Now." *Hypatia: A Journal of Feminist Philosophy* 24.1 (Winter): 70–80.

Card, Claudia. 1990. "Caring and Evil." *Hypatia* 5.1: 101–6.

Card, Claudia. 1996. "Against Marriage and Motherhood." *Hypatia* 11.3: 1–23.

Card, Claudia. 2000. "Women, Evil and Gray Zones." *Metaphilosophy* 31.5 (Oct.): 509–28.

Card, Claudia. 2002. *The Atrocity Paradigm: A Theory of Evil*. New York: Oxford University Press.

Card, Claudia. 2007. "Gay Divorce: Thoughts on the Legal Regulation of
    Marriage." *Hypatia* 22.1: 24–38.
Chan, Alan K. L. and Sor-hoon Tan, eds. 2004. *Filial Piety in Chinese Thought
    and History*. London: Routledge.
Chan, Joseph. 2013. *Confucian Perfectionism: A Political Philosophy for Modern
    Times*. Princeton: Princeton University Press.
Chan, Sin-Yee. 2016. "Would Confucianism Allow Two Men to Share a Peach?
    Compatibility between Ancient Confucianism and Homosexuality." In *The
    Bloomsbury Research Handbook of Chinese Philosophy and Gender*, ed. Ann
    Pang-White, 173–202. New York: Bloomsbury.
Chan, Sin-Yee. 2023. "Confucianism and Gender." In *The Oxford Handbook
    of Confucianism*, ed. Jennifer Oldstone-Moore, 408–22. New York: Oxford
    University Press.
Chang, I-Jen, William G. Boltz, and Michael Loewe. 1993. *Kuo yu*. In *Early
    Chinese Texts: A Bibliographical Guide*, ed. Michael Loewe, 263–8. Berkeley:
    University of California Press.
Chang, Wonsuk and Leah Kalmanson, eds. 2010. *Confucianism in Context:
    Classic Philosophy and Contemporary Issues, East Asian and Beyond*.
    Albany: SUNY.
Chen, Ya-Chen. 2011. *The Many Dimensions of Chinese Feminism*. New York:
    Palgrave Macmillan.
Cheng, Anne. 1993. *Ch'un ch'iu, Kung yang, Ku liang and Tso chuan*. In *Early
    Chinese Texts: A Bibliographical Guide*, ed. Michael Loewe, 67–76. Berkeley:
    University of California Press.
Chiu, Yvonne. 2017. "Democracy without Autonomy: Moral and Personal
    Autonomy in Democratic Confucianism." *Philosophy East and West* 67.1
    (January): 47–60.
Chunqiu fanlu 春秋繁露 (*Luxuriant Drew of the Spring and Autumn*). *Chinese
    Text Project*. http://ctext.org/chun-qiu-fan-lu, (accessed 22 April 2024); for a
    partial translation, see Csikszentmihalyi, 2003.
Clark, Lorenne M. G. 2003. "Women and John Locke; Or, Who Owns the
    Apples in the Garden of Eden?" In *Social and Political Philosophy: Classical
    Western Texts in Feminist and Multicultural Perspectives*, ed. James P. Sterba,
    207–21. Belmont, CA: Wadsworth.
Clarke, J. J. 1997. *Oriental Enlightenment: The Encounter between Asian and
    Western Thought*. New York: Routledge.
Cline, Erin M. 2015. *Families of Virtue: Confucian and Western Views on
    Childhood Development*. New York: Columbia University Press.
CNN. 2015. "Still Missing: Female Business Leaders," by Matt Egan, March
    24. http://money.cnn.com/2015/03/24/investing/female-ceo-pipeline-
    leadership/ (accessed 22 April 2024).
Coblin, W. South. 1993. *Erh Ya*. In *Early Chinese Texts: A Bibliographical Guide*,
    ed. Michael Loewe, 94–9. Berkeley: University of California Press.
Collins, Stephanie. 2015. *The Core of Care Ethics*. London: Palgrave Macmillan.

Connolly, Tim. 2012. "Friendship and Filial Piety: Relational Ethics in Aristotle and Early Confucianism." *Journal of Chinese Philosophy* 39.1: 71–88.

Cooper, John M., ed. 1997. *Plato: Complete Works*. Indianapolis: Hackett.

Craig, Edward. 2002. *Philosophy: A Very Short Introduction*. New York: Oxford University Press.

Crittenden, Ann. 2001/2010. *The Price of Motherhood: Why the Most Important Job in the World Is Still the Least Valued*. New York: Picador.

Csikszentmihalyi, Mark, intro. & trans. 2003. "*Luxuriant Gems of the Spring and Autumn* (*Chunqiu fanlu*), Dong Zhongshu." In *Images of Women in Chinese Thought and Culture: Writings from the Pre-Qin Period through the Song Dynasty*, ed. Robin R. Wang, 162–9. Indianapolis: Hackett.

Dai, Yuanfang. 2019. *Transcultural Feminist Philosophy: Rethinking Difference and Solidarity through Chinese—American Encounters*. New York: Lexington Books.

Dalmiya, Vrinda. 2009. "Caring Comparisons: Some Thoughts on Comparative Care Ethics." *Journal of Chinese Philosophy* 36.2: 192–209.

Daly, Mary. 1978/1990. *Gyn/Ecology: the Metaethics of Radical Feminism*. Boston: Beacon Press.

Daodejing 道德經 (*Classic of Dao and De*). *Chinese Text Project*. http://ctext.org/dao-de-jing, (accessed 22 April 2024); for trans., see Ames and Hall, 2003.

Daxue 大學 (*Great Learning*). *Chinese Text Project*. http://ctext.org/liji/da-xue, (accessed 22 April 2024); for translation, see Legge, 1885.

Denis, Lara. 2001. "From Friendship to Marriage: Revising Kant." *Philosophy and Phenomenological Research* 63.1: 1–28.

Deresiewicz, William. 2007. "Thomas Hardy and the History of Friendship between the Sexes." *Wordsworth Circle* 38.1/2: 56–63.

Deutsch, Eliot, ed. 1997. *Introduction to World Philosophies*. Upper Saddle River: Prentice Hall.

Dixon, Nicholas. 1995. "The Friendship Model of Filial Obligations." *Journal of Applied Philosophy* 12.1: 77–87.

Dworkin, Andrea. 1974. *Woman Hating*. New York: Penguin.

EIA (US Energy Information Administration). 2016. April 4. http://www.eia.gov/tools/faqs/faq.cfm?id=92&t=4 (accessed 22 April 2024).

English, Jane. 1979 [1989]. "What Do Grown Children Owe Their Parents?" In *Vice and Virtue in Everyday Life: Introductory Readings in Ethics*, ed. Christina Sommers and Fred Sommers, 682–9. San Diego: Harcourt Brace Jovanovich Publishers.

Epley, Kelly. 2015. "Care Ethics and Confucianism: Caring through *Li*." *Hypatia* 30.4 (Fall): 881–96.

Erya 爾雅 (*Glossary*). https://ctext.org/er-ya (accessed 22 April 2024).

Eze, Emmanuel Chukwudi, ed. 1997. *Race and the Enlightenment: A Reader*. Malden: Blackwell.

Farr, James. 2008. "Locke, Natural Law, and New World Slavery." *Political Theory* 36.4 (August): 495–522.

Fingarette, Herbert. 1972 [1998]. *Confucius: The Secular as Sacred*. Prospect heights: Waveland Press.

FiveThirtyEight. 2023. "Trump Leads DeSantis in Our 2024 Republican Primary Polling Average," by Nathaniel Rakich, April 12. https://fivethirtyeight.com/features/trump-desantis-national-polls/ (accessed 22 April 2024).

Flikschuh, Katrin and Lea Ypi, eds. 2014. *Kant and Colonialism*. New York: Oxford University Press.

Forbes. 2023. "New Year, New Glass Heights: Women Now Comprise 10% of Top U.S. Corporation CEOs," by Liz Elting, January 27. https://www.forbes.com/sites/lizelting/2023/01/27/new-year-new-glass-heights-for-the-first-time-in-history-over-10-of-fortune-500-ceos-are-women/?sh=531f2f67e77f (accessed 22 April 2024).

Forke, Alfred. 1907/1911 [1962]. *Lun-Heng: Philosophical Essays of Wang Ch'ung*. New York: Paragon.

Forster, Eckart, ed. 1993. *The Cambridge Edition of the Works of Immanuel Kant: Opus postumum*. New York: Cambridge University Press.

Fortune. 2015. "America Is the Richest, and Most Unequal, Country," by Erik Sherman, September 30. http://fortune.com/2015/09/30/america-wealth-inequality/ (accessed 22 April 2024).

Foust, Mathew and Sor-hoon Tan, eds. 2016. *Feminist Encounters with Confucius*. Boston: Brill.

Fracasso, Riccardo. 1993. *Shan hai ching*. In *Early Chinese Texts: A Bibliographical Guide*, ed. Michael Loewe, 357–67. Berkeley: University of California Press.

Friedman, Marilyn. 1993. *What Are Friends For? Feminist Perspectives on Personal Relationships and Moral Theory*. Ithaca: Cornell University Press.

Fullam, Lisa. 2012. "Toward a Virtue Ethics of Marriage: Augustine and Aquinas on Friendship in Marriage." *Theological Studies* 73: 663–92.

Fuller, Steve. 2018. "'China' as the West's Other in World Philosophy." *Journal of World Philosophies* 3 (Summer): 157–64.

Fuller, Timothy. 2008. "Plato and Montaigne: Ancient and Modern Ideas of Friendship." In *Friendship and Politics: Essays in Political Thought*, ed. John von Heyking and Richard Avramenko, 197–213. Notre Dame: University of Notre Dame.

Garfield, Jay L. and Bryan W. Van Norden. 2016. "If Philosophy Won't Diversify, Let's Call It What It Really Is." *The New York Times*, May 11. https://www.nytimes.com/2016/05/11/opinion/if-philosophy-wont-diversify-lets-call-it-what-it-really-is.html (accessed 22 April 2024).

Gilligan, Carol. 1982. *In a Different Voice: Psychological Theory and Women's Development*. Cambridge: Harvard University Press.

Goldberg, David Theo. 2002. "Liberalism's Limits: Carlyle and Mill on 'The Negro Question.'" In *Philosophers on Race: Critical Essays*, ed. Julie K. Ward and Tommy L. Lott, 195–204. Malden: Blackwell.

Goldthwait, John T, intro. & trans. 1960. *Kant: Observations on the Feeling of the Beautiful and Sublime*. Berkeley: University of California Press.

Graham, A. C., intro. & trans. 1960/1990. *The Book of Lieh-tzu: A Classic of Tao*. New York: Columbia University Press.

Greenhalgh, Susan. 1977. "Bound Feet, Hobbled Lives: Women in Old China." *Frontiers: A Journal of Women Studies* 2.1 (Spring 1977): 7–21.

Gregor, Mary, trans. & ed. 1996. *The Cambridge Edition of the Works of Immanuel Kant: Practical Philosophy*. New York: Cambridge University Press.

Grimshaw, Jean. 1986. *Feminist Philosophers*. Brighton: Wheatsheaf Books.

Groenhout, Ruth. 2014. "Virtue and Feminist Ethics of Care." In *Virtues and Their Vices*, ed. Kevin Timpe and Craig A. Boyd, 482–501. New York: Oxford University Press.

Guanzi 管子 (*Master Guan*). *Chinese Text Project*. https://ctext.org/guanzi, (accessed 22 April 2024); for trans., see Rickett, 1998.

Guoyu 國語 (*Discourses of the States*). *Chinse Text Project*. http://ctext.org/guo-yu (accessed 22 April 2024).

Haass, Richard. 2023. *The Bill of Obligations: The Ten Habits of Good Citizens*. New York: Penguin.

Hanfeizi 韓非子 (*Master Hanfei*). *Chinese Text Project*. http://ctext.org/hanfeizi, (accessed 22 April 2024); for translation, see Watson, 2003.

Hanshi waizhuan 韓詩外傳 (*Outer Commentary on the Book of Songs by Master Han*). *Chinese Text Project*. http://ctext.org/han-shi-wai-zhuan (accessed 22 April 2024).

Hanshu 漢書 (*History of Han*). *Chinese Text Project*. https://ctext.org/han-shu (accessed 22 April 2024).

Harvard Business Review. 2014. "Rethink What You 'Know' About High-Achieving Women," by Robin J. Ely, Pamela Stone, and Colleen Ammerman, December. https://hbr.org/2014/12/rethink-what-you-know-about-high-achieving-women (accessed 22 April 2024).

He, Yuanguo. 2007. "Confucius and Aristotle on Friendship: A Comparative Study." *Frontiers of Philosophy in China* 2.2: 291–307.

Held, Virginia. 2006. *The Ethics of Care: Personal, Political, and Global*. New York: Oxford University Press.

Henry, Eric. 1987. "The Motif of Recognition in Early China." *Harvard Journal of Asiatic Studies* 47: 5–30.

Henry, Eric, intro. & trans. 2022. *Garden of Eloquence/Shuoyuan* 說苑. Seattle, WA: University of Washington Press.

Herr, Ranjoo Seodu. 2003. "Is Confucianism Compatible with Care Ethics? A Critique." *Philosophy East and West* 53.4: 471–89.

Hill, Thomas E. Jr. and Bernard Boxill. 2001. "Kant and Race." In *Race and Racism*, ed. Bernard Boxill, 448–71. New York: Oxford University Press.

Hoagland, Sarah Lucia. 1991. "Some Thoughts about 'Caring.'" In *Feminist Ethics*, ed. Claudia Card, 246–64. Lawrence: University Press of Kansas.

Hochschild, Arlie Russell. 1989. *The Second Shift*. New York: Quill.

Holzman, Donald. 1998. "The Place of Filial Piety in Ancient China." *Journal of the American Oriental Society* 118.2: 185–99.

Huang, Martin W. 2007. "Male Friendship in Ming China: An Introduction." *Nan Nu* 9: 2–33.

Hume, David. 1739–40 [1969]. *A Treatise of Human Nature*. In *David Hume: A Treatise of Human Nature*, ed. Ernest C. Mossner. New York: Penguin.

Hume, David. 1748/1754/1777 [1985]. "Of National Characters." In *David Hume Essays: Moral, Political, and Literary*, ed. Eugene Miller, 196–215. Indianapolis: LibertyClassics.

Infield, Louis, trans. 1930/1963. *Kant: Lectures on Ethics*. Indianapolis: Hackett.

Ing, Michael David Kaulana. 2012. *The Dysfunction of Ritual in Early Confucianism*. New York: Oxford University Press.

Jaggar, Alison. 1995. "Caring as a Feminist Practice of Moral Reason." In *Justice and Care: Essential Readings in Feminist Ethics*, ed. Virginia Held, 179–202. Boulder: Westview Press.

Jin, Yutang. 2020. "Confucian Justifications of Democracy: A Critique of Joseph Chan's Democratic Theory." *Philosophy East and West* 70.2 (April): 374–94.

Johnston, Ian, intro. & trans. 2010. *The Mozi: A Complete Translation*. New York: Columbia University Press.

Judge, Joan and Hu Ying, eds. 2011. *Beyond Exemplar Tales: Women's Biography in Chinese History*. Berkeley: University of California Press.

Kant, Immanuel. 1764 [1960]. *Observations on the Feeling of the Beautiful and Sublime*, trans. John T. Goldthwait. Berkeley: University of California Press.

Kant, Immanuel. 1775 [2007]. "Of the Different Human Races." In *The Cambridge Edition of the Works of Immanuel Kant: Anthropology, History, and Education*, ed. Gunter Zoller and Robert B. Louden, 81–97. New York: Cambridge University Press.

Kant, Immanuel. 1775–1780 [1930/1963]. *Lectures on Ethics*, trans. Louis Infield. Indianapolis: Hackett.

Kant, Immanuel. 1784 [2007]. "Idea for a Universal History with a Cosmopolitan Aim." In *The Cambridge Edition of the Works of Immanuel Kant: Anthropology, History, and Education*, ed. Gunter Zoller and Robert B. Louden, 107–20. New York: Cambridge University Press.

Kant, Immanuel. 1788 [2007]. "On the Use of Teleological Principles in Philosophy." In *The Cambridge Edition of the Works of Immanuel Kant: Anthropology, History, and Education*, ed. Gunter Zoller and Robert B. Louden, 81–97. New York: Cambridge University Press.

Kant, Immanuel. 1790 [1987]. *Critique of Judgment*, trans. Werner S. Pluhar. Indianapolis: Hackett.

Kant, Immanuel. 1793 [1996]. *Religion within the Boundaries of Mere Reason*. In *The Cambridge Edition of the Works of Immanuel Kant: Religion and Rational Theology*, trans. & ed. Allen W. Wood and George Di Giovanni, 39–216. New York: Cambridge University Press.

Kant, Immanuel. 1797 [1996]. *The Metaphysics of Morals*. In *The Cambridge Edition of the Works of Immanuel Kant: Practical Philosophy*, trans. & ed. Mary Gregor, 353–604. New York: Cambridge University Press.

Kant, Immanuel. 1798 [2007]. *Anthropology from a Pragmatic Point of View*. In *The Cambridge Edition of the Works of Immanuel Kant: Anthropology, History, and Education*, ed. Gunter Zoller and Robert B. Louden, 227–429. New York: Cambridge University Press.

Kant, Immanuel. 1802 [2012]. *Physical Geography*. In *The Cambridge Edition of the Works of Immanuel Kant: Natural Science*, ed. Eric Watkins, 434–679. New York: Cambridge University Press.

Kant, Immanuel. 1882–1884 [1993]. *Opus postumum*. In *The Cambridge Edition of the Works of Immanuel Kant: Opus postumum*, ed. Eckart Forster. New York: Cambridge University Press.

Kangxi zidan 康熙字典 (*Kangxi Dictionary of Qing Dynasty*). *Chinese Text Project*. http://ctext.org/kangxi-zidian (accessed 22 April 2024).

Keller, Simon. 2006. "Four Theories of Filial Duty." *The Philosophical Quarterly* 56.223: 254–74.

Kierkegaard, Soren. 1846–47 [1991]. *Works of Love*. In *Other Selves: Philosophers on Friendship*, ed. Michael Pakaluk, 233–47. Indianapolis: Hackett.

Kim, Sungmoon. 2014. *Confucian Democracy in East Asia: Theory and Practice*. Cambridge: Cambridge University Press.

Kim, Sungmoon. 2017. "Confucian Authority, Political Right, and Democracy." *Philosophy East and West* 67.1 (January): 3–14.

Kim, Young Kun. 1978. "Hegel's Criticism of Chinese Philosophy." *Philosophy East and West* 28.2: 173–80.

Kinney, Anne Behnke. 2004. *Representation of Childhood and Youth in Early China*. Stanford: Stanford University Press.

Kinney, Anne Behnke, trans. 2014. *Exemplary Women of Early China: The Lienu zhuan of Liu Xiang*. New York: Columbia University Press.

Kirkpatrick, Kate. 2019. "Was Simone de Beauvoir as Feminist as We Thought?" *The Guardian*, August 20. https://www.theguardian.com/books/2019/aug/20/was-simone-de-beauvoir-as-feminist-aswe-thought (accessed 22 April 2024).

Kittay, Eva Feder. 1999. *Love's Labor: Essays on Women, Equality, and Dependency*. New York: Routledge.

Kittay, Eva Feder. 2002. "Love's Labor Revisited." *Hypatia* 17.3: 237–50.

Kleingeld, Pauline. 2007. "Kant's Second Thoughts on Race." *The Philosophical Quarterly* 57.299 (October): 573–92.

Knapp, Keith N. 1995. "The *Ru* Reinterpretation of *Xiao*." *Early China* 20: 195–222.

Knoblock, John and Zhang Jue, intro. & trans. 1999. *Xunzi*, 2 vols. Hunan: Hunan People's Publishing.

Kongzi jiayu 孔子家語 (*School Sayings of Confucius*). *Chinese Text Project*. http://ctext.org/kongzi-jiayu, (accessed 22 April 2024); for translation, see Kramers, 1950.

Knox, T. M. and A. V. Miller, trans. 1985. *Hegel's Introduction to the Lectures on the History of Philosophy*. New York: Oxford University Press.

Kramers, Robert Paul, trans. 1950. *K'ung Tzu Chia Yu: The School Sayings of Confucius*. Leiden: Brill.

Kristeva, Julia. 1977. *About Chinese Women*, trans. Anita Barrows. New York: Urizen.

Kukathas, Chandran. 2003. *The Liberal Archipelago*. New York: Oxford University Press.

Kutcher, Norman. 2000. "The Fifth Relationship: Dangerous Friendships in the Confucian Context." *American Historical Review* 105.5: 1615–29.

Lai, Whalen. 1996. "Friendship in Confucian China: Classical and Late Ming." In *Friendship East and West: Philosophical Perspectives*, ed. Oliver Leaman, 215–50. Richmond: Curzon.

Lai Tao, Julia Po-Wah. 2000. "Two Perspectives of Care: Confucian *Ren* and Feminist Care." *Journal of Chinese Philosophy* 27.2: 215–40.

Langton, Rae. 2000. "Maria von Herbert's Challenge to Kant." In *Ethics: Classical Western Texts in Feminist and Multicultural Perspectives*, ed. James P. Sterba, 201–11. New York: Oxford University Press.

Larrimore, Mark. 2008. "Antinomies of Race: Diversity and Destiny in Kant." *Patterns of Prejudice* 42.4–5: 341–63.

Lau, D. C., intro. & trans. 1970. *Mencius*. New York: Penguin.

Legge, James, intro. & trans. 1879. *The Shu King*. Oxford: The Clarendon Press.

Legge, James, intro. & trans. 1882. *The Yi King*. Oxford: The Clarendon Press.

Legge, James, intro. & trans. 1885. *Li Chi: Book of Rites*, 2 vols. New York: The Union Theological Seminary.

Levi, Jean. 1993. *Shang chun shu*. In *Early Chinese Texts: A Bibliographical Guide*, ed. Michael Loewe, 368–75. Berkeley: University of California Press.

Li, Chenyang. 1994. "The Confucian Concept of *Jen* and the Feminist Ethics of Care: A Comparative Study." *Hypatia* 9.1: 70–89.

Li, Chenyang. 2002. "Revisiting Confucian *Jen* Ethics and Feminist Care Ethics: A Reply to Daniel Star and Lijun Yuan." *Hypatia* 17.1: 130–40.

Li, Chenyang. 2006. "The Confucian Idea of Harmony." *Philosophy East and West* 56.4: 583–603.

Li, Chenyang. 2015. "Confucian Ethics and Care Ethics—The Political Dimension of a Scholarly Debate." *Hypatia* 30.4: 897–903.

Li, Feng. 2012. *Bureaucracy and the State in Early China Governing the Western Zhou*. New York: Columbia University Press.

Lienu zhuan 列女傳 (*Biographies of Exemplary Women*). *Chinese Text Project*. http://ctext.org/lie-nv-zhuan, (accessed 22 April 2024); for translation, see Kinney, 2014.

Liezi 列子 (*Master Lie*). *Chinese Text Project*. http://ctext.org/liezi, (accessed 22 April 2024); for translation, see Graham, 1960/1990.

Liji 禮記 (*Book of Rites*). *Chinese Text Project*. http://ctext.org/liji, (accessed 22 April 2024); for translation, see Legge, 1885.

Locke, John. 1689 [1988]. *Two Treatises of Government*, ed. Peter Laslett. Cambridge: Cambridge University Press.

Louden, Robert B. 2000. *Kant's Impure Ethics: From Rational Beings to Human Beings*. New York: Oxford University Press.

Louden, Robert B. 2011. "'The Play of Nature': Human Beings in Kant's Geography." In *Reading Kant's Geography*, ed. Stuart Elden and Eduardo Mendieta, 139–59. Albany: SUNY.

Lu, Xiufen. 2007. "Rethinking Confucian Friendship." *Asian Philosophy* 20.3: 225–45.

Lunheng 論衡 (*Discursive Weighing*). *Chinese Text Project*. https://ctext.org/lunheng, (accessed 22 April 2024); for translation, see Forke, 1907/1911.

Luo, Shirong. 2007. "Relation, Virtue, and Relational Virtue: Three Concepts of Caring." *Hypatia* 22.3: 92–110.

Lushi chunqiu 呂氏春秋 (*Lu's Spring and Autumn Annals*). *Chinese Text Project*. http://ctext.org/lv-shi-chun-qiu (accessed 22 April 2024).

MacIntyre, Alasdair. 2004. "Questions for Confucians: Reflections on the Essays in Comparative Study of Self, Autonomy, and Community." In *Confucian Ethics: A Comparative Study of Self, Autonomy, and Community*, ed. Kwong-loi Shun and David B. Wong, 203–18. New York, NY: Cambridge University Press.

Mackerras, Colin. 1989. *Western Images of China*. New York, NY: Oxford University Press.

Mahoney, Patricia and Linda M. Williams. 1998. "Sexual Assault in Marriage: Prevalence, Consequences, and Treatment of Wife Rape." http://www.ncdsv.org/images/nnfr_partnerviolence_a20yearliteraturereviewandsynthesis.pdf (accessed 22 April 2024).

Mahowald, Mary Briody. 1978/1994. *Philosophy of Woman: An Anthology of Classic to Current Concepts*. Indianapolis: Hackett.

Margalit, Avishai and Joseph Raz. 1995. "National Self-determination." In *The Rights of Minority Cultures*, ed. Will Kymlicka, 79–92. New York: Oxford University Press.

Martin, Fran. 2016. "'From Sparrow to Phoenix': Imagining Gender Transformation through Taiwanese Women's Variety TV." *Positions: Asian Critique* 24.2 (May): 369–401.

McLaughlin, Eleanor. 2000. "Equality of Souls, Inequality of Sexes: Women in Medieval Theology." In *Ethic: Classical Western Texts in Feminist and Multicultural Perspectives*, ed. James P. Sterba, 137–44. New York: Oxford University Press.

Mencius 孟子 (*Master Meng*). *Chinese Text Project*. http://ctext.org/mengzi, (accessed 22 April 2024); for translation, see Lau 1970.

Mendus, Susan. 2003. "Kant: 'An Honest but Narrow—Minded Bourgeois'?" In *Social and Political Philosophy: Classical Western Texts in Feminist and Multicultural Perspectives*, ed. James Sterba, 300–11. Belmont, CA: Wadsworth.

Mill, John Stuart. 1848 [1891]. *Principles of Political Economy*, ed. J. Laurence Laughlin. New York: D. Appleton & Co, scanned by Jerome S. Arkenberg, Cal. State Fullerton. https://sourcebooks.fordham.edu/mod/1849jsmill-colonies.asp (accessed 22 April 2024).

Mill, John Stuart. 1859 [1995]. *On Liberty and Other Writings*, ed. Stefan Collini. Cambridge: Cambridge University Press.

Mill, John Stuart. 1869 [1994]. "The Subjection of Women." In *Philosophy of Woman: An Anthology of Classic to Current Concepts*, ed. Mary Briody Mahowald, 151–70. Indianapolis: Hackett.

Mill, John Stuart. 1869 [2003]. "The Subjection of Women." In *Social and Political Philosophy: Classical Western Texts in Feminist and Multicultural Perspectives*, ed. James P. Sterba, 340–51. Belmont: Wadsworth.

Miller, Eugene, ed. 1985. *David Hume Essays: Moral, Political, and Literary*. Indianapolis: LibertyClassics.

Moellendorf, Darrel. 1992. "Racism and Rationality in Hegel's Philosophy of Subjective Spirit." *History of Political Thought* XIII.2 (Summer): 243–55.

Mohanty, Chandra Talpade. 2003. *Feminism without Borders: Decolonizing Theory, Practicing Solidarity*. Durham: Duke University Press.

Montaigne, Michel de. 1580 [1991]. *Of Friendship*. In *Other Selves: Philosophers on Friendship*, ed. Michael Pakaluk, 185–99. Indianapolis: Hackett.

Mossner, Ernest G, ed. 1969. *David Hume: A Treatise of Human Nature*. New York: Penguin.

Mozi 墨子 (*Master Mo*). *Chinese Text Project*. http://ctext.org/mozi, (accessed 22 April 2024); for translation, see Johnston, 2010.

Mulgan, Richard. 1990. "Aristotle and the Value of Political Participation." *Political Theory* 18.2 (May): 195–215.

Mungello, D. E. 1999. *The Great Encounter of China and the West, 1500–1800*. New York: Rowman & Littlefield.

Murr, Dimitri El. 2014. "*Philia* in Plato." In *Ancient and Medieval Concepts of Friendship*, ed. Gary Gurtler and Suzanne Stern-Gillet, 3–34. Albany: SUNY.

Nagel, Thomas. 1979. *Mortal Questions*. New York: Cambridge University Press.

Nagel, Thomas. 1989. *The View from Nowhere*. New York: Oxford University Press.

Narayan, Uma. 1997. *Dislocating Cultures: Identities, Traditions, and Third-world Feminism*. New York: Routledge.

National Review. 2023. "A Fifth of Americans Want a 'National Divorce' Between States," by John Fund, March 19. https://www.nationalreview. com/2023/03/a-fifth-of-americans-want-a-national-divorce-between-states/ (accessed 22 April 2024).

NBC News. 2021. "U.S. Presidential Election Results 2020: Biden Wins." February 8. https://www.nbcnews.com/politics/2020-elections/president-results (accessed 22 April 2024).

Nichols, Mary P. 2009. *Socrates on Friendship and Community: Reflections on Plato's Symposium, Phaedrus, and Lysis*. New York: Cambridge University Press.

Noddings, Nel. 1984. Caring: *A Feminine Approach to Ethics and Moral Education*. Berkeley: University of California Press.

Noddings, Nel. 2010. *The Maternal Factor: Two Paths to Morality*. Berkeley: University of California Press.

Norden, Bryan W Van. 2017. *Taking Back Philosophy: A Multicultural Manifesto*. New York: Columbia University Press.

NPR. 2014. "GOP Politicians from Texas Agree: It's a Great State," by Wade Goodwyn, Nov. 5. https://www.npr.org/2014/11/05/361676911/gop-politicans-from-texas-agree-its-a-great-state (accessed 22 April 2024).

NPR. 2019. "This Woman Fought to End Minnesota's 'Marital Rape' Exception, and Won," by Briana Bierschbach, May 4. https://www.npr. org/2019/05/04/719635969/this-woman-fought-to-end-minnesotas-marital-rape-exception-and-won (accessed 22 April 2024).

NPR. 2020. "Stuck-At-Home Moms: The Pandemic's Devastating Toll on Women," by Pallavi Gogoi, October 28. https://www.npr.org/2020/10/28/928253674/stuck-at-home-moms-the-pandemics-devastating-toll-on-women (accessed 22 April 2024).

NPR. 2021. "Senate Acquits Trump in Impeachment Trial—Again," by Domenico Montanaro, February 13. https://www.npr.org/sections/trump-impeachment-trial-live-updates/2021/02/13/967098840/senate-acquits-trump-in-impeachment-trial-again#:~:text=The%20U.S.%20Senate%20on%20Saturday,results%20that%20certified%20Trump's%20loss (accessed 22 April 2024).

Nussbaum, Martha C. 1986. *The Fragility of Goodness: Luck and Ethics in Greek Tragedy and Philosophy*. New York: Cambridge University Press.

Nylan, Michael, trans. 2013. *Exemplary Figures: Fayan* 法言. Seattle: University of Washington University Press.

Obergefell et al. v. Hodges, Director, Ohio Department of Health, et al. 2015. Supreme Court of the United States, No. 14-556. Argued April 28, 2015–Decided June 26, 2015. http://www.supremecourt.gov/opinions/14pdf/14-556_3204.pdf (accessed 22 April 2024).

Okin, Susan Moller. 1989. *Justice, Gender, and the Family*. New York: Basic Books.

Okin, Susan Moller. 1994. "Gender Inequality and Cultural Differences." *Political Theory* 22.1 (February): 5–24.

Okin, Susan Moller. 1995. "Response to Jane Flax." *Political Theory* 23.3 (August): 511–16.

Okin, Susan Moller. 1999. "Is Multiculturalism Bad for Women?" In *Is Multiculturalism Bad for Women?*, ed. Joshua Cohen, Matthew Howard, and Martha C. Nussbaum, 7–24. Princeton: Princeton University Press.

Okin, Susan Moller. 2002. "'Mistresses of Their Own Destiny': Group Rights, Gender, and Realistic Rights of Exit." *Ethics* 112 (January): 205–30.

Olberding, Amy. 2004. "The Consummation of Sorrow: An Analysis of Confucius' Grief for Yan Hui." *Philosophy East and West* 54.3 (July): 279–301.

Olberding, Amy. 2019. *The Wrong of Rudeness: Learning Modern Civility from Ancient Chinese Philosophy*. New York: Oxford University Press.

Oltermann, Philip. 2014. "Heidegger's 'black notebooks' Reveal Antisemitism at Core of His Philosophy." *The Guardian*, March 12. https://www.theguardian.com/books/2014/mar/13/martin-heideggerblack-notebooks-reveal-nazi-ideology-antisemitism (accessed 22 April 2024).

Pakaluk, Michael, ed. 1991. *Other Selves: Philosophers on Friendship*. Indianapolis: Hackett.

Pang-White, Ann A., intro. & trans. 2018. *The Confucian Four Books for Women: A New Translation of the Nu Sishu and the Commentary of Wang Xiang*. New York: Oxford University Press.

Papadaki, Lina. 2010. "Kantian Marriage and Beyond: Why It Is Worth Thinking about Kant on Marriage." *Hypatia* 25.2: 276–94.

Parekh, Bhikhu. 1999. "A Varied Moral World." In *Is Multiculturalism Bad for Women?* ed. Joshua Cohen, Matthew Howard, and Martha C. Nussbaum, 69–75. Princeton: Princeton University Press.

Park, Peter K. J. 2013. *Africa, Asia, and the History of Philosophy*. Albany: SUNY.

Pateman, Carole. 2003. "Hobbes, Patriarchy and Conjugal Right." In *Social and Political Philosophy: Classical Western Texts in Feminist and Multicultural Perspectives*, ed. James P. Sterba, 167–80. Blemont: Wadsworth.

Perkins, Franklin. 2007. *Leibniz and China: A Commerce of Light*. New York: Cambridge University Press.

Pew Research Center. 2016. "5 Ways Americans and Europeans Are Different," by Richard Wike, April 19. http://www.pewresearch.org/fact-tank/2016/04/19/5-ways-americans-and-europeans-are-different/ (accessed 22 April 2024).

Phillips, Anne. 2007. *Multiculturalism without Culture*. Princeton: Princeton University Press.

Pines, Yuri, trans. 2017. *The Book of Lord Shang: Apologetics of State Power in Early China*. New York: Columbia University Press.

Plato. 1997. *Plato: Complete Works*, ed. John M. Cooper. Indianapolis: Hackett.

Pluhar, Werner S., trans. 1987. *Immanuel Kant: Critique of Judgment*. Indianapolis: Hackett.

Politico. 2017. "The Greying World." January 11. https://www.politico.com/agenda/story/2017/01/the-graying-world-000276 (accessed 22 April 2024).

Quinn, Patrick. 1996. "St. Thomas Aquinas and the Christian Understanding of Friendship." In *Friendship East and West: Philosophical Perspectives*, ed. Oliver Leaman, 270–9. Richmond: Curzon Press.

Raphals, Lisa. 2002. "A Woman Who Understood the Rites." In *Confucius and the Analects: New Essays*, ed. Bryan W. Van Norden, 275–302. New York: Oxford University Press.

Raphals, Lisa. 2004. "Reflections on Filiality, Nature and Nurture." In *Filial Piety in Chinese Thought and History*, ed. Alan K. L. Chan and Sor-hoon Tan, 215–25. London: Routledge.

Rickett, W. Allyn, intro. & trans. 1998. *Guanzi: Political, Economic, and Political Essays from Early China*. Princeton: Princeton University Press.

Rosemont, Henry Jr. 2015. *Against Individualism: A Confucian Rethinking of the Foundations of Morality, Politics, Family and Religion*. Lanham: Lexington Books.

Rosenlee, Li-Hsiang Lisa. 2006. *Confucianism and Women: A Philosophical Interpretation*. Albany: SUNY.

Rosenlee, Li-Hsiang Lisa. 2009. "What Is the Use of Philosophy in General and Asian Philosophy in Particular to Feminism?" *American Philosophical Association* Newsletters (Fall) 9.1: 3–4.

Rosenlee, Li-Hsiang Lisa. 2012. "Review of Femininity and Feminism: Chinese and Contemporary [A Special Issue of the *Journal of Chinese Philosophy*, vol. 36, no. 2, June 2009]." *Hypatia* 27.2 (Spring): 449–55.

Rosenlee, Li-Hsiang Lisa. 2014. "Confucian Care: A Hybrid Feminist Ethics." In *Feminist-Asian Comparative Philosophy: Liberating Traditions*, ed. Ashby Butnor and Jen McWeeny, 187–202. New York: Columbia University Press.

Rosenlee, Li-Hsiang Lisa. 2020. "A Revisionist History of Philosophy." *Journal of World Philosophies* 5.1: 121–37.

Rosenlee, Li-Hsiang Lisa. 2023a. "Confucianism and the Lives of Women." In *The Oxford Handbook of Confucianism*, ed. Jennifer Oldstone-Moore, 423–34. New York: Oxford University Press.

Rosenlee, Li-Hsiang Lisa. 2023b. "Gender in Confucian Philosophy." *Stanford Encyclopedia of Philosophy*, February, open access. https://plato.stanford.edu/entries/confucian-gender/ (accessed 22 April 2024).

Ruddick, Sara. 1980. "Maternal Thinking." *Feminist Studies* 6: 342–67.

Ruether, Rosemary Radford. 2000. "Misogynism and Virginal Feminism in the Fathers of the Church." In *Ethic: Classical Western Texts in Feminist and Multicultural Perspectives*, ed. James P. Sterba, 103–6. New York: Oxford University Press.

Rupp, George. 2015. *Beyond Individualism: The Challenge of Inclusive Communities*. New York: Columbia University Press.

Russell, Bertrand. 1922. *The Problem of China*. London: Allen and Unwin.

Salkever, Stephen. 2008. "Taking Friendship Seriously: Aristotle on the Place(s) of *Philia* in Human Life." In *Friendship and Politics: Essays in Political Thought*, eds. John Von Heyking and Richard Avramenko, 53–83. Notre Dame: University of Notre Dame Press.

Sandberg, Sheryl with Nell Scovell. 2013. *Lean In: Women, Work, and the Will to Lead*. New York: Alfred A. Knopf.

Schindler, Jeanne Heffernan. 2008. "A Companionship of *Carita*: Friendship in St. Thomas Aquinas." In *Friendship and Politics: Essays in Political Thought*, ed. John von Heyking and Richard Avramenko, 139–62. Notre Dame: University of Notre Dame Press.

Schott, Robin May. 2003. *Discovering Feminist Philosophy: Knowledge, Ethics, Politics*. New York: Rowman & Littlefield.

Schwartz, Daniel. 2007. *Aquinas on Friendship*. New York: Oxford University Press.

Shangjun shu 商君書 (*Book of Lord Shang*). *Chinese Text Project*. http://ctext.org/shang-jun-shu, (accessed 22 April 2024); for translation, see Pines, 2017.

Shanhai jing 山海經 (*Classic of Mountains and Seas*). *Chinese Text Project*. http://ctext.org/shan-hai-jing (accessed 22 April 2024).

Sherman, Nancy. 1997. *Making a Necessity of Virtue: Aristotle and Kant on Virtue*. New York: Cambridge University Press.

Shiji 史記 (*Records of the Grand Historian*). Chinese Text Project. http://ctext.org/shiji, (accessed 22 April 2024); for translation, see Watson, 1961/1993.

Shijing 詩經 (*Book of Songs*). *Chinese Text Project*. http://ctext.org/book-of-poetry, (accessed 22 April 2024); for translation, see Waley, 1996.

Shlam, Shosh and Hilla Medalia. 2020. *Leftover Women*, film premiered on *PBS*, Feb. 10. https://www.pbs.org/independentlens/films/leftover-women/ (accessed 22 April 2024).

Shulman, Alix Kates. 1993. "A Marriage Agreement." In *Feminist Frameworks: Alternative Theoretical Accounts of the Relations between Women and Men*, ed. Alison M. Jaggar and Paula S. Rothenberg, 367–70. New York: McGraw-Hill.

Shun, Kwong-loi. 2003. "*Xiao* (*hsiao*): Filial piety." In *Encyclopedia of Chinese Philosophy*, ed. Antonio S. Cua, 793–5. New York: Routledge.

Shun, Kwong-loi and David B. Wong, eds. 2004. *Confucian Ethics: A Comparative Study of Self, Autonomy, and Community*. New York: Cambridge University Press.

Shuowen jiezi 說文解字 (*Discussing Writings and Explaining Characters*). *Chinese Text Project*. http://ctext.org/shuo-wen-jie-zi (accessed 22 April 2024).

Shuoyuan 說苑 (*Garden of Persuasions*). *Chinese Text Project*. http://ctext.org/shuo-yuan, (accessed 22 April 2024); for translation, see Henry 2022.

Shujing 書經 (*Book of Documents*). *Chinese Text Project*. http://ctext.org/shang-shu, (accessed 22 April 2024); for translation, see Legge, 1879.

Sim, May. 2007. *Remastering Morals with Aristotle and Confucius*. New York: Cambridge University Press.

Slaughter, Ann Marie. 2012. "Why Women Still Can't Have It All." *The Atlantic*, July/August. http://www.theatlantic.com/magazine/archive/2012/07/why-women-still-cant-have-it-all/309020/ (accessed 22 April 2024).

Slote, Walter H. 1998. "Psychocultural Dynamics within the Confucian Family." In *Confucianism and the Family*, ed. Walter H. Slote and George A. Devos, 37–52. Albany: SUNY.

Solomon, Robert C., Kathleen M. Higgins, and Clancy Martin, eds. 2012. *Introducing Philosophy: A Text with Integrated Readings*. New York: Oxford University Press.

Sommers, Christina. 1989. "Philosophers against the Family." In *Vice and Virtue in Everyday Life: Introductory Readings in Ethics*, ed. Christina Sommers and Fred Sommers, 728–54. San Diego: Harcourt Brace Jovanovich Publishers.

Star, Daniel. 2002. "Do Confucians Really Care? A Defense of the Distinctiveness of Care Ethics: A Reply to Chenyang Li." *Hypatia* 17.1: 77–106.

Stewart, Mary White. 2014. *Ordinary Violence: Everyday Assaults against Women Worldwide*. Santa Barbara: Praeger.

Sullivan, Eileen P. 1983. "Liberalism and the Imperialism: J. S. Mill's Defense of the British Empire." *Journal of the History of Ideas* 44.4: 599–617.

Swann, Nancy Lee, intro. & trans. 1932 [2001]. *Pan Chao: Foremost Woman Scholar of China*. Preface by Susan Mann. Ann Arbor: University of Michigan Press.

Tan, Sor-hoon. 2004. *Confucian Democracy: A Deweyan Reconstruction*. Albany: SUNY.

Taylor, Charles. 1992. *Sources of the Self: The Making of the Modern Identity*. Boston: Harvard University Press.

Taylor, Charles. 1995. *Philosophical Arguments*. Cambridge: Harvard University Press.

Taylor Mill, Harriet. 1852 [1994]. "Enfranchisement of Women." In *Philosophy of Woman: An Anthology of Classic to Current Concepts*, ed. Mary Briody Mahowald, 170–85. Indianapolis: Hackett.

The Atlantic. 2016. "I Alone Can Fix It," by Yoni Appelbaum, July 21. http://
www.theatlantic.com/politics/archive/2016/07/trump-rnc-speech-alone-fix-
it/492557/ (accessed 22 April 2024).

The Guardian. 2017. "How does the US Healthcare System Compare with Other
Countries?" by Josh Holder, Paul Torpey, and Feilding Cage, July 25. https://
www.theguardian.com/us-news/ng-interactive/2017/jul/25/us-healthcare-
system-vs-other-countries (accessed 22 April 2024).

The Guardian. 2019. "French Publishing Boss Claims She was Groomed at Age
14 by Acclaimed Author," by Angelique Chrisafis, December 27. https://www.
theguardian.com/world/2019/dec/27/french-publishingboss-claims-she-was-
groomed-at-age-14-by-acclaimed-author (accessed 22 April 2024).

The New York Times. 2012. "Jobs Where Gender Segregation Persists," by Bill
Marsh, September 30. http://www.nytimes.com/imagepages/2012/09/30/
opinion/30coontz-gr1.html (accessed 22 April 2024).

The New York Times. 2015. "Donald Trump Says He'd 'Absolutely' Require
Muslims to Register," by Trip Gabriel, November 20. http://www.nytimes.
com/politics/first-draft/2015/11/20/donald-trump-says-hed-absolutely-
require-muslims-to-register/?_r=0 (accessed 22 April 2024).

The New York Times. 2021a. "'Our President Wants Us Here': The Mob
That Stormed the Capitol," by Dan Barry, Mike McIntire, and Matthew
Rosenberg, January 9. https://www.nytimes.com/2021/01/09/us/capitol-
rioters.html (accessed 22 April 2024).

The New York Times. 2021b. "More Than One-Third of U.S. Coronavirus Deaths
Are Linked to Nursing Homes," February 2. https://www.nytimes.com/
interactive/2020/us/coronavirus-nursing-homes.html (accessed 22 April
2024).

The New York Times. 2021c. "Coronavirus World Map: Tracking the Global
Outbreak," February 9. https://www.nytimes.com/interactive/2020/world/
coronavirus-maps.html (accessed 22 April 2024).

The New York Times. 2021d. "The World 'Has Found a Way to Do This': The
U.S. Lags on Paid Leave," by Claire Cain Miller, November 3. https://www.
nytimes.com/2021/10/25/upshot/paid-leave-democrats.html (accessed
22 April 2024).

The Washington Post. 2016a. "Trump Reveals How He Would Force Mexico to
Pay for Border Wall," by Bob Woodward and Robert Costa, April 5. https://
www.washingtonpost.com/politics/trump-would-seek-to-block-money-
transfers-to-force-mexico-to-fund-border-wall/2016/04/05/c0196314-fa7c-
11e5-80e4-c381214de1a3_story.html (accessed 22 April 2024).

The Washington Post. 2016b. "Trump Recorded Having Extremely Lewd
Conversation about Women in 2005," by David, Fahrenthold, October 8.
https://www.washingtonpost.com/politics/trump-recorded-having-
extremely-lewd-conversation-about-women-in-2005/2016/10/07/3b9ce776-
8cb4-11e6-bf8a-3d26847eeed4_story.html?utm_term=.602ef7f55258
(accessed 22 April 2024).

Time. 2009. "What Women Want Now," by Nancy Gibbs, October 14. http://content.time.com/time/specials/packages/article/0,28804,1930277_1930145_1930309-2,00.html (accessed 22 April 2024).

Time. 2016. "Read George W. Bush's Speech at the Dallas Shooting Memorial Service," by Julissa Higgins, July 12. http://time.com/4403510/george-w-bush-speech-dallas-shooting-memorial-service/ (accessed 22 April 2024).

Tjan, Tjoe Som, intro. & trans. 1949 /1952. *Po Hu T'ung, The Comprehensive Discussions in the White Tiger Hall*. Leiden: Brill.

To, Sandy. 2015. *China's Leftover Women. Late Marriage among Professional Women and Its Consequences*. Oxon: Routledge.

Tongdian 通典 (*Comprehensive Encyclopedia*). *Chinese Text Project*. https://ctext.org/tongdian (accessed 22 April 2024).

Tronto, Joan C. 1993. *Moral Boundaries: A Political Argument for an Ethic of Care*. Oxon: Routledge.

Tronto, Joan C. 2013. *Caring Democracy: Markets, Equality, and Justice*. New York: New York University Press.

Tu, Wei-ming. 1985. *Confucian Thought: Selfhood as Creative Transformation*. Albany: SUNY.

Tu, Wei-ming and Wm. Theodore De Bary, eds. 1998. *Confucianism and Human Rights*. New York: Columbia University Press.

US News. 2016. "The Kids Are Still Not Alright: It's Time for the United States to Expand Early Childhood Education Programs," by Arne Duncan, July 21. http://www.usnews.com/opinion/articles/2016-07-21/universal-preschool-would-boost-the-economy (accessed 22 April 2024).

US News. 2022. "Wealthy Countries Are Outpacing Poor Nations in COVID-19 Vaccination Rates," by Christopher Wolf, Alex Leeds Matthews, and Horus Alas, Nov. 7. https://www.usnews.com/news/best-countries/articles/covid-19-vaccination-rates-by-country (accessed 22 April 2024).

USA Today. 2015. "Judge Dismissed Domestic Charges against Ray Rice." May 21. http://www.usatoday.com/story/sports/nfl/2015/05/21/judge-dismissed-domestic-violence-charges-against-ray-rice/27709875/ (accessed 22 April 2024).

Uzgalis, William. 2002. "An Inconsistency Not to Be Excused: On Locke and Racism." In *Philosophers on Race: Critical Essays*, ed. Julie K. Ward and Tommy L. Lott, 81–100. Malden: Blackwell.

Uzgalis, William. 2017. "John Locke, Racism, Slavery, and Indian Lands." In *The Oxford Handbook of Philosophy and Race*, ed. Naomi Zack, 21–30. New York: Oxford University Press.

Valls, Andrew. 2005. "'A Lousy Empirical Scientist': Reconsidering Hume's Racism." In *Race and Racism in Modern Philosophy*, ed. Andrew Valls, 127–49. Ithaca: Cornell University Press.

Veltman, Andrea. 2014. "Aristotle and Kant on Self-disclosure in Friendship." In *Ancient and Medieval Concepts of Friendship*, ed. Gary M. Gurtler and Suzanne Stern-Gillet, 271–87. Albany: SUNY.

Vervoorn, Aat. 2004. "Friendship in Ancient China." *East Asian History* 27 (June): 1–32.

Waldron, Jeremy. 1995. "Minority Cultures and the Cosmopolitan Alternative." In *The Rights of Minority Cultures*, ed. Will Kymlicka, 93–119. New York: Oxford University Press.

Waley, Arthur, trans. 1996. *The Book of Songs, Shijing: The Ancient Chinese Classic of Poetry*. New York: Grove Press.

Watson, Burton, intro. & trans. 1961/1993. *Records of the Grand Historian by Sima Qian*, Vol. I & II. New York: Columbia University Press.

Watson, Burton, intro. & trans. 1963. *Hsun Tzu: Basic Writings*. New York: Columbia University Press.

Watson, Burton, intro. & trans. 1968. *The Complete Works of Chuang Tzu*. New York: Columbia University Press.

Watson, Burton, intro. & trans. 2003. *Han Feizi: Basic Writings*. New York: Columbia University Press.

Watkins, Eric, ed. 2012. *The Cambridge Edition of the Works of Immanuel Kant: Natural Science*. New York: Cambridge University Press.

WHO (*World Health Organization*). 2023. "WHO Coronavirus (COVID-19) Dashboard." April 4. https://covid19.who.int/ (accessed 22 April 2024).

Wielenberg, Erik. 2006. "I Think, Therefore I Am Misunderstood." *Newsweek*, October 16.

Williams, Bernard. 1981. *Moral Luck: Philosophical Papers 1973–1980*. New York: Cambridge University Press.

Wimmer, Franz, Robert Bernasconi, Paul Hountondji, and Thomas Norton-Smith. 2015. "Symposium: How Are Histories of Non-Western Philosophies Relevant to Intercultural Philosophizing?" *Journal of World Philosophies* 3 (November): 126–67.

Wolf, Eric R. 1984/1997. *Europe and the People without History*. Berkeley: University of California Press.

Wolff, Jonathan. 2016. "Why Do Philosophers Make Unsuitable Life Partners?" *The Guardian*, March 15. https://www.theguardian.com/education/2016/mar/15/why-philosophers-make-unsuitable-life-partners (accessed 22 April 2024).

Wollstonecraft, Mary. 1792 [2003]. "A Vindication of the Rights of Woman." In *Social and Political Philosophy: Classical Western Texts in Feminist and Multicultural Perspectives*, ed. James Sterba, 263–70. Belmont: Wadsworth.

Woo, Terry. 1999. "Confucianism and Feminism." In *Feminism and World Religions*, ed. Arvind Sharma and Katherine K. Young, 110–47. Albany: SUNY.

Wood, Allen W. and George Di Giovanni, eds. 1996. *The Cambridge Edition of the Works of Immanuel Kant: Religion and Rational Theology*. New York: Cambridge University Press.

Xiaojing 孝經 (*Book of Filiality*). *Chinese Text Project*. http://ctext.org/xiao-jing, (accessed 22 April 2024); for translation, see Ames and Rosemont, 2009.

Xinshu 新書 (*New Book*). *Chinese Text Project*. http://ctext.org/xin-shu (accessed 22 April 2024).

Xinxu 新序 (*New Order*). *Chinese Text Project*. http://ctext.org/xin-xu (accessed 22 April 2024).

Xunzi 荀子 (*Master Xun*). *Chinese Text Project*. http://ctext.org/xunzi, (accessed 22 April 2024); for translation, see Knoblock and Zhang, 1999.

Yalom, Marilyn. 2001. *A History of the Wife*. New York: Harpercollins.

Yangzi fayan 揚子法言 (*Exemplary Sayings by Master Yang*). *Chinese Text Project*. https://ctext.org/yangzi-fayan, (accessed 22 April 2024); for translation, see Nylan, 2013.

Yanshi jiaxun 顏氏家訓 (*Yan's Family Instructions*). *Chinese Text Project*. http://ctext.org/yan-shi-jia-xun (accessed 22 April 2024).

Yantielun 鹽鐵論 (*Discourses on Salt and Iron*). *Chinese Text Project*. http://ctext.org/yan-tie-lun (accessed 22 April 2024).

Yanzi chunqiu 晏子春秋 (*Master Yanzi's Spring and Autumn Annals*). *Chinese Text Project*. http://ctext.org/yanzi-chun-qiu (accessed 22 April 2024).

Yijing 易經 (*Book of Changes*). *Chinese Text Project*. http://ctext.org/book-of-changes, (accessed 22 April 2024); for translation, see Legge, 1882.

Yuan, Lijun. 2002. "Ethics of Care and Concept of *Jen*: A Reply to Chenyang Li." *Hypatia* 17.1: 107–29.

Yuan, Lijun. 2005. *Reconceiving Women's Equality in China: A Critical Examination of Models of Sex Equality*. New York: Lexington Books.

Yuan, Lijun. 2019. *Confucian Ren and Feminist Ethics of Care: Integrating Relational Self, Power, and Democracy*. New York: Lexington Books.

Zhonglun 中論 (*Balanced Discourses*). *Chinese Text Project*. http://ctext.org/zhong-lun (accessed 22 April 2024).

Zhongyong 中庸 (*Centrality and Commonality*). *Chinese Text Project*. http://ctext.org/liji/zhongyong, (accessed 22 April 2024); for translation, see Ames and Hall, 2001.

Zhouli 周禮 (*Rites of Zhou*). *Chinese Text Project*. http://ctext.org/rites-of-zhou (accessed 22 April 2024).

Zhuangzi 莊子 (*Master Zhuang*). *Chinese Text Project*. http://ctext.org/zhuangzi, (accessed 22 April 2024); for translation, see Watson, 1968.

Zoller, Gunter and Robert B. Louden, eds. 2007. *The Cambridge Edition of the Works of Immanuel Kant: Anthropology, History, and Education*. New York: Cambridge University Press.

Zuozhuan 左傳 (*Zuo's Commentary*). *Chinese Text Project*. http://ctext.org/chun-qiu-zuo-zhuan (accessed 22 April 2024).

Index